D1084210

POLITICAL CHANGE
IN THE UNITED STATES:
A Framework for Analysis

Useful as a whipping boy maybe, but not really very good

POLICY IMPACT
AND POLITICAL CHANGE
IN AMERICA
KENNETH M. DOLBEARE, Consulting Editor

Designed as brief supplements for American Government and other undergraduate political science courses, books in this series confront crucial issues of public policy in the United States. The primary goal of the series is to demonstrate the utility of analytical concepts of political science for understanding the most pressing social and political problems of our time. Some books will be addressed to the question of how adequate present policies are to cope with current problems, and others will deal with questions of political change. Each book will be published in both soft- and cloth-cover editions.

POLITICAL CHANGE IN THE UNITED STATES: A Framework for Analysis

KENNETH M. DOLBEARE

The University of Washington

McGraw-Hill Book Company

*New York   St. Louis   San Francisco   Düsseldorf   Johannesburg
Kuala Lumpur   London   Mexico   Montreal   New Delhi   Panama
Paris   São Paulo   Singapore   Sydney   Tokyo   Toronto*

3649-G

This book was set in Press Roman by Creative Book Services,
division of McGregor & Werner, Inc.
The editor was Robert P. Rainier;
the designer was Creative Book Services;
and the production supervisor was Sally Ellyson.
The printer was The Murray Printing Company;
the binder, The Book Press, Inc.

POLITICAL CHANGE IN THE UNITED STATES:
A Framework for Analysis

1 2 3 4 5 6 7 8 9 0 B P B P 7 9 8 7 6 5 4 3

Library of Congress Cataloging in Publication Data

Dolbeare, Kenneth M
    Political change in the United States.

    (Policy impact and political change in America)
    Bibliography: p.
    1. United States—Politics and government—1945—
—Addresses, essays, lectures. 2. United States—Social
conditions—1960-   —Addresses, essays, lectures.
3. Elite (Social sciences)—Addresses, essays, lectures.
I. Title. II. Series.
JK271.D635   301.5'92'0973   73-11263
ISBN   0-07-017403-2
ISBN   0-07-017402-4 (pbk.)

FEB.   1978

CONTENTS

PREFACE

This essay was not written for any particular "audience." It is not intended for my professional colleagues, but neither can I exculpate myself by defining the audience as "undergraduates" or "literate non-professionals." I have learned far too much from both of the latter to be condescending—and many of them know it. Rather, it is an effort to apply a version of political science to four major arguments concerning political change in the United States today. One, held by the great majority, is that the orthodox political channels are capable of re-forming our politics and solving our problems if only people will (a) become more actively concerned and involved, and (b) accept the inevitability and propriety of accommodation and compromise, with each other and with evolving technological capitalism. The second is at the opposite pole: Marxist revolutionary socialism, the various factions of which have recently grown in strength and numbers. The third is still more popular, probably because it involves neither traditional nor revolutionary routes—indeed, no effort at all. This is the counterculture route, symbolized by Charles Reich's *Greening of America,* rock music, and religious revivalism. It promises that the pursuit of maximally individualistic self-indulgence will somehow solve social problems. Fourth is the view that special interests, such as minorities, youth, or militant feminists can combine either explicitly or tacitly to transform the society. I shall also keep constantly in mind perhaps the largest and fastest growing argument of all, that of those who have seriously tried one or more of these routes and who now have concluded, sadly but completely, that there is no way in which fundamental change can be accomplished in the United States today.

With the greatest respect, I think each of these arguments is wrong in major respects. Reform *cannot* solve today's problems. But, although Americans have a great deal to learn from the Marxist tradition, the mechanistic application of nineteenth-century European models can only be a disservice both to the cause of change *and* the memory of Marx. No instantaneous or individualistic route can accomplish social change, least of all our apolitical and antipolitical counterculture. Emphasis on what divides people rather than on what they share in the way of needs and hopes is more likely to bring about conflict over the leavings of the larger system—or mutual cancellation—than significant change in that system. But there is something to be learned from each of these arguments, and a synthesis and raising of sights that should be cause for cautious optimism. Fundamental political change is possible, although it will be very difficult and a modern American brand of fascism may be more likely.

Perhaps, like many of my colleagues, I compulsively take refuge in either equivocal middle-of-the-road positions or antiseptic calls for further analysis and development of more comprehensive theory. Indeed, although I deny it, this essay may be an example of both forms of escape. But I do not think advocates of any of these arguments can be or should be persuaded of the parochialism or error of their views unless a general, if rudimentary, theory of political change in the United States can be set forth. Nor can interested citizens intelligently judge them without a clear sense of what the process of change might actually look like.

Thus the task of this essay is to construct such a rudimentary theory of political change in the United States, to draw on the lessons of the past and analysis of the present to state the conditions, contingencies, and potentialities that make fundamental change more, and less, likely in the foreseeable future. When we have identified the crucial threshold and the relevant questions to be asked, we shall proceed to critically evaluate a number of contemporary prescriptions and strategies for change. Although we shall find them seriously lacking, the experience will move us toward clearer understanding of what is desirable and workable.

Two words of warning seem appropriate. One is that I am a political scientist. This essay, therefore, will no doubt appear unnecessarily complex and pessimistic to many readers, both left and right. To be comprehensive, a theory of change must pay systematic and serious attention to a wide variety of possibilities, some of which—such as fascism or revolution—may seem unlikely or undesirable. I believe that each of these, given the right combination of circumstances, is a real possibility—and I shall treat them with appropriate respect. But the ultimate result is optimistic, not pessimistic.

The second is that this essay is only a beginning. It is merely a framework, an itemization of the questions that must be asked in order to understand the process of change. It is emphatically *not* a cookbook or set of procedures for accomplishing fundamental change in the United States. Rather, it is a necessary preliminary to the formulation of any such strategy—a primer on *how to think* and *what to think about* in order to understand the problem and process of fundamental change. Most Americans merely *do*, without benefit of much analysis or theory about the probable consequences or relative utility of their acts. Change-seekers are no exception. Impatiently, they ask what to *do*, not how to understand a total process of intervention into history so as to purposefully redirect its course. And the cost is very high: the lack of any such theory is the major reason for the evaporation of the New Left of the 1960s, and for the general sense of frustration and hopelessness that many feel today. The right questions are more important than facile answers masquerading as solutions to the deeply serious problem of political change. Therefore, I shall not apologize, either for the brevity of this framework, or for my temerity in grappling with this amorphous and frankly intimidating problem.

It is not an apology, however, to note quite consistently that I expect others (both professional social scientists and political activists) to find this essay lacking in important ways. It is, but perhaps it is not entirely my fault. We simply do not know very much about political change, partly because we have not asked systematic and careful questions about it. Nostrums abound, but knowledge is scarce. Too many (scholars and activists) treat political change as if it were either so complex and idiosyncratic that analysis is hopeless or so simple a matter that it can readily be brought about by all groups just going out and "doing their own thing." This is an attempt to enter and, perhaps, to expand a dialogue about change, and I have no doubt that the framework offered can soon be transcended by subtler and more comprehensive approaches. But I am not now aware of any that are available to beginning students, and so I have taken the self-exposing step of recording these notes and questions in this form. To make the book more generally readable, I have omitted the usual academic footnoting. Both specific references and background sources are cited, however, in the bibliographical essay.

I want to thank the many students and other friends who have helped develop, test, and refine both me and the framework set forth here. Many, perhaps most, of the ideas were not originally mine, and only I know the true scope and depth of my debts to them. My primary debt is to Pat, for showing me the way in so many respects, including some I could not follow. Other major debts are owed to Barbara, David, Linda, Marty, Phil, and Ray. Michael's review forced me to re-think and improve somewhat, but generally to cling stubbornly to the argument I make. Special thanks go to Lee, the supertypist.

K.M.D.

POLITICAL CHANGE
IN THE UNITED STATES:
A Framework for Analysis

CHAPTER ONE

Introduction:
The Problem of Thinking about Political Change

Unlike other advanced industrial societies, the United States has neither experienced fundamental political change nor known a viable tradition that advocated such change. Perhaps for these reasons, Americans show little capacity to think about political change. Amid multiplying images—and ample reality—of accelerating change in all other spheres of life, most Americans simply assume that available channels will produce appropriate political change. But even those few who know better also fail to come to grips with the admittedly staggering problems involved in achieving fundamental political change. All Americans, whatever their location on the political spectrum, appear inhibited by history, culture, and consciousness from coping creatively with what is, in the first instance, a *conceptual* problem.

For some, of course, socioeconomic standing or ideological acquiescence foreclose interest in political change. Many who do see or sense problems in our present, however, are so steeped in unrecognized self-limitations, flowing from our orthodox way of thinking, that they are helpless. We are presently almost submerged, for example, by a flood of works critical of the American economic and political systems. Typically, these works paint a picture of decaying conditions, corrupt or ineffective institutions, and archaic or morally indefensible values. They then follow this devastating critique with a final five pages in which readers are exhorted to write their Congressmen, elect wiser leaders, or otherwise "get involved." The prescription falls so far short of the analysis in part because we do not normally see that problems often have their roots in basic social and economic causes. But it is also because, after "analyzing" a problem, the liberal reform tradition conceptualizes no remedial channels except the same existing routes that have previously generated or tolerated the problem. Unable to imagine alternative political strategies or goals, such reformers then exhaust themselves vainly within the infinitely absorbing canyons of prescribed procedures.

But more radical change-seekers display the same conceptual limitation, albeit in different forms. The dominant style is avoidance. For some, the only answer lies in escape, which may occur as utopian individualism or various styles of counterculture self-indulgence. Others place their faith in a process of change that is effortless and automatic. Charles Reich's *Greening of America*,[1] for example, assures us that we need never face the realities of power and interest; an irresistible process of change in values and goals is sweeping all before it, and generating a new society quite without the need for serious reflection or social action. Still others, to their credit, have discovered that nineteenth-century Europe knew conceptual and philosophic traditions that can lead to critical insight about our present and creative alternatives for our future. But they have, for the most part, merely seized and applied such principles or models—as if they were automatically transferable to a distinctive society in a subsequent century. In today's world, they are often either romantic revolutionaries or reactionary oligarchs—and sometimes both. In very few cases have they managed to deal creatively or credibly with the problem of accomplishing their goals.

Thus, despite a deeply and sincerely felt need for profound change, neither liberals nor radicals have produced very satisfactory prescriptions for achievement. Some prescribe routes that are self-defeating or illusory, while others reluctantly conclude that real change is impossible. In both cases, much of the problem is traceable to societally generated limitations on our way of thinking about the relationship between man and his social order and how all three evolve through time. One major task of this essay, therefore, is a critical assessment of the narrow and self-limiting way we think—in the course of which we shall see that much that passes for strategies of change is misconceived.

To the superficial reader, it may seem that I am merely denigrating the sincere (and often self-sacrificing) efforts of change-seekers. The import of the essay may appear pessimistic.

But such is not my intent at all. Properly understood, the essay is soberly optimistic, given our current social context and prospects. For example, I insist that the beginnings of a viable approach to change are already with us. Consistently, they are at this stage only (*only*!) conceptual germs. Some draw on nineteenth-century European ways of thinking that, once they have transcended their particular contexts and social constraints, may offer critical distance and creative potential for Americans. Others draw on the way of thinking characteristic of some American minorities. Pressed by such totally non-American world views and concepts, we can begin to develop the missing capacity to think beyond the limits of our orthodoxy and social context.

I have few illusions about how far this particular effort can go, of course; I would consider it a dramatic advance to merely lay a brick on the foundation that has been so long in rising. But it is extremely important to direct attention to this joint task. I see several dangerous, and perhaps destructive, prospects if we do not come to grips more seriously and effectively with the problem of change. One is that sincere and potentially constructive people may be lost (in one way or another), and simultaneously the last real opportunity for fundamental political change. Another is that frustration, hopelessness, and cynicism give rise to a significant potential for mobilization in support of leaders or movements that offer illusory and progressively more repressive "solutions." Because I see a modern American brand of fascism as a real prospect, I think the task of learning to think about political change is urgent indeed. That task begins, familiarly enough, with some basic definitions.

WHAT IS POLITICAL CHANGE?

Political change is an independent process. It does not necessarily follow with every change in social or economic institutions and practices. For example, the United States has experienced vast changes in many areas of life in the last two centuries, but by comparison, very little change in the basic structures, rules, or processes of government. Time and again, there have been waves of reform washing up from below, matched by dramatic rhetoric from above. But when the waters recede, the basic contours of power and advantage remain essentially as before. Symbolic reassurance is sufficient, until the next wave of frustration and resentment builds up, eventually spills its banks again, and the process is repeated. Such stability may be due to the fact that only certain key changes in other areas can force political change. Or it may be because some elements in the society apply their power to arrest or prevent change, or because masses of people fear and likewise resist change. Political institutions and decisions are highly visible and potentially threatening, after all, and holding them constant may serve as a source of security in a very insecure world. Meaning no sacrilege (in either direction), the depth and character of Americans' attachment to their Constitution, institutions, and traditions may be summarized in a stanza from a well-known Protestant hymn:

> Change and decay
> In all around I see,
> O Thou who changest not
> Abide with me!

But recognition of the power of permanence only opens the subject of its opposite, change. What do we mean by *political change*? I shall use the term in connection with a single basic concept, that of a *structure of authority.* The latter has two dimensions. One is the *power structure* of a society. The other is the acceptance by the general public of that power structure's management of the society, or *legitimacy.* Legitimacy is what converts a power structure to a structure of authority. Each of these terms must now be defined.

Power denotes a capability in people, each of whom possesses certain resources (money, talent, reputation, institutional position, etc.) that may affect the thoughts and action of others in various ways. *Politics* is a system of relationships in which power is employed, consciously and unconsciously (in the sense that some anticipate the preferences of others whom they view as more powerful than they), to gain ends and to condition the behavior of others in ways deemed desirable. Where such effects are unperceived, subtle, or acceptable, they are often termed *influence.* At the opposite end of the continuum, effects that are crude, sweeping, or unwelcome may be viewed as *coercion.*

Where the major resources that give rise to power are concentrated in a relatively few people in the society, and this condition is static, we may speak of a *power structure.* There may be disagreement over precisely who has how much power, or how to weight various resources at various times. But there can be no question that these resources are very unequally distributed in all advanced industrial societies, and we may therefore speak of the resulting hierarchy as a power structure.

Because the resources of power may take various forms, including *economic* (wealth, ownership of societally significant property), *social* (status, reputation) and *cultural* (the values and expectations held by others), an effective power structure may coalesce independently of the expressly political institutions of the society. Ordinarily its needs and preferences would also suffuse the political system, for the latter is essentially the economic and social systems viewed from another perspective. But the goal of democratization has been to open the political decision-making process to participation by those with fewer power resources, and thus domination by those with the most may be incomplete. Accordingly, the extent to which the crystallization of power resources in a society results in a *governing* power structure must be acknowledged to be in some respects an empirical question. In other words, where what we accept has facts demonstrate impact by the relatively powerless, we must see limits to the scope of control wielded by those whose resources locate them without the society's power structure.

The basic point is, however, that the conditions and quality of life for most people are either established or strongly shaped by the interests and actions of the society's combined economic, social, and political power structure. The values, beliefs, and expectations of the general public contribute significantly to making this process a peaceful one. The power structure, therefore, has a compelling interest in seeing that such values, beliefs, and expectations are formed in ways that are consistent with its needs and preferences. Its governing role may then be only dimly perceived by the general public, whose attention is focused chiefly on the expressly political institutions and practices. These institutions, and the officials, procedures, and traditions associated with them, are viewed generally as the right or legitimate ones for the society. People thus confer authority on such institutions, accepting their existence and acts as legitimate and (normally) obeying them. In effect, popular acquiescence achieved through attachment to political institutions converts the structure of power to a *structure of authority.*

Political Change: Nature and Scope

It is this structure of authority—the merger of operative power structure and authoritative institutions accepted as legitimate—that contains the key to the definition of political change. *Fundamental* political change involves change in the structure of authority—in the basic distribution of power in the society *and* the expectations of people concerning its uses in the form of political decision making and major public policies. Associated with it or resulting from it will be major shifts in the patterns of distribution of the benefits and burdens of public policies and in the dominant political values of the society. (Implied are fundamental changes in economic and social structures as well, but these are not the identifying political indicia of political change in its independent form.)

Marginal political change involves the incorporation of new groups or strata of the population into a larger role within the system, perhaps even the inclusion of a few members into the penumbra of the existing structure of authority; the modification of existing policies so as to direct fewer burdens or more benefits at particular groups or strata; and the incremental evolution of political values. But it does *not* involve change in the basic makeup or goals of the existing structure of authority. Nor does it imply major shifts in the distribution patterns accomplished by major policies, or more than linear, step-by-step changes in political values.

This distinction is the basis of my opening assertion that there have been no occasions of fundamental political change in the nearly two centuries since the Constitution was ratified. Such changes as the extension of the right to vote to women or the 18 to 21 year age group are clearly not fundamental change. They were not changes in the operative structure of authority, but merely the inclusion of new strata in marginally larger participatory roles. Other constitutional amendments and such major policies as the Wagner Act or the Marshall Plan represent at most instances of marginal change, in the sense of increased participatory rights or reallocation of benefit-burden patterns. They involved neither significant change in then-existing structures of authority nor in the expectations of people about how and why power should be employed in politics. I am not suggesting that they were unimportant, of course, but merely that they do not constitute fundamental change properly conceived.

The decade of the 1930s was a period when fundamental change might have occurred, but it did not. What changes took place were at levels below that of the structure of authority itself. Several marginal changes in policy allocations, the inclusion of some labor bureaucrats at the peripheries of power, much symbolic reassurance, and the coming of the Second World War apparently forestalled fundamental change. (Some other important reasons why this period did not eventuate in fundamental change will be examined later.) The closest we have come to fundamental political change was in the era of the Civil War. But the victory of the North makes that period better understandable as the consolidation of the long-continuing advance of industrial capitalism. If the South had succeeded, there would have been undeniably significant change in the structure of authority in both emerging nations. But, despite drastic social and economic changes before, during, and after the Civil War, the extent of political change—at the level of the structure of authority and the basic values of expectations of people regarding its actions—was relatively slight. It is more accurately seen as marginal than fundamental.

An enduring dilemma in defining and analyzing political change is the equation to be struck between quantities of identifiable change and the duration of time in which they occurred. How much change must occur within how short a time period, to constitute fundamental rather than merely marginal change? Lively disagreements exist about the proper time frame to be used in analysis, and for some the issue hinges entirely on the choice of time span. The threshold I employ, however, emphasizes the *character* of the change rather than quantities or time. No matter how much of what I have defined as marginal change occurs in a very short time, it would not constitute fundamental change; the latter is identifiable only qualitatively, by change of a certain level and kind. (The prospect of much marginal change in a very short period of time is so unprecedented and so unlikely—and so likely to be accompanied by change in the structure of authority in any event—that the issue seems exclusively one of definition. I raise it here only to stress the nature of the distinction being made between fundamental and marginal change.)

The Civil War illustration makes clear, however, that there remains the question of how much change in the structure of authority and popular expectations must occur in what period of time to constitute an occasion of fundamental change. Again, the answer is better cast in qualitative terms than by attempting to specify terms of years. I reserve the label *fundamental change* for clearly visible alterations of the basic makeup and goals of the structure of authority which are accompanied by widespread popular recognition of that change and of its implications for the future use of political power. This implies a relatively short time span, without specifying it more precisely. It may also suggest a further distinction between fundamental and marginal change, having to do with the subjective response of the mass public. Fundamental change is first a *de*legitimating process, and then legitimation of a new structure of authority and associated political institutions and purposes. Marginal change is a *re*legitimating process, in which the existing structure of authority and institutions draw new support in exchange for limited reconstruction. Applied to the experience of most Americans at the time, the Civil War cannot be called an occasion of fundamental change.

There are, of course, many important distinctions to be made between degrees and kinds of marginal change, as well as between that huge category and the elusive one of fundamental change. But my purpose here is to understand fundamental change, why it has not occurred in the past, and whether and how it may come about in the United States in the late twentieth century. For that reason, we focus only on kinds of fundamental change, and certain characteristics of the processes associated with it.

Political Change: Direction and Process

Change may take either of two very broad directions. One is toward wider distribution of the material products of the society, greater sharing of political power, and expanded opportunities for human development. The other is toward narrower distribution and stronger constraints in each of these categories, or increasingly rigid defense of the status quo. The former is the possibility on which our primary attention will be concentrated. But, just as much can be learned about change through the study of stability, so can the analysis of reactionary or fascist tendencies yield insight into the nature and problems of human liberation.

The direction of change is not foreordained by evolving social conditions or events. Circumstances do not place only one form of fundamental change on the agenda at a time: the same forces that make possible the most equalitarian and liberating reconstruction of our society also raise the probably more likely prospect of a modern American brand of fascism. The actual outcome—once basic social forces have set the stage—depends on how wisely and effectively people act to bring about the society they prefer. The stage is not often set. Fundamental change has not been on the American agenda since the 1930s, for example. But when it is, when deep-running economic and social forces converge to force change of some kind upon a society—as is the case in the decade of the 1970s—men and women who understand their opportunities can intervene and make their history. Once the inertia of the status quo is overcome and fundamental change becomes possible, the direction of that change becomes an issue to be decided in major ways by purposeful human actors.

For this reason, it is essential to focus on certain key characteristics of the process by which fundamental change occurs. Almost by definition, fundamental change assumes a major role for people not now included within the structure of authority—i.e., a bottom-up process of change. Actions by people now in power will be important, of course, perhaps in provoking popular outbreaks, ineptly failing to contain thrusts toward change, or contributing to governmental paralysis and delegitimization. But elite-initiated, top-down processes of change are much more likely to be associated with marginal change results.

The necessity that numbers of people be involved does not resolve the issue of how or to what end. It does make continuingly possible that form of mobilization and submission to organization that can lead to fascism, hierarchical socialism, or other totalitarianisms. Indeed, there are many opportunities all along the way for the most sincere and compassionate seekers of fundamental change to become the mirror images of the worst qualities of those whom they would replace—as the history of such movements amply documents.

The process by which change is sought is absolutely crucial to the prospect of achieving something better than that which now exists. Moreover, it is the only clue that we have to what may be in store. We cannot know for sure the characteristics or quality of life of a society that has not yet been brought into being. But we can gain a glimpse of it in the process of its becoming—in the kinds of people involved in seeking to achieve it and in the character of their actions. With due regard for the exigencies of the struggle and the fact that improvement on the character traits of this society requires time and effort, such people must exhibit intellectual and moral grounds for our respect and confidence. If they are no different from those whom they struggle against, there is little prospect that the society they would create will be either.

In this context, we may note the relationship between revolution and fundamental change. Revolution is one form of attempted fundamental change, the effort to seize state power—thereby altering the structure of authority—by means of force. Of all revolutionary attempts at fundamental change, very few succeed in acquiring state power, still fewer in accomplishing fundamental change, and only a handful in achieving desirable forms of such change in the long run. To alter the structure of authority in our sense requires not just substituting new members for the old. It requires also that the goals of that structure of authority be altered and that masses of people recognize, accept, and confer legitimacy upon the new political purposes, institutions, and uses of power. Thus, a coup d'etat, which normally only replaces one ruling group with another, would not fall within this definition of revolution. Nor would mere rebellions, no matter how violent or destructive, because they are essentially protests which do not seek to acquire state power or alter the structure of authority.

There is no necessary connection between fundamental change and revolution. The latter is only one form that the process of fundamental change may take. It may seem the dominant or even the only such process, because it is obvious that ruling groups normally do not submit gratefully to their own replacement. But there are other routes, involving various levels and kinds of both purposeful and spontaneous violence, which we shall explore later. That some Americans see no alternatives between utter hopelessness and full-scale violent revolution is attributable once again to our inexperience and innocence concerning political change. So is the tendency to seize upon some nineteenth-century European (or twentieth-century Cuban or Chinese) model of change and uncritically apply it to the United States today.

Thus our immediate goal is to develop the capacity to think more creatively, systematically, and theoretically about political change. We need to be able to select the viable methods and insights from other times and other places, combine them with careful analysis of the conditions and potential of the present, and emerge with an understanding of the opportunities for fundamental change in the United States today. This capability is only one part of the larger task of developing ways of thinking that take us outside the current boundaries of American orthodoxies and enable us to see and become a society far better than we are. A start on this task is sketched in the next section.

A STRATEGY OF CONCEPTUAL RECONSTRUCTION

The basic thesis of this book is that the indispensable prerequisite to constructive fundamental change is reconstruction of the way we think, both about change and more generally. We are, individually and collectively, locked into a particular set of concepts, language, and logic that nurtures one specific way of understanding and interpreting the world. That way of knowing, thinking, and understanding is deeply rooted in our culture, and serves to blind us to all that is not consistent with the particular form of social order that we live in. No constructive or liberating fundamental change in that social order can be accomplished unless we can first develop the concepts and other mental tools that enable us to imagine another social order *and* how it might come about. Without this, we shall inevitably find that the result of the most favorable conditions and strenuous efforts is sheer frustration, marginal change, or something worse than we now have. The failure of fundamental change in the past, and the lack of viable programs for fundamental change today, are directly attributable to the failure to break the conceptual chains laid upon us by our way of thinking and knowing.

The appropriate summary term for the culturally grounded concepts, language, logic, and other basic mental tools and style just referred to as "way of thinking" is *consciousness*. It is a deeply meaningful term with a long and respectable history, signifying the mental processes involved at the earliest stages of human self-awareness, concept formation, perception, and cognition. But it has recently been drastically mis- and overused, effectively trivialized by the forces and current tendencies of our status quo. Various counterculturalists, starting with Charles Reich's innocent superficialities, have joined with facile revolutionaries to make it an empty slogan. At a subsequent stage, I shall try to rehabilitate the term and recapture the heritage. For the present, I stress only the crucial significance that reconstruction of conceptual capability—ways of thinking and knowing—carries for the possibility of fundamental change.

Is it possible for us to deliberately and fundamentally reconstruct the way we think? I think it is, and that coming to grips with the problem and process of political change provides a unique opportunity to do so. Thinking about *change* forces us to examine many of the basic tools with which we now think, for they too might be different within a different social order. We shall be forced to ask what is *true*, and how we *know* what is true or false, and perhaps even whether such categories make sense. We shall have to be sensitive to possibilities and potentialities, to a wide variety of unmeasurable forces at work to shape and reshape our evolving world. Seeing all in motion, emphasizing what might be instead of only what now is, and employing a wide variety of "evidence," we may well break some of the bounds of our familiar, empirical social science. In short, to think about change is to think *differently*, and that is the goal of this essay.

The exploration of political change in the United States that follows thus proceeds on two levels. The first consists of plain facts and familiar styles of analysis, applied to the problem of change so as to generate some sense of when, why, and how it does and may occur. The second, however, is a continuing series of questions and speculations about the conceptual reconstruction necessary to understand and achieve fundamental change. Readers will be asked to become increasingly self-conscious about how they think or know, and how this is related to understanding social and political change. It may be that complete conceptual reconstruction can occur only through acceptance or development of a whole new way of thinking or consciousness. But that is not attempted here. I seek only to establish the basic thesis just set forth, that fundamental change depends on such conceptual reconstruction, and to provide some opportunity for alert and purposeful readers to gain that insight and experience such understanding for themselves.

The plan of the essay reflects these two levels or goals. In Part 1, I shall state in a summary fashion some of the most basic facts and interpretations about the circumstances of the United States today. I do this primarily to show the premises from which I begin, the understanding of what is wrong and why that serves as a starting point for all that follows. I do not think it necessary to argue this case in great detail. This is well done in many sources referred to in the bibliography, and most readers probably already *feel* the existence of crisis-level problems and the approaching societal and personal crossroads in any event. But we must have some base from which to proceed.

Part 1, therefore, looks at current conditions—at the American political economy and structure of authority, at our supportive political values, ideology, and consciousness, and at what the trend of present problems, forces, and conditions offers us in the way of alternatives for the immediate future. We shall see that our rigidifying politico-economic system is undergoing destructive pressure from an unprecedented number of economic and social problems. Circumstances have converged to forestall solutions or adaptation, and we have been set at a crossroads where basic change of some kind is inevitable. We cannot hold on to our present, and perhaps not even to evolutionary projections from it. Fundamental change is on the agenda, for the first time in two generations.

A further purpose of Part 1, however, is to show the intimate connection between *objective conditions* (the apparent reality of things and forces external to us) and *subjective interpretations* (the personal understanding that we have of such conditions, grounded in the concepts and expectations we hold). What we see as social reality is powerfully affected by what is in our heads to begin with, and we must analyze both together. In each chapter, therefore, we look both at the "facts" and at how we understand those facts, at the objective and subjective sides of our world and the significance of the connection between them.

In the case of the conditions analyzed in Part 1, the prospects of change are powerfully affected by subjective interpretations. Many Americans sense the inability of our politico-economic system to cope with current conditions and problems. But, locked within our present system of thought, they do not know how to articulate their concerns or conceive of viable solutions. Some manifest their malaise in the grossest forms of self-indulgence, from drugs to pornography to hedonism. Others turn to religious revivals, rock music, or other absorbing, escapist, pseudosocial activities. Still others reach for the most rigid versions of fundamentalist values and ideology, often demanding that the defects of our current lives be cured by governmentally coerced compliance with such orthodoxy. Meanwhile, problems remain unsolved if not deliberately ignored, the society continues to disintegrate, and tensions build ever closer to the ultimate crossroads. Within the confines of our current way of thinking, however, the only alternatives are a much more highly organized and controlled version of the state capitalism with which we have begun to flirt, a modernized and Americanized brand of fascism, or sheer chaos.

The implications of this intimate connection between objective conditions and subjective understanding should become steadily clearer as we proceed. For example, we shall analyze the structure of power in the United States today. But we shall see that it is connected to a particular way of thinking, which in effect justifies and helps us sustain that power structure. To achieve fundamental change, therefore, it will first be necessary to develop a way of thinking that not only denies the legitimacy of that power structure but provides ways of ordering a society so that neither it nor similar power structures are necessary, and also suggests the kinds of actions amidst today's concrete social reality that can move the society in that direction.

In Part 2, I take up the exploration of the subjective component, in particular the crucial threshold of consciousness and consciousness change, in an intensive manner. Our present consciousness serves as a second line of defense for the status quo, backing up our more explicitly political ideology in ways that prevent us—when we *do* see the contrast between ideology and reality—from conceiving of real alternatives. Instead, it leads us into vain reform efforts or equally self-limiting radicalism. The fact that radicalism can be no more than another version of the existing consciousness can be understood only through some extended exploration of the nature and implications of our current consciousness.

The central issue of bringing about constructive fundamental change is the question of how consciousness change can be accomplished, first for some and then for all. My argument is that it is a social process involving the most painful readjustment of the individual's personal identity. People are in effect learning to identify with, and live in terms of, a social order that has not yet come into being, while they still exist physically within *this* society. Such consciousness change is made possible in the first instance by the character of social conditions, but achieved in part through hard effort and full investment of one's life in particular forms of social process with like-minded others. We shall also explore a variety of ways in which larger and larger numbers of people may experience the same basic consciousness change. The essence, once again, is learning to think quite differently than we do now—to employ a whole new frame of reference, judge with different values and standards, and generally experience a new world with entirely different potentialities and prospects. Merely to enumerate the scope of change involved is to stress the difficulty and improbability of achieving it, and perhaps to imply that some change-seekers will be tempted to realize mass-consciousness change primarily through some form of post-revolutionary coercion. But we shall examine several other possibilities as well.

Once the question of consciousness change has been dealt with in some way, constructive fundamental change becomes possible. And the remaining issues, while important in their own right, are strictly secondary by comparision. One issue has to do with the identity of the primary agency expected to fuel the process of change. For at least the last century, many have assumed that the working class had to be the source of any thrust toward fundamental change. More recently, the impression has grown that industrial working classes are essentially satisfied and no longer potentially capable of societal reconstruction. Those who subscribe to this view see either a new working class of white-collar people, minorities, or leading layers of cultural change movements, such as militant young people, as the modern agents.

Another issue that must be explored is that of the need for, and character of, the organization(s) required to bring about constructive fundamental change. Some deny the need for any organization, or insist that there be as many small units as possible. Others argue for one massive national organization representing all elements of the currently dispossessed, both as a means of bringing people together and of mobilizing the necessary force to overturn this system and defend the new one against reaction from the right. Other issues will also be considered, including the problem of justifying alternative systems and avoiding the failings of other fundamental change movements.

Third (Part 3), we shall concretize and refine our developing image of how constructive fundamental change can occur, and further develop our insight into the requisite conceptual reconstruction process, through critical evaluation of several contemporary prescriptions for change. In essence, we shall begin with certain principles derived from Part 2, and add to or more fully understand their nature by contrasting them with the often very different assumptions, concepts, and ways of thinking involved in proposals made by others. Two categories of fundamental-change prescriptions will be examined: those which identify themselves as or with particular versions of the Marxist-socialist tradition, and all the other home-grown varieties that currently fill our bookshelves and streets. Much that is valid will be drawn from these prescriptions, and we shall see both convergence and contrast with the growing body of principles which we are working into a rudimentary theory of political change. But much will also have to be rejected as utopian, archaic, proto-fascist, self-destructive, or simply support for the current status quo under cover of flaming rhetoric. The latter category, a sort of sheep-in-wolf's-clothing, is by far the largest.

The fundamental change process which I envision requires the growth of a new culture, and associated social relationships and structures, inside and along with the old society. Of course, there will be conflict with that existing social order; it cannot tolerate serious challenge, and will seek to incorporate, insulate, or crush its rising replacement. The struggle, however, poses options visible to more and more people. At this stage, it is essential that the form of the future be visible in at least some ways in the present—in the human relationships, or in the program, of the change-seekers, for example. If it is *not,* there will be neither ethical nor (I think) practical claims *or* prospects of becoming the new society. If it *is,* social conditions, progressive delegitimization of the present structure of authority, and timely human intervention may in time transform such pockets of potential into a new social order.

Notice that this cannot be an instantaneous process. No cataclysmic moment brings about social transformation; at the most, such a moment follows a period in which basic undermining forces have been eating away at the status quo and its supports. There must be time during which the multiple elements of fundamental change converge, escalate, and generate the social process that can culminate in transformation. This suggests a crucial role for the defense of the traditional civil liberties, a point that seekers of fundamental change would do well to keep in mind. The process envisioned above depends on the availability of certain basic rights. Constructive fundamental change is inevitably vulnerable to repression, and fascism can always intervene and stamp out its future. Only the vigorous defense of civil liberties makes possible the day when the need for them is past.

A SUMMARY NOTE

On the *first* level of exploration referred to on page 12, we are in effect synthesizing two broad approaches to achieving fundamental change to produce a version or theory which combines the best of each. The first of these approaches is that which emphasizes the structure of the political economy today, as the system of power with points of vulnerability, and attempts to mobilize people to attack it and transform it. The second is the cultural or value change route, which argues that social action against the current power structure is bound to fail, or at best to result in no more than a transfer of power to some new group of oppressors, and that only cultural and value change can—but will, more or less automatically—transform the society. It should be obvious that each of these, by itself, is incomplete; and that only synthesis of the two offers any real prospect. Such an effort thus provides a useful, if rather mechanical, service to understanding and perhaps action within our present social reality and consciousness.

But, on the *second* level of exploration referred to earlier, some more demanding and potentially rewarding effort is involved. There is a threshold to be first conceptualized and then crossed. On *this* side, politics and political change are conceived of as processes occurring in an objective world which can be observed and understood by man through detached analysis. On the *other*, the observer merges with those processes, becoming an integral part of them, and they in turn become extensions or projections of the observer-participant's conceptual capabilities. The subjective-objective distinction dissolves, as man and world are understood as interacting parts of a larger whole—a totality of people and things in motion toward a future now unknown but potentially open to being shaped by appropriate conscious action.

The task of conceptual reconstruction is first to see this threshold; next, to develop the conceptual capabilities to envision what human relationships and social systems might be, given other social conditions; and finally to understand how today's social "reality" can enter upon a process of becoming such an ultimate future. Patently, it is neither possible nor desirable for one book to do all of these things. It is not possible, if only because one cannot do it for and by oneself, or through any nonsocial process. One real step would be quite enough. In a crucially important sense, to see one's world differently *is* to change it. Perhaps we shall break through to the point of self-consciousness about what reconceptualization means, intellectually and socially, and what the next steps involve and imply.

In my eyes, it would not be desirable to even attempt more. This is because of the absolutely fundamental and uniquely personal nature of the combined epistemological-and-value choice that individuals may be able to open and make for themselves—if they are successful in the struggle for conceptual reconstruction. Education-as-it-should-be involves becoming aware of the nature and sources of one's values and way of thinking, and of their implications for the development of human potential. The goal is to peel off layer after layer of accumulated assumptions, values, concepts, and premises, in hopes of reaching the point where the elements of and values implied in one's way of thinking are laid bare. At this point, and I think only at this point, individuals can experience a moment of truly self-directive capability. They can choose among the available packages of (combined) values and ways of knowing, an act of autonomy denied to all but a few by the inevitable effects of the society we live in. This is the essence of what it means for human beings to intervene consciously in history.

I shall return to this theme in the final chapter. If the point were entirely clear now, there would be no need for this book. With confidence in my unclarity, therefore, if not in the difficulty of the point itself, there are eight chapters between us and that stage.

NOTE

1. Charles Reich, *Greening of America* (New York: Bantam Books, Inc., 1970).

1

System in Crisis:
Seeing It Clearly

CHAPTER TWO

The Structure
of Authority
in the United States

To speak sensibly to change, we must first have some idea of the basic outlines of the present, and of the major forces at work to subvert it. We can hope to catch a glimpse of its vital features today, in order to better understand its problems and the potential new forms toward which it is being propelled.

This chapter analyzes the social sources and basic character of the structure of authority in the United States today. A structure of authority consists in part of the people who are at the top of a society's power stratification system, together with the social and economic structures from which they derive and sustain their power resources. But its other side is the legitimacy accorded to the political institutions and purposes associated with that power structure—the popular values, ideology, and acquiescence that convert power into authority. Thus we shall also examine the nature of such support in the United States today, and its grounding in our ideology and consciousness. Throughout our analysis, for example, we shall repeatedly see that the latter insulate us against recognition of reality and cover our real political world with a most benevolent gloss.

No effort will be made to present either a new or an elaborately detailed analysis of the distribution and usage of power in the United States. That has been well done many times, and the doubtful reader is welcome to refer to the many works discussed in the bibliographical essay. Such studies are familiar to many, and many readers intuitively sense the validity of their conclusions in any event. My purpose in this chapter is to highlight certain primary features of that power system, such as its roots in the economic system and the imperatives that flow from that fact, and to show how certain myths and characteristics of our way of thinking combine to provide defenses or even support for that status quo. In a sense, I am merely stating the premises from which the book begins.

But I am also sketching the basic background from which we can begin to understand our current social, economic, political, and intellectual crisis. What characterizes the power base of our current structure of authority, the American political economy, is only partly the size of its corporate units, and only partly the thorough integration of the "private" economy with state power. The most significant comment to be made is that it is still a *capitalist* system, with associated needs (growth, investment opportunities, government support) and weaknesses (tendencies toward inflation or depression, maldistribution of income and wealth, rigidity).

In the next chapter, we shall see that we face some quite intractable problems of staggering consequence. These problems stem to an extent from late twentieth-century conditions, but their character and the range of possible solutions to them are shaped in fundamental ways by the nature of our (capitalist) political economy. The combination of this system with these problems is the basic building block of the contemporary crisis. To put it bluntly, there can be no real solution to these problems that does not imply fundamental change in this system, for system and problems are extensions of each other; they are locked together in unwelcome but necessary and inextricable embrace.

THE CHARACTER OF THE AMERICAN POLITICAL ECONOMY

Popular images of one's own society tend to lag well behind the actual facts. This is certainly true in the case of our ideology, symbolism, and public rhetoric, most of which has barely made it past the New Deal. But so much has been written about the "post-industrial state" in recent years that we may wrongly believe that some totally new system has come into existence. When it comes to talking about the economy and its workings, we turn futuristic. Science and technology, computerization and automation, mergers, growth, and internationalization are taken to have converted the economy to some wholly new and not yet understood system.

Let us grant immediately that the individualistic, property-oriented, profit-seeking farmers and small businessmen of the early nineteenth century have given way to an economy dominated by massive corporations. In scale of organization and scope of activities, these giants far exceed many states and countries, and in some respects the United States government itself. General Motors, the world's largest, is often cited in illustration. A former counsel for the Senate Antitrust Subcommittee[1] describes GM and the large corporate world in typical fashion:

> General Motors' yearly operating revenues exceed those of all but a dozen or so countries. Its sales receipts are greater than the *combined* general revenues of New York, New Jersey, Pennsylvania, Ohio, Delaware, and the six New England States. Its 1,300,000 stockholders are equal to the population of Washington, Baltimore, or Houston. GM employees number well over 700,000 and work in 127 plants in the United States and 45 in countries spanning Europe, South Africa, North America, and Australia.... General Motors ... should not be thought of as unique. Some 175 other manufacturing, merchandising, and transportation companies now have annual sales of at least a billion dollars. One, rivalling GM in the grandeur of its operations, is Standard Oil of New Jersey. With more than a hundred thousand employees around the world (it has three times as many people overseas as the U.S. State Department), a six-million ton tanker fleet (half again bigger than Russia's), and $17 billion in assets (nearly equal to the combined assessed valuation of Chicago and Los Angeles), it can more easily be thought of as a nation-state than a commercial enterprise.

There is no end to ways of characterizing the size and significance of the corporate economy. Another route is to contrast the assets, sales, or activity of the 100, 200, or 500 largest firms with the remaining 99-plus percent of the more than 300,000 firms that exist in the country. Still another is to show the extent of dominance of the leading one, two, or three companies in nearly all the major industries. Whatever the route taken, the result is the same image of vast size, concentration of power, and domination of markets.

But what does all this mean? Size, complexity, interdependence, and technological advancement are tangible features of considerable importance. They have not, however, changed the basic nature of the system, nor its fundamental operating principles and imperatives. Individualistic, property-oriented, profit-seeking giant corporations have replaced the farmers and small businessmen of 150 years ago, *changing the players but not the rules or goals of the game.* Despite admittedly great changes in form and operating characteristics, this is still a capitalist economy, in which the only real measure of success is *profit.* This crucial principle—the single most important motive force underlying the whole American political economy—is often lost sight of amidst our fascination for what is new and, presumably, significant.

These very changes in form and operating characteristics, of course, are both revealing in their own right and indicative of possible directions of future evolution. For example, there have been vast changes in the occupational characteristics of the population in the last century. Literally millions of farmers have been forced off the land and into the industrial work force. Independent small businessmen have declined drastically as a proportion of employed persons and in share of business activity. Vast increases have occurred in white collar fields, such as professional, managerial, and service workers; government services in particular have shown one of the most dramatic increases of all occupational categories. A technological economy and burgeoning sales, advertising, and office worker needs have spurred great advancement in educational levels of the population, to the point where nearly half of all high school graduates enter some kind of further training.

Once again, however, it is possible to be carried too far by evidence of change. Nearly half of all working people remain in blue-collar jobs, on assembly lines, in mines, in municipal services, in construction, and so forth. For the most part, they are engaged in menial physical labor, at hourly wages, and subject to layoff on short notice. Still more millions are unemployed or underemployed. Others are held on welfare. About half of all Americans are either below the "poverty line" or so close to it that they are "marginal"—i.e., could drop below it in the event of an accident, serious illness, or long-term layoff. Nor has there been significant change in the distribution of income in the twentieth century. According to the U.S. Census Bureau, the lower *half* of all income-earners still receives only slightly more than 20 percent of the income generated within this economy, while the top *tenth* receives almost 50 percent more, or 30 percent of all income. About half of all families earn less income per year than is required for the U.S. Department of Labor's official "modest but adequate" family budget. For many people, the smug characterization "Affluent Society" is a cruel joke.

The Integration of Economy and Polity

Perhaps the most significant change, one with profound implications for our purposes, has been the nearly complete integration of the new corporate economy with the political system. This integration has three dimensions. The *first* is internal integration within the corporate and financial sectors of the economy itself. Not only do a handful of giant firms dominate whole markets, but they also dominate their suppliers and subcontractors. The sweeping wave of mergers in the 1950s and 1960s created new holding companies with interests in broadly diversified areas, and many large firms now own others in totally different fields.

Where integration is not achieved through such direct domination or outright ownership, it may come about through ownership of controlling shares of stock. Mutual funds, pension funds, and insurance companies are in a position to exercise significant control over many major corporations. But an even more important source of integration are the trust department assets and loan capabilities of the major commercial banks. Through control of the voting rights of great blocks of stocks held in trust and the leverage involved in providing expansion capital, a few key banks develop influence over wide sectors of the corporate system.

Thus, ownership and control flow back and forth between the major units of the economy. Extensive interlocks, in which officers or members of the board of directors of one bank or manufacturer sit on the board of directors of one or several other corporations or banks, sew the system firmly together. Initiative is not easy to locate, given the hidden nature of much stock ownership and the reluctance of insiders to reveal secrets of control. Pinning down the locus of control precisely may not be crucial; the degree of integration is such that decision makers so fully share interests and experience that coherent judgment and action are likely without conscious direction. But most close observers, such as the House Banking Committee, tend to see the top ten banks of the nation at the nerve center of the system.

The *second* type of integration is the complete meshing of the "private" economy with government. The separation of the economic and political spheres was always more rhetoric than reality. From the early days of Hamilton's efforts to promote manufacturing, government was used to aiding specific industries. But government was only sporadically used, because it was not necessary to profitable operation of most businesses.

The nineteenth century's collection of ad hoc land and franchise grants, tariff provisions, etc., began to be balanced in the early twentieth century by regulatory measures, as reformers sought to use government to regain control of the economy. Although business resisted at first, the more forward-looking sectors saw that some government action was inevitable, and that cooperation could be turned to advantage. Cooperation not only bought reduced public clamor, but it provided opportunities to more subtly shape government actions as they developed. With the New Deal, such innovations as NIRA codes, subsidies, war expenditures, and a variety of emergency measures enlisted the support of other elements of the business world because they provided immediate tangible benefits. World War II provided the final stage in business' recognition of the uses of government. Massive government borrowing and spending finally brought the country out of the Depression. The many businessmen then in government, as well as others, soon realized that fiscal policy management and government spending could serve many desirable goals.

Three decades later, the boundaries between the economic and political spheres are only arbitrarily distinguishable. And what used to be "government" is clearly the junior partner in the newly combined firm. Government is the revenue-raising agent, the rationalizer, and the stabilizer of the society. But its priorities, its personnel, and its policies are either those of the economic system, or ones consistent with the imperatives of that system. Patterns of tax breaks, subsidies, grants, and direct purchases support broad sectors of the economy. Fiscal and monetary measures are adapted to serve the growth and inflation-managing needs of its major components. An elaborate system of social welfare provisions mutes complaints and provides a floor of sorts under aggregate demand. An equally elaborate network of regulatory measures symbolically reassures a potentially anxious public while it rationalizes competition. The policies of government and of business are so intertwined and mutually supportive that no citizen can tell where one ends and the other begins.

In a sense, this is a completely natural product of the evolution of the American economy *and* the apparent preferences of the American people. Regulation of business, social welfare measures, and efforts to prevent depression and inflation are all activities of government that were sought and are approved by broad segments of the general public. But this is just the point. They were designed with the characteristics and needs of this particular—capitalist—economic system in mind. They are limited to those types of things and funding levels that are acceptable to the major elements of this economy. They are managed now by businessmen in government, and by politicians whose values and vision are the same. When they threaten to impinge upon business in important ways, they are cut back or ignored.

Thus the first priority that underlies the entire pattern of government activity, social welfare and regulatory measures included, is the furtherance of the growth and other needs of the economic system. This is a matter of sheer necessity: no politician, and particularly no President, can face the prospect of serious unemployment—and his only alternative is to do what is best for the development of the economy. Government has no choice but to play the junior partner role. Speaking bravely of its capacity to manage the economy and handle the problems of the day, it must meanwhile hope devoutly that the needs of the corporate capitalist economy will permit such things.

The United States as the Center of the World Political Economy

The *third* form that ongoing integration has taken is the merger of the American political economy with that of the world as a whole. Since the end of World War II, from which the United States emerged as the world's leading economic power, American dollars—often followed by military power—have penetrated and affected every corner of the globe. Vast aid programs first restored European demand for export products, and then became vehicles of political influence in the Cold War. Simultaneously, the American currency became the world's standard, and American policy makers became dominant in the World Bank and the International Monetary System. Investments overseas leaped forward, principally in Europe and Canada but also in Latin American and other Third World countries. Most major corporations became international in scope, acquiring plants and other productive facilities in several countries. In most cases, profit margins on overseas investments, raw material extraction, manufacturing, and trade are much higher than on domestic activities. Indeed, production overseas for sale in the United States is increasingly common practice for American corporations.

Although much of the initiative for this process was taken by large corporations and major investors, the United States government played its partnership role. All departments of the federal government maintain aggressive business-promoting staffs abroad, and the consistent policy of the United States is to persuade and pressure other countries into granting new opportunities for American trade and investment. Aid, grants, and loans are normally conditioned on recipients following practices acceptable to American capitalist priorities. Military power stands ready to help maintain friendly governments, if necessary against the efforts of their own people for self-determination.

As a result, the United States now stands at the center of the world economy. The advanced capitalist world is tightly linked into the American system through American ownership of many major businesses, other American investments, the presence of American corporations in their midst, competition from American products shipped in from the United States, and American pressure applied through the international monetary system. The socialist world can trade with the West only on terms set or approved by the United States, and is under constant competitive pressure from the more fully-developed American capabilities. The Third World is in debt to American and world bankers, and has only a firmly-maintained unfavorable balance of trade with which to seek to better itself. In the meantime, American investments in raw material extraction and single-crop production return great profits to the United States. Thus, what the American political economy needs, it is in a position to try to get. At the same time, integration is such that the health of each major national economy, including the United States', is intimately linked to the health of every other major economy. Inflation or depression can be exported in just the same manner as any other product, and a downturn in a major capitalist system can precipitate tremors through the world.

The American Power Structure

Power, as we defined it earlier, means the possession of resources (money, time, fame, institutional position, knowledge, oratorical skill, strength, etc.) which enable some people to influence the behavior of others. All persons have a certain amount of one or another of these resources, and thus some power. But obviously some have much more than others. The exercise of power involves transactions between people, in which those with relatively more resources cause those with less to adapt their behavior to the former's preferences. We may view society—any society, but here the United States—as a social pyramid, in which those few with the most resources are at the top and others are ranged below in layers according to the resources at their disposal. What results is a loose hierarchical arrangement, in which power is stratified and a relative few are in a position to manage the many. The latter, taken together, have much greater political power than those at the top, but they are neither self-conscious of their strength, inclined to use it, or coherently organized to do so if they were.

In this sense, there is obviously and remarkably a *power structure* in the United States—just as there is in most societies. We might logically now proceed to the much more important issues concerning the *nature* of that power structure (who rules, how did they get there, in whose interest do they act, what difference does it make?). But the concept of power stratification, indeed, the very idea of power itself, is immensely troubling to some Americans. Our ideology insists that the United States is a democracy, and that because all persons have one vote there can be no power disparities among them that are relevant to government. Our political consciousness deflects us away from confrontation with the realities of power in a variety of ways. These effects of ideology and consciousness are so important that we shall have to consider them in detail in a later chapter. But we can illustrate the nature of this conceptual obstacle by digressing for a moment to consider and dismiss two contemporary versions of this peculiarly American penchant for avoiding the facts of power.

The first of these rests on the premise that current conditions of social, economic, and political life are so new and distinctive that *power* no longer has its old meaning, and in particular there can be no stratification of power between the few and the many.

The central fact of contemporary life, this argument notes, is large-scale organization. Corporations, governments, churches, universities, etc., are impersonal bureaucratized machines overlapping each other and giving rise to a mindless, technological, "organizational society." Within this vast mechanism, there is no opportunity for purposeful, inner-directed action. There are only roles to be played—roles that are fixed by the organization's needs. Thus, no persons or groups of persons, no matter what their location within the apparatus, have real discretion over their actions. Those at the top of an apparent social pyramid are as trapped and powerless in their roles as anybody else in the society. *Nobody* is in charge of the great organizational machine, no matter what people at the top (or the bottom) may think. Thus, *nobody* can be said to have power in the sense of discretionary capacity to deliberately manage the society. Its only motive force stems from the self-maintenance needs that are built into the organizations themselves. The concept of a power structure is thus meaningless.

What this objection completely overlooks is nothing less than the foundation of the system itself. In effect, it raises a contextually valid insight (the importance of large-scale organization) to the level of an utterly exclusive societal interpretation. Ignored is the *basis* of the American social order and the *direction* and *purpose* of all its organizations—individualism, materialism, property, and profit—or, in a word, capitalism. The web of organizational structures is just that—a web, or coherent. It is purposeful, not random. It responds to the imperatives built into it from its inception, and to those who own it. It requires (and receives) the direction of those who sit at the nerve centers, the points where choices regarding uses of its lifeblood—capital—are made. The *needs* of these organizations, conceded by this objection to be the only motive force in society, are themselves shaped to provide the opportunity (the power) to some to control it.

The society does not run automatically, nor has modern capitalism become self-correcting. Peoples' demands, unforeseen events, and social problems require deliberate and rationally calculated management. Adaptation of the industrial system to its changing environment and solution of its periodic crises require purposeful actions. In neither case is the system's response pre-programmed, although the boundaries of what it can tolerate are clearly marked. Choices must be made, in which some will gain and some will suffer. Certain real people, some of whom are in particular positions, make these choices. Others suffer the consequences. No amount of ideological unwillingness to face the fact of power in action should prevent us from seeing this preliminary truth.

The other objection to the concept of power stratification as it is used here is a prescriptive one. Again, it proceeds from a valid and important insight, but employs that insight exclusively and non-contextually. The argument is simply that to use *power* as an analytic construct in the manner here proposed is to perpetuate the principle of hierarchy and dominance inherent in it. If we are ever to reach a society where people are truly equal, we must start by creating new ways of thinking about personal relationships, and the language we use is a key to that new mode of thinking. Thus, power must either be totally redefined, or better, abandoned and a new concept developed that would express equality and mutual trust and assistance in personal relationships.

The insight is valuable: our understanding *is* shaped by the meanings attached to the words with which we think. And clearly, reconstruction of our vocabulary and basic thought patterns would be necessary to a fundamentally altered and truly egalitarian society. But action to achieve such a society must nevertheless deal with the tangible realities of the present, insofar as those realities affect the prospects of achieving that future society. To put it bluntly, *who holds the guns, and whether they will fight,* are relevant questions. We do not analyze the present for the purpose of justifying it, nor merely in its own terms. We use those analytical constructs which free us from disabling myths and illusions, and which cut most revealingly to the core of those characteristics which are relevant to fundamental change. We do so from the perspective of a morally and socially justifiable future, with the focus on seeing the potential that the present has to become that future. Thus, the objection is well-intended, will ultimately be of central importance, but is currently inapplicable.

Each of these objections to the concept of power structure has shed useful light on the part played by subjective factors in understanding objective conditions. The American political consciousness erects many defenses on behalf of the existing social order, including surface ideologies, particular uses of logic, evidence, and other tools of thinking, and the meanings of words themselves. To understand the objective world, we must first wrench free of the political consciousness or system of thought which is associated with a specific social order. But we must keep contact with some "reality." This is a process which requires us to shift back and forth between the objective and subjective sides of our understanding, always conscious of the implications of one while apparently engaged with the other. Let us return now to our unfolding analysis of the structure of power in the United States.

A Ruling Class?

If some Americans balk at the concept of *power structure*, many are totally derailed by the thought of a *ruling class*. It sounds un-American, foreign, or archaic, and its use with respect to the United States appears imprecise, incongruous, or "ideological." Enough has just been said to indicate the sources of such aversions. Perhaps we can now exorcise the evil spirits from the term and calmly give it concrete meaning. In this way, we may be able to communicate succinctly about power stratification in the United States without resorting to a wholly new, unique (and euphemistic) vocabulary.

A *class* is a social grouping identifiable by certain objective characteristics, such as occupation, education, wealth, income, status, or relationship to sources of power in the society. When members of that social stratum share values, interests, goals, and orientations toward the society—and are aware that they share them with other like-situated persons—they are *class-conscious*. When a body of class-conscious persons from a single social grouping so dominates the levers of government, as well as the other sources of power, such that it can and does work its will on the major issues of the society, we have a ruling class.

Now for the hard parts (challenges are already audible). Is there such a ruling class in the United States? Of course there is. There is no requirement that every member be named, nor that the precise number of members be fixed exactly. Its boundaries are blurred and permeable (in both directions), and it is necessarily arbitrary to draw them at any given point in the upper reaches of the social pyramid. Moreover, certain intangibles of personality and style and attitude are conditions of full membership. But the existence of such a grouping is real and its impact is profound.

The American ruling class today consists of those persons whose ownership of, or positions within, the organizations and institutions of the combined econopolitical system grant them significant discretionary influence over the basic policy directions of that integrated system. Thus, membership may be grounded in certain types of great wealth, such as stockholdings. Or it may be grounded in institutional position, such as the presidency of a key bank or corporation, or a major post in the executive branch of the national government. Where membership is grounded in institutional position, it must also have an additional base, either in great wealth or in ample wealth plus complete psychosocial integration with the ruling class; our definition is *not* circularly dependent upon mere institutional office.

In either case, another precondition of membership is that individuals recognize their mutual interests and responsibilities, display regard for the furtherance of the class' interests in their actions, and operate consciously, coherently, and systematically—but with sophistication—to orchestrate societal acquiescence to action in accordance with the needs of the class. The ruling class is small, but its leverage is easily extended. Upper class persons have the very same interests and goals, there are many willing agents at hand, and the orthodox ideology prepares the middle class to come promptly to the support of ruling class needs and measures.

Can this ruling class be empirically discovered? Again, the answer seems obviously affirmative. Study after study documents the vastly disproportionate wealth of the upper one percent of Americans, the great stockholdings of a tiny share of even this group, the existence of distinctive cultural, attitudinal, and life-style characteristics of this group, and the population of major economic and political institutional positions of persons from, or closely associated with, this group. The functional linkages within the combined econopolitical system, already described, serve to enhance the influence-generating capabilities of a relative few well-placed persons.

But do they use this capability, and in ways that are different from what majorities in the country would prefer? Once more: yes, and yes. But can we prove it? Only if the dogged questioner can be separated at least temporarily from his or her democratic mythology and ideological insistence upon only certain kinds of logic and evidence. The latter is the task of later chapters. For the moment, it seems enough to point out that the actions of government—the patterned, tangible consequences of what government has done and not done over the years—have consistently and heavily favored the interests of the ruling class. Dozens of opportunities to serve the interests of lower classes—well over half the population—have not been taken. The United States lags well behind other advanced industrialized societies in proportion of gross national product devoted to social welfare purposes. Substantial proportions of the American population, as already indicated, live in poverty or precarious financial circumstances. Wealth and power are becoming more concentrated, not less so.

Majorities cannot be assumed to prefer such conditions. If their acquiescence seems demonstrated, it can only be for lack of perceived alternatives, the failure of leaders and institutions, symbolic manipulation and distraction, ideological quiescence, the perhaps deliberate management of educational and communication media, or similar causes and combinations of causes. However, we have not proved ruling-class action contrary to majority preferences through exhaustive factual evidence in a particular case. Must we split-screen videotape and simulrecord Mr. David Rockefeller of the Chase Manhattan Bank instructing President Nixon by telephone on a major policy move at the precise instant that Mr. George Gallup conducts a national survey that reveals a contrary public preference? Suppose we did. Undoubtedly, defensive ideology would leap to provide a dozen or more rationalizations: Rockefeller was right, Nixon had vital secret information, the survey was poorly constructed, the people didn't really understand or care much about the issue, Nixon was elected by the people to make such decisions, only the long run can tell, it's the whole system that counts, etc., etc. The point is that the nature of the evidence deemed appropriate and sufficient is dictated in major ways by our ideology, expectations, and general way of thinking and knowing.

As may be more than apparent, I see no serious obstacle to using the "ruling class" characterization in the United States. With reference to major questions and basic policy directions (*not* in regard to every bill before the Congress), a ruling class primarily exerts influence, normally gets its way, and orchestrates popular acquiescence besides. This ruling class operates coherently, but not necessarily consciously; often no consultation is necessary, because of its shared values, interests, experiences, and goals. Thus, it is neither all-pervading nor all-controlling. Nor is it a conspiracy managed through daily conference telephone calls. Perhaps readers would be more comfortable viewing the ruling class as a literary fiction useful for personifying the control mechanism of the integrated political economy. If so, they are welcome to do so. The distinction is not important, for it is the consequences of their (or such) action for the rest of the system and its people that count. But, whether ruling class or control mechanism, there *is* an effective, conscious manifestation of the views and interests of the dominant social grouping of the society.

THE AMERICAN STRUCTURE OF AUTHORITY

The picture we have sketched here is one of dominance by a very few, grounded in the major economic institutions. Wealth and power are very unequally distributed. And yet most Americans sense this only dimly, if at all; they have ample justification ready when they do, or else consider the fact only marginally relevant. For the most part, what they know to be wrong about social life and individual situations is attributed to personal failings, irresistible forces or fate, or the (correctable) mistakes or malfeasance of particular office-holders. Very few Americans blame their economic or combined econopolitical systems for the shortcomings of their life situations.

This phenomenon of trust in the basic rightness and competence of economic and political institutions and purposes is partly due to the favorable circumstances of American national development. In relative terms, most Americans are better off than other people of the world. But it is also attributable—as we have already seen in two illustrations in this chapter—to the support-generating power of our ideology and consciousness. These are the major sources by which the structure of power has, over time, cloaked itself in legitimacy and authority. That the latter are now genuine and powerful cannot be doubted, although later analysis will indicate that they are permeable and subject to fragmentation.

Ideology is a particular set of beliefs in the minds of some people about how some aspect of the social system does and should work. It is cast up out of the deeper realm of consciousness, and though it may be false or contradictory to another ideology in the same society, is nevertheless grounded in that consciousness. Political consciousness is comprehensive and pervasive, suffusing all areas of thought and action, individual and social. It encompasses ways of thinking—the underlying frame of reference, the subjects, the tools, and the style with which minds work—as well as the specific substance of beliefs. It sets parameters, provides purposes, and generally envelops and directs our understanding in a manner which is particular to a given society or culture. Ideology and consciousness frequently articulate with each other so that they become the first and second lines of defense of a given social order. How and why they do this are keys to our analysis of the subjective aspects of politics.

Ideology and Consciousness: Democratic Pluralism and Its Rationale

In our discussion of power stratification, we noted that much American resistance to that concept was attributable to strongly held democratic mythology. It is certainly possible for some, perhaps through frequent contact with reality, to come to the point of challenging the validity of dominant democratic ideology. But that ideology flows from and is supported by what we understand as knowledge, our sense of whether, how, and which specific questions can be answered by facts and logic, what premises are to be accepted as given and which are false, etc. From the latter, our political consciousness, there can be no appeal—it is the way we think. And it does not offer us many alternatives to our present society. Let us see how it supports the ideological refusal to see power as concentrated or used in nondemocratic ways.

Simple town-meeting, democratic mythology proceeds from "one-man, one-vote" principles to insist that all people are equal—i.e., equally powerful in political terms—and can therefore control their government and, through it, the entire range of forces that affect their lives. To talk of power structures, therefore, is to focus on nonexistent or irrelevant images, except as government officials represent the "agents" of the people. What such thinking rests on, of course, is a set of long-lived illusions. One is that politics is sufficiently separate from the social and economic systems that the obvious disparities in the latter spheres play no part in the former. Another is that elected representatives act in ways that accurately reflect popular preferences, and that such officials possess exclusive power and discretion over the actions of the national government. Thus, government policies are by definition the expression of the public interest, or at least the best possible accommodation among disparate interests that can be made under the circumstances. No amount of logic, evidence, or common sense observation has succeeded in laying to rest these benevolent beliefs.

The democratic-mythology objection, however, does not normally come forth in quite such bold and vulnerable fashion. It often takes more subtle forms, particularly in the hands of academic social scientists and journalists.

The most often used, and most effective, ideological barrier to real power structure analysis is that of *democratic pluralism.* This doctrine imposes democratic-mythology premises and assumptions upon description and interpretation of American politics. It starts by assuming that all people are or can be represented by interest groups, and that these groups will carry their constituents' claims into the halls of government, where all decisions are made, with a fully accurate reflection of the desires of the various groups, with regard to the merits of the situation—and without the intrusion of any other factors. This is democracy in action. Elites work out the right solution to conflicting popular wants and needs.

Much research can be undertaken, particularly with respect to the Congress and the administrative agencies, in which these assumptions can be "seen" as reality. They are at least plausibly true in some instances at this level. Of course, even where verifying cases are found, it is a highly elitist version of democracy that has been identified. But the democratic pluralists promptly leap to the (ideological) generalization that the workings of the entire political system have now been fully and evidentially characterized, and conclusively demonstrated to be "democratic." Starting with assumptions about the democratic nature of the system, they conclude, not surprisingly, that it is such. If it does not appear from the evidence to be thus open and democratic for certain individuals or particular groups, it is at least true of the system as a whole, which is what counts.

Political consciousness operates in a variety of ways to support democratic ideology. Sometimes the realities of power and its usage in the larger sense are ignored entirely, and description focuses exclusively on the most limited aspects of decision making within an institution of government. Thus, policy is made to appear as the product of two aberrant personalities. Or the rules and procedures of decision making are described as having operated mechanically to produce the outcome. Inevitably, consensus and practicality are major diversions, alternatives to analyzing power as such. Descriptions emphasizing policy makers' helplessness in the face of compelling conditions, the depth and breadth of their agreement, or their conformity with principles of the American political style, all are deflections from the real issue of power and its usage. So is the premise that politics is too complex to be effectively understood through the idea of power. So is the argument that power is too "vague" a concept for rigorous empirical analysis. Each of these amounts to consciousness-generated refusal to look at anything beyond the tip of the iceberg.

A supporting set of premises is methodological, and reflects the consciousness-fixed method of thinking noted earlier. The only appropriate evidence to sustain interpretations contrary to democratic pluralism are tangible and verified facts sufficient to exclude every other possibility at every necessary stage of the decision-making process. Because certain ways of thinking are so obviously "right," they are socially enforced by the arbiters of truth—the scholarly professions. If interpretations at odds with the already assumed democratic-interplay-of-groups model do not rest on this almost impossibly high standard of proof, for example, they are dismissed as "unproved" and "lacking in rigor." If some sociologists employ evidence about the upper-class social backgrounds or interests of decision makers, or some political scientists point to consistent patterns of policy outcomes favoring the same people or interests, another tactic is employed. The status and social-control pressures of the academic disciplines are invoked, and those same sociologists or political scientists are labelled "unprofessional" or "ideological." A similar process occurs in editorial newsrooms in the case of journalists.

Both the methodology and the standard of proof involved here, like the ideological premises before, are reflections of the dominant political consciousness. What cannot be demonstrated, by empirical research into one small aspect of a vast total process, cannot responsibly be considered an alternative to the "established" understanding of politics. What it would be an alternative *to,* that established understanding of politics, is of course none other than the democratic mythology—itself *assumed* from non-empirical sources, and thereafter "confirmed" by scraps of research and description undertaken under those same assumptions.

Academics and journalists, and through them students and the general public, are thoroughly imbued with this set of democratic pluralist assumptions and approaches. Sometimes their bestowal of a democratic gloss on American institutions and practices is deliberate, but probably more often it is quite unconscious. Even where untenable aspects of ideology are perceived and denied, the methods and standards of analysis remain those of the dominant political consciousness. Exhaustive fact-gathering, within the *existing frame of reference* about their nature and probably meaning, about *one small slice* of the governmental decision-making process, is still the only approach taken.

Where there is no capacity to think critically, or to connect visible shortcomings and unsatisfactory conditions with the character or workings of the basic economic and political systems, it is hard to resist the massive symbolic appeals to which all are subject. Nationalism, patriotism, materialism, religion, and democracy routinely surround and dissolve into our political institutions and purposes. The vast reservoir of legitimacy and authority on which they draw is constantly being refilled, with the result that the American structure of authority is threatened only under special circumstances. That exactly those conditions now obtain, however, is the argument of the next chapter.

NOTE

1. Richard J. Barber, *The American Corporation: Its Money, Its Power, Its Politics* (New York: E. P. Dutton & Co., Inc., 1970), pp. 1-2.

CHAPTER THREE

The Current Crisis and Our Real Alternatives

The United States is well into a process of economic decline and social disintegration that, together with evolving world conditions, is steadily building up to a crisis at least as severe as that of the 1930s and perhaps unprecedented in our history. Twenty-first century historians will probably date the beginning of the American decline from 1958, when unchallenged American economic hegemony ended in a severe recession, trade and payments difficulties, and dollar drainage. This was also the time in which the Soviet Union achieved scientific and technological (and nuclear) parity, the Third World was thereby freed to follow relatively independent courses, and Castro was about to seize power in Cuba. Internally, the civil rights movement was beginning the process that would ultimately place that most divisive of all American issues, race relations, insistently upon the political agenda. By 1958, the Alabama bus boycott and the first lunch-counter sit-ins had already indicated blacks' determination to achieve full citizenship by means appropriate to the character of white resistance.

Of course the date from which disintegration began is less important than the fact that it is proceeding, and at an increasing rate. The reasons are multiple, as is the case in all major social crises. We are faced with a convergence of so many destructive—and mutually reinforcing—conditions, problems, and forces that there are no remedies, or at least none which retain the basic outlines of our present economic and political systems. Not that we yet explicitly recognize that fact: some sense it dimly, but most continue complacently and others stridently reassert the validity of fading vestiges of outmoded values and ideology.

In this chapter, we shall first survey the range of problems that currently confront us, and show how they are both linked together and rooted in the basic structural features of our political economy. As such, they are insoluble without change in that system. Such change, of course, would not only require reconstruction of the entire basis of economic organization and activity in the United States, but also undermine the power base of the American power structure itself. Next, we examine the more explicitly subjective effects of ongoing disintegration, finding a general malaise that is loosening the grip of basic ideology for some, while inducing others to search more and more desperately for validation of it. Finally, we look at the real alternatives that lie ahead. Inevitably worsening problems and continuing deterioration in the legitimacy and authority of political institutions, combined with our present way of thinking and knowing, yield only three major possibilities. In order, we take up fascism, superorganized state capitalism, sheer chaos; the latter two, I argue, may be only way-stations en route to the first.

PROBLEMS OF THE AMERICAN POLITICAL ECONOMY

This is no place, and indeed there is little need, to engage in a detailed description of contemporary American problems. That task is accomplished, exhaustively if not well, by the lives we lead and the vast literature on the subject to which we can hardly avoid exposure. We shall consider here only certain underlying linkages among some major problems that are often treated as distinct sets of conditions and issues.

The analysis of linkage among tangible social problems leads toward a coherent theme. Just as the economic, social, and political systems have become integrated into a single political economy, so may (a) the sources of most problems, and (b) the constraints upon their solutions, be traced to the needs of that system for continued profit. This is the single most revealing and unifying interpretation of American problems that can be offered.

This and associated imperatives of the American political economy set the context, and fix the margins of possible solutions, for every social problem that exists. But it is neither the *only* nor a *complete* explanation. We shall touch upon other, less directly economic causes of problems and bases of linkage among them. This is not sinister or simpleminded "economic determinism." It is quite simply recognition that coherent understanding of a society's problems must begin with that framework which does the most to explain them. Other interpretive dimensions and secondary explanatory themes can then be woven into and around that basic framework, to reach ultimately toward full understanding. This section is therefore organized by the relationship of problems to the character and needs of the American political economy. The nonexclusivity of such a causal base, however, will be seen with increasing clarity as we proceed, although it remains of great significance even in the case of the status of minorities and women.

The Economic Crisis: Inflation and Depression

The paramount problem of the present decade is to avoid a depression. The necessary corollary is to maintain steady growth while managing inflation. These are in themselves massive tasks, and in many respects they may be mutually contradictory. The special circumstances of the post-World War II decades permitted rapid growth and relative prosperity, leading to a general euphoria about the capacity of built-in stabilizers and Keynesian principles to tame the business cycle. Then came the recession of the late 1960s, with simultaneous unemployment and inflation, and the recurring monetary crises of the early 1970s. Suddenly, complacency gave way to anxiety again. The greatest problem of them all was back. Once more, the threat of world depression hung over wage freeze, world trade, and monetary negotiations. What happened? How serious is this threat?

Surface manifestations suggest that it is real enough. Never before in history had there been such rapid inflation during a period of substantial (over six percent) unemployment. According to orthodox Keynesian economics, the two phenomena are mutually inconsistent. That is, inflation is associated with high employment, and unemployment with depressed prices. Moreover, the remedy for one is to promote the other—a tactic which seems bizarre when the economy already has too much of both. Thus, it appeared that something new was at work in the economy, something not understood and for which the orthodox analysis and remedies were inapplicable.

Moreover, the United States soon began to run unprecedented deficits in its balance of payments. The net outflow of American dollars rose to several billions per year, and gold reserves began to drain away. The dollar, once the world's standard of value, its "hardest" currency, began to seem inflation-eroded in the eyes of the world's speculators and central bankers. Devaluation with respect to other world currencies appearing necessary, both speculators and multinational (American) corporations dumped their dollar holdings and sought other ("harder") currencies. Soon the central banks of Europe were no longer able to support the dollar by using their reserves to keep purchasing them, and the United States was unable to redeem them in gold. Established exchange rates were thus abandoned (or the dollar was floated) for a period. Subsequently, the dollar was repeatedly revalued downward, and new exchange rates set.

But it soon became clear that these arrangements were only temporary, and that recurring monetary crises on this order were becoming standard. The great danger inherent in continuing uncertainty about the future values of various currencies with respect to each other is that world trade, upon which the economies of all advanced capitalist sector countries depend, may be paralyzed. Profitability of any such transactions, of course, depends upon predictability as to the value of the currencies in which payments are to be made some time in the future. And one of the first tactics employed by national decision makers faced with internal economic difficulties is the use of protective tariffs, which threaten to set off mutually destructive trade wars.

Wage controls are one of the more extreme measures available to a government which seeks to control inflation and assure other countries that it is determined to maintain the value of its currency. Although wage increases follow, rather than cause, inflation in prices—and have relatively little price-spurring impact by contrast with other factors in any event—the Nixon administration imposed wage controls as part of its efforts to cope with inflation and the world monetary crisis. At the same time, it was incurring record peacetime budget deficits in an effort to pump up the economy again, and thus contributing to the continuing inflationary spiral. In this context, wages were effectively held while inflation continued and prices kept rising—the result being that the *real* wages of working people began to decline.

The situation appears to be one of continuing long-term dilemma. Inflation seems necessary to spur the economy and reduce unemployment. But inflation undermines the value of the dollar, sparks monetary crises, and threatens world trade, on which all economies depend. And inflation reduces the real wages of the working classes, reducing not only their standard of living but also their demand for the products of the economy. Meanwhile, bondholders insist upon their returns, and speculators seek out the weakest parts of the system from which the quickest and greatest profits can be made. The credit system's postponement of the day when accounts must be settled is purchased at the cost of risking the collapse of all upon failure of any significant component—or upon mere failure of long-term confidence on the part of some. Clearly, a new instability and uncertainty has entered the picture, and efforts to avoid a depression must take precedence over all else on the public agenda.

The Economic Crisis: Distribution and Services

We have already noted that the structure of the American political economy skews the distribution of wealth and income so that a few at the top receive far more than the many at the bottom. The top 1 percent of the population, for example, owns 25 percent of the nation's wealth, including 76 percent of all corporate stock. Income distribution is only somewhat less skewed, and the pattern has been essentially fixed for the last seventy years. Poverty, or the immediate threat of poverty in the event of illness, accident, or prolonged layoff, are facts of life for about half the population. In 1970, unemployment or underemployment were experienced by nearly 30 percent of the population nationally, with higher levels in some cities and for minorities.

It need hardly be said that the causes of these conditions do not lie in the personal character or preferences of the people who are poor, unemployed, or underemployed. The causes are structural, i.e., they are rooted in characteristics of the political economy itself. The processes of mechanization of agriculture and industry, coupled with the principles of cost-cutting and profit-maximizing, have for the past decades steadily reduced the number of less-skilled jobs. Recent advances in technology have heightened this effect for several industries. Thus, literally millions of people are left behind, without the education or training to occupy the types of positions that the new economy requires.

Perhaps it is too costly to invest in the kinds of education and training necessary to prepare people for such jobs. More likely there are simply not enough jobs available. The labor force is growing every year, as new generations of better-educated persons begin seeking employment. The less skilled, older persons, and minorities are thus increasingly expendable. They have few or no means of defense against this process; less than 25 percent of working people are unionized, and the pressures upon unions to yield to efficiency in this sort of situation are very heavy. Moreover, the general wage level and any developing movement among employed workers for better working conditions are held down by the availability of this large pool of unskilled labor, so there is little incentive within the system itself to change this pattern.

But the economic as well as the social and human costs are very high. Approximately fifteen million Americans were on welfare in 1972, and probably more than twice that many were being maintained, either preceding or following their working years, through government assistance. Social security benefits went to more than 25 million persons, mostly retired workers and the children or families of deceased workers. Several millions of young persons are held out of the labor force annually in educational institutions or in some combination of underemployment and public assistance. Unemployment rates are highest among persons under 25, ranging up to 40 percent in some areas, and higher still for minority youth.

The problems of the welfare system in particular have recently appeared to be reaching crisis proportions, and it has drawn much attention. Despite the most stringent and often demeaning limitations and investigations, welfare rolls have climbed drastically and costs have skyrocketed. In particular, dramatic increases have occurred in the category of aid to families with dependent children, in most cases women with children but without means of support. Despite general agreement that "something must be done," and much talk of eliminating the costly administering bureaucracy in favor of either a negative income tax or guaranteed annual wage, nothing substantial has yet been done. The general principle continues to be that welfare recipients are personally responsible for their plight, and that if they only had more character or tried harder they would not need public assistance. This punitive attitude, perhaps supplemented by a desire to deflate public-service employees' wages, led in 1972 to the only innovation in recent welfare administration: the requirement that welfare recipients work a specified number of hours per week at state-assigned jobs in order to "earn" their checks.

The skewed pattern of distribution of the income and other rewards of the economy, however, is not the only dimension of this problem. The provision of basic social services also presents a crisis of major proportions. The physical condition of American cities is an oft-noted, but little acted-upon, condition of American life. In the area of housing, for example, decay and overcrowding in central city slums, particularly the ghettoes into which racial discrimination locks minorities, have been documented repeatedly—and sometimes underlined by riots. But it would take massive sums of money to make a dent on these conditions—to buy the land and buildings, and remodel or build new housing—sums that profit-maximizing large corporations and hard-pressed individual taxpayers alike resist strongly. And the current situation is highly profitable to the successful speculators and landlords who own the packed if crumbling ghettoes, and to the banks and insurance companies whose billions of dollars in loans, mortgages, and other financing depend upon their continued existence.

There is thus neither public nor private incentive, given the current political economy, to do anything about worsening housing conditions. The one initiative undertaken in this area, the federal urban renewal program, soon established itself as applicable chiefly for the purpose of removing urban residents, usually minorities, from areas of central cities where the expansion of business, educational, or cultural institutions was desired. The same situation exists with respect to other social services, such as urban transportation. Billions have been spent for the freeways that would move suburbanites into and out of the cities, carry commerce efficiently, and support the construction industry. But few cities have a transit system with the capacity to move their citizens with speed and comfort and reasonable cost.

Other social services also operate with the same truncated priorities and patterns of financing. Health care through government insurance, long resisted by the medical profession, proved to be an income-producing bonanza after it was finally enacted. Prices of both professional and hospital services shot up, sometimes doubling and tripling in the space of a year, in one of the great raids of all time on the federal treasury. But patients found themselves waiting in long lines for brief moments of attention, or paying vast sums for rooms in overcrowded and understaffed hospitals. Duplicative new medical technology, immensely expensive given its limited use, is much more likely to be found in the average hospital than an adequate number of beds or services.

Education feels the same effects and presents the same problems. Public school buildings are among the oldest and least functional structures in most large cities. Patchwork financing, resting primarily on property taxes from local homeowners, leads to limited flexibility, large classes, and low salaries for teachers. After a period of expansion to fill the needs of the new technological economy, higher education is being substantially cut back. If the urgings of the prestigious Carnegie Commission are followed, cutbacks will be at the expense of minorities and lower-class students who are "not taking full advantage" of their new opportunities.

To what extent do skewed income patterns, costly blocs of unemployable workers, physical decay of cities' facilities, and generally limited social services represent problems? In and of themselves, they probably are not measurable as problems. Many of them have been familiar parts of the American landscape for some time, and are only somewhat worse now. The United States has always trailed other industralized nations in social services, and does not now lag much further behind than before. The answer to this question must wait exploration of the American political consciousness, and of current and possible changes in it. Whether these conditions are serious problems depends on subjective factors—on one's expectations and one's sense of what is fixed or given versus what can and should be changed.

New Problems: Technology and Ecology

Less familiar problems have newly been raised by distinctive late twentieth-century developments. Starting with the many technological innovations generated by research and development undertaken during World War II, the last decades have seen more rapid scientific and technological advance than any other period in American history. Government support of public and private research and development (particularly that related to weapons and space travel) has been steady, and the pace of innovation is increasing. But technical capability far outstrips both our knowledge of how best to use it and our understanding of its possible effects on organizational forms and social attitudes. Capacity to modify weather patterns, for example, does not tell us where to direct hurricanes or how to compensate regions for lack of rainfall. Some recent decisions as to how technology would be employed may have caused as much damage to the society as aid in the solution of its problems. And many have begun to see the character of American life as powerfully affected by the presence of new technological capabilities, and even the wants and desires of people being shaped in the image of what such technologies are capable of producing.

But the problem with the most media attention in the 1970s has been that of ecology and environment. In part, both media and middle class may have turned to this subject with relief at being able to get away from the strife produced in the 1960s by the demands of racial minorities and antiwar activists. The objective part of the ecology-environment situation can be summed up briefly in two parts. One is the simple exhaustion of resources under the pressure of an insatiable industrial system and growing population. It is easy, for example, to project a severe energy crisis in ten or more years, if no new sources of energy are found or developed and demand continues to rise at the present rate. Other similar catastrophes can be projected, given the twin assumptions of fixed demands and increasing population. Much concern therefore has focused on limiting population growth, and (together with the availability of new contraceptive devices) this has already resulted in drastic alteration of the American birthrate. Very little has been done to modify the types or approaches to production and use of energy sources.

The other aspect of the ecology-environment problem has to do with the destruction of the earth's ecosystem. Pollution of the air and water by industrial waste, for example, threatens by itself to destroy the capacity of nature to provide life for man within the foreseeable future. Not only the pleasant rural streams visited by middle-class vacationers, but the lakes and oceans and waterways necessary to sustain industrial production and life itself are affected. For perhaps the first time, sober forecasts of a finite end to man's existence on this planet have entered serious political discussion. But there are drastic contrasts in the meaning and interpretation placed on this crisis, and in the remedies proposed for its solution. Once again, subjective factors take over, as we shall illustrate in a later chapter.

Newly Perceived Problems: The Status of Minorities and Women

There is nothing new about the deprived and exploited condition of minorities and women in the United States. What is new is the fact that, through their own efforts, these conditions have been made visible. The objective fact probably is that conditions are somewhat better now than they have been in past decades; but suddenly these facts have been forced onto the political agenda as a problem to be dealt with by the public. Because minorities and women have defined their situations and problems as of sufficient reality and magnitude to be worth fighting for, they have become real problems for others.

But there are important objective components to the conditions of minorities and women also, and they set the context in which action can be taken on these issues. Blacks who constitute 11 percent of the American population, are now isolated in large city ghettoes and Southern enclaves. Torn from their native continent and sold as slaves in America four centuries ago, blacks nevertheless have survived the decimation of their family structures and the systematic destruction of their cultural heritage. But the price has been heavy in terms of acculturation to the American value system. In important ways, blacks are Americans, thinking and acting in ways established by the dominant white society—even though these ways often contribute to their second-class status.

Other racial minorities make up much smaller proportions of the population. They also have quite different origins and claims upon the larger society. Chicanos, a mixture of Spanish, Aztec, and other Indian cultures, were once owners of a large portion of what is now the American Southwest. Their lands and capacity to control their own communities have been taken from them in a variety of ways despite the contrary assurances of the treaty which ended the Mexican-American War. Although they make up significant proportions of the electorate of California, New Mexico, Colorado, and Texas, they have found no ways of gaining equal status with the Anglo newcomers. The other major Spanish-speaking minority, the Puerto Ricans, have little else in common with Chicanos. They are relatively recent arrivals on the mainland, although Puerto Rico was acquired in 1898. They are located chiefly in East Coast cities, where they have been immediately assigned residence and jobs (if any) alongside blacks at the bottom of the status ladder.

American Indians, or at least the tiny number now remaining sequestered in shrinking reservations, are the heirs of a quite distinctive culture totally at odds with any of the European influences. Once the occupants of a continent, they base their citizenship and property claims upon a series of treaties between tribes as sovereign nations and the United States government. But neither the courts nor other remedies have proved capable of gaining the rights promised therein. The other noteworthy racial minority, the Asian-Americans, have found it possible to bifurcate themselves in such ways as to survive relatively well in the economic world of the dominant society while retaining aspects of their own community and culture. It has not been easy, as repeated riots, removals, and other discrimination have occurred primarily in the Western states, but in relative terms Asians have preceded other minorities into the dominant society's economic mainstream.

All of these minorities are currently pressing demands for full citizenship in white American society. Their numbers are small, but the coupling of their clear moral claim with the evident facts of discrimination and their own militancy have created severe tensions and serious dilemmas within the American political economy. With the exception of the Asians, none asked to be Americans, and the record of conquest, dishonored treaties, mistreatment, and exploitation is too clear to be dismissed.

This does not mean that white resistance is any less determined. The roots of racism go very deep, and the status anxieties and precarious economic position of the immediately-involved white lower classes make them bitterly resentful of measures to give minorities things they have only recently and barely won themselves. A sense of guilt on the part of some upper- and middle-class white liberals, together with significant social and economic distance from minorities, leads them to suspend their usual concern for standard procedures and offer compensation or preferment to minorities. This can only come at the cost of opportunities for lower-class whites, of course, provoking understandable tension and conflict and effectively dividing those who have much in common with respect to the political economy as a whole.

Nor is the position of minorities strong in any but moral terms. They are few in number, isolated, very poor, and systematically discriminated against in both blatant and subtle ways. No group is really well organized, even internally, in part because each is torn between the pervasive and compelling dominant system and their indigenous culture. They can accept the opportunities provided by the dominant society only at the price of yielding to its values, standards, and practices and submerging their own cultural identities. There is not much prospect of any but limited alliances between them, for their goals and claims are different and in some respects conflicting. In short, their political leverage, however measured, is minimal.

Thus the dilemma is acute. Deeply frustrated, holding an irrefutable moral claim, minorities confront intransigent white resistance grounded not only in centuries of prejudice but also in the basic characteristics of the social order itself. There seem no remedies within the existing political economy for the conditions which minorities experience. The result has been, and must continue to be, enduring tension, frequent outbreaks of violence, and continuing refutation of the American self-image of "justice for all."

At first glance, the claims of women for full citizenship appear to be similar, except for the fact that women constitute an absolute majority of the population. A similarly systematic discrimination has kept women either totally dependent upon men or in secondary economic and social roles where their income and status trail those of men. In recent years, and inspired in part by the militance of minorities, several women's movements have vigorously and variously challenged the male dominance and established sex roles that have so long been part of this and other cultures. The potential for change inherent in the numbers of women and the fundamental nature of the demands that can be made on their behalf is undeniably vast.

But two factors suggest that, at least for the present, the situation of women is not analogous to that of minorities, and the potential inherent in the movement is not yet being mobilized. First, women occupy all levels of the social class structure, and have access to many resources (money, education, status, etc.) that minorities do not. They are not concentrated at the lowest levels and denied access as a group, and there are fewer practical barriers to their moving into a wide variety of occupational slots at all levels of the system. Second, the women's movement is still at what may be an early stage and, for the most part, the demands being made are for no more than those rights to which women are already legally entitled. Such demands can be satisfied to a considerable extent, and it remains to be seen whether this will so blunt the movement that its larger potential will go unrealized.

The demands, strategies, and prospects of both minority and women's movements will be considered in detail in later chapters. What we have seen here, however, should be enough to portray the nature of the problems placed on the political agenda by their conditions and claims. For example, it seems clear that there is not really very much in common between them. But the nearly-simultaneous awakening of the two sets of claims for full citizenship does suggest the depth and scope of the underlying value change that may be underway in the United States. We shall have to probe this subterranean and perhaps un-recognized process as a potentially vital factor in a long-term process of change. First, however, we must expand our survey by examining the subjective elements of the current crisis and the prospects immediately ahead for the political economy.

OUR SUBJECTIVE MALAISE

We explicitly recognize at least some of the symptoms of societal problems, and *feel* many more. Many may seem disconnected. Others appear as petty annoyances. But they are busily working their way into our consciousness, undermining our ideology, and shaking some of the foundations of our ways of thinking—the normally unexamined assumptions, premises, and expectations with which we address our world. When things are demonstrably not as they are supposed to be, people react in a variety of different ways: by refusing to acknowledge the facts, by seeking scapegoats to blame and punish, by withdrawal, by trying to force the facts back into the mold prescribed by ideology, by taking refuge in escapist activities, or by undergoing conscious or unconscious change. Some Americans vividly display these and other responses. But for most the developing crisis is still characterizable only as a malaise, a sense that things are wrong and that solutions are not forthcoming and perhaps are not possible. Such a malaise is the essential precondition for loosening the grip of ideology and consciousness and reducing the legitimacy and authority of political institutions. The same precondition, of course, makes possible quite different kinds of change—from the most liberating to the most repressive.

The malaise that grips the United States today has several components. One surely is the wide sense of powerlessness that individuals feel in the face of the massive corporate economy, the organizational society, and their related technological and governmental bureaucracies. This vast system, so firmly locked together and moving so ponderously yet swiftly into an unknown future, appears to leave no room for the individual. No compensating opportunities for the exercise of personal impact upon the world seem available. Alone, adrift, passive, the citizen must either seek solace in business or some other cause, or drop out to seek a world that he or she can affect.

Another major element in today's malaise flows from the ambiguity of change and stability. On the one hand, everything seems to be changing. Science and technology advance rapidly, material conditions change as quickly, new events occur on the international scene, and the future seems to be assaulting us. At the same time, so many things do not change at all. Our social problems endure—race tensions, decaying environment, demands by the poor, economic insecurities—all these remain the same. So does the inadequate performance of our institutions, leaders, and other problem-solving instruments. The ambivalence goes further for some: at one moment, there are no serious problems, but at the next our problems are too difficult to solve at all. Out of all this there seems to be a disjunction between material progress, in the clear sense of technological capability, and the capacity of our values and traditions to provide directions and purpose for these developments. The old values lead neither to solution of problems nor to the wise use of new capabilities. But no new or better values seem widely accepted, and only bitterness and conflict ensue. What seemed so right—both our material achievements and our old values—now bring only misery, uncertainty, and increasing conflict.

The loss of a sense of social purpose is linked to a general loss of moral principle throughout the society. Few broadly accepted standards endure, as all forms of belief and practice appear equally valid. To each his own, and if it produces income or pleasure, what principle is there that can show that it is wrong? Surely not the old values in this fast-changing and complex world of threat and pressure. Added to this loss of moral standard is a widespread cynicism toward leaders. Decades of widening gap between promises and performance, and the continuing desire to receive the promises and reassurances without facing the drastic tasks involved in realizing them, have led to deep distrust of political and economic leadership.

Nor is there confidence in any intellectual leadership, or in intellect itself. The universities have contributed substantially to the degradation of intellect in the United States, through their market orientation and ready subservience to research and prestige goals. Those who pass through them *know* they are frauds, mechanical certifiers of readiness for corporate somnolence, and agents of whatever power source holds their purse strings. Those who know them less well nevertheless resent their posturing and self-aggrandizement at public expense. For none do they play the part of creatively critical analysis and guidance for the society; instead, they assiduously aid in the justification and perpetuation of the very conditions that are so patently unsatisfactory.

These factors—and many others along with them—lead to a situation of deepening malaise. At the lowest social levels of minorities and working-class whites, quiet desperation is broken only by occasional riots and similar outbreaks. At middle-class levels, there is frenetic casting about for some new style or possession or fad that will provide satisfaction and prevent confrontation with reality. Young people drop out, return to nature, or become plastic revolutionaries. At all levels, personal relationships sink into despairing, self-gratifying, objective transactions lacking in fulfillment. Expectations for the future include economic insecurity, personal lack of identity and purpose, and generally worsening social conditions. Wild fads break out, absorbing millions for brief periods of time with their promise of identity and sense of belonging to something with some direction or purpose. Rock music festivals and the Jesus People's movement draw on the same profound and unfilled needs, and offer equally empty solutions.

What is distinctive about our society in the mid-1970s is not just the presence of this potentially destructive malaise. It is the combination of these subjective conditions with the objective realities that have helped to bring them about. It is the convergence of subjective and objective conditions into a conjunctural crisis of proportions as yet unknown. And this comes at a time when the conditions leading to the crisis are worldwide in scope. There is simply no avoiding the massive impact of ecological, economic, racial, and other insoluble problems that overlap and reinforce each other. And nowhere in the world is there confidence in man's capability to survive and maintain human relationships.

In the United States, there is a growing, although unacknowledged, recognition that the present system is not working. In various subterranean ways, people sense that this social order is doomed. Ongoing social fragmentation is visible all around us. But because people see no alternatives—because they cannot or have not yet broken out of this political consciousness—there can be no explicit acknowledgement of the implication of what people see and feel. Much energy and hope is invested in self-deluding activity, particularly in efforts at political reform. In desperately groping for a solution, people come to believe that reform is possible because it is so necessary, and that the only real barrier to reform is the failure of more people to work for the candidates and issues of their choice. Other forms of escape include group sex, pornography, countercultural life-styles, and similar self-indulgences. For some, the solution lies in returning to the old values with even greater rigidity than in the past.

Overall, the situation is one which promises great change, and soon. Both objective and subjective conditions are right—indeed overdue—for significant upheaval in the system itself. What is lacking, however, is any really new and different political consciousness that might show the way to a new and better social order. All we have is our malaise, and our unacknowledged recognition that our society is doomed. All we see is a program-less series of protest movements, some promising reform through one of the major political parties and others around them. All, of course, think and act solely within the existing consciousness and the limits it imposes.

OUR REAL ALTERNATIVES

What lies ahead? What is implied by the problems and forces at work in our society, given the dominant motivations and way of thinking that now exist? Our problems cannot be solved, because the basic motivation and character of our political economy cannot permit it. They can only get worse, with subsequent escalation of social malaise and disintegration. With no basic change in consciousness, the logical end point is fascism—with certain Americanized features, mostly rhetorical, and much real popular support. Two alternatives, both of which might well ultimately end in an even harsher fascism, are what I have been calling superorganized state capitalism and sheer chaos. Let us consider each of these assertions in turn.

The form that our problems take, and the range of possible solutions to them, are shaped in important ways by the character and imperatives of the American political economy. This is true of *all* of them, not just those involving depression avoidance, income distribution, and social services. The key to understanding the problem of wise use of technology, for example, lies in the realization that the currently-dominant criterion of decisions regarding such use is the maximization of profit by major firms and industries with an interest in that technology. Neither long-range or social consequences carry much weight against that standard. Similarly, the key to understanding the dilemma of ecology lies in seeing that the profits of business and the provision of jobs for workers may be possible only at the cost of pollution and environmental destruction.

Even in the areas of the status of minorities and women, the character and imperatives of the economic system are vital factors. If jobs for unskilled workers are not available, if it seems too costly to educate and train the lowest levels, if it is an aid to the system to have some available workers unemployed or in uncompensated household services—then minorities and women will suffer most. Other factors also affect these problems, of course, particularly in the latter case, where racism and sexism obviously play a major part—as they do in so many societies. But the pervasive effects of the economic dimension seem clear.

These problems are related to each other, and grounded in the needs and character of the economic system. This means that they cannot be temporarily or superficially "solved," or even deferred so that things can go on for a while longer as they are. In the first place, the American political economy may not even be able to address them. The possibility of serious depression, or of combined stagnation and inflation, may make it impossible to do anything except desperately seek ways to get things moving again. If this happens, of course, there will be neither resources nor energy to apply to other problems, conditions will be much worse, and we might well move directly to the crossroads.

Even if modest growth or a temporary boom occurs, these problems will remain insoluble—growing sources of infection and disease leading to continued social fragmentation. The vast sums needed to rebuild the cities or remedy the welfare crisis or restore the environment are simply not available. Not only is there bitter ideological and economic resistance against redirection of existing war expenditures or other subsidies, but not even these huge sums would be sufficient. Great new revenues would have to be taken out of corporate profits or the limited incomes of middle- and lower-class taxpayers. Moreover, efforts to do such things would amount to an attack upon the elaborate system of investment and profits that now depends upon maintenance of slums, dumping of wastes, etc. And even if such massive efforts were made, they would be undertaken by private entities operating for profit and with little regard for the achievement of social goals.

Beyond mere money, obstacles arise from the multiplicity and contradictory character of problems, as well as the flat-out opposition of the dominant ideology to the complete reversal of standards and purposes that would be required to undertake efforts at solution. There are just too many problems converging upon the society, its antiquated machinery and its sense of purpose all at once. As the decisional process grinds along, framing a marginal solution to the symptoms of one problem and tentatively looking for painless ways of financing it, a myriad other crises dig deeper into the social fabric. And efforts to solve one problem exacerbate others. Tangible advances for minorities mean bitter resentment from lower-class whites. Or women and minorities are forced to compete with each other for limited opportunities. Or new jobs are created and growth spurred by subsidies and contracts which call for projects (e.g., the construction of supersonic aircraft) which destroy the environment. And standing solidly against full-scale efforts to deal with these problems is the dominant ideology's insistence upon individualism, self-help, private initiative, profit-seeking, anticommunism, and limited government.

It is not just pessimism, but hard analysis of the range of the possible, that finds these problems insoluble under present circumstances. Conditions can only worsen, as all the causes remain and their effects escalate. At some point, large numbers of people will conclude that things are intolerable, and others will perceive a variety of threats to their status and opportunities. Protest movements will become larger and more numerous, aimed at a variety of targets but all expressing profound dissatisfaction with the status quo. Some will be of the left, some fundamentalist right, but most will be merely populist outrage with little or no coherent program in mind.

Fascism and Its Way Stations

Fascism is a term originally applied by Mussolini to his "corporate state," but which has since loosely covered a range of politico-economic systems from Hitler Germany and Franco Spain to Peronist Argentina. (It is applied even more loosely as an epithet to describe a variety of government tactics disliked by the speaker.) My definition is intended to be stricter, but to modernize the essence of the concept used in the 1930s for application in the 1970s. It has three components. First is the joining of big capital—the ruling class or major segments of it—in a formal alliance with the state for the purpose of preventing capitalist collapse, organizing the work force to endure austerity, increasing productivity and profitability, and preserving social order. Second, the state in this alliance is represented by a leader or small group of leaders with an already-mobilized popular following. Such leaders represent no coherent ideology. They are distinguished by sheer power-seeking opportunism, and acknowledge no democratic procedural or civil libertarian limits to what should be done to gain or hold power. Their following has been mobilized chiefly around discontent with the way in which the current order is working. Radical anticapitalist and fundamentalist (racist, nationalist, anticommunist, patriotic, etc.) appeals may alternate ambivalently in drawing the discontented to the support of the leader or group promising dramatic change in exchange for sacrifice and support. Third, consolidation implies totalitarian organization, surveillance, and repression in the society. Scapegoating and provocation are deliberately employed to divide potential opponents from each other, and police state tactics are proudly and visibly used to crush dissent in the name of the people. Enough enemies are found at home and abroad to justify extensive organization of the population, which nevertheless continues to give substantial support to their leaders.

Our analysis so far suggests that we may not be far from the point at which the necessary preconditions for fascism will have matured. In the last section, for example, we described a malaise with many characteristics of the soil from which fascism springs. Let us now run a plausible scenario of what might occur in the next several years.

Americans see and feel intransigent problems, threatening prospects of change, powerlessness—but nothing seems to work anymore. There is no moral principle worth standing behind, and existing leaders appear venal or self-aggrandizing. We yearn for a return to the old values, which made for solid personal lives and real social achievement in a decent world; a variety of vocal leaders cater to this desire by constant strident appeals to fundamentalist values and ideology. At the same time, militant minorities and other protest groups continually press their claims for more of everything—all those things that most people have worked long and hard for, and barely achieved. At the same time, inflation and hard times seem to be taking away exactly those things for which entire lives have been invested. The American dream, in effect, is falling apart before our very eyes. Big business and big labor seem to be working hand in hand to milk the little man. Anti-intellectualism, cynicism, and relativism are widespread. Many are alienated from their work, from their fellows, from themselves. Hardly anybody enjoys personally fulfilling relationships with other human beings. In this context, the shift from protest to protofascist followership is but a small step.

The crossroads at which fascism rises to nascent reality would be reached when problems are at crisis proportions, a variety of protest movements casting about, frequent violent clashes, restive stirrings among the working class as well as divisions among established elites, and the general prospect of social disintegration. From once-serene fortieth floor corporate board rooms and exclusive country clubs, the situation may appear one in which serious threats are posed to the continued existence of the economic and social systems themselves. It is beyond the stage of ideological management, repression is neither reliable nor practical, and there is a real risk of losing all. Tentatively at first, overtures are made to opportunistic incumbent politicians or to leaders of major protest movements, in hopes that their demonstrated capacity to mobilize followers can be turned to preservation of the basic outlines of the system and effective management of the disruptive forces.

For their part, the nationalist or populistic leaders were never encumbered by coherent ideology or program, being about equally fundamentalist, opportunist, and anti-establishment. Their principal achievement lay in identifying the discontent and protest surge, mobilizing it, and employing demagogic skills to keep ahead of it. The opportunity to keep or acquire power through joining forces with key segments of the industrial and financial systems, therefore, seems highly attractive, and the alliance is made. With millions of followers, and the acquiescence and cooperation of such elites, control of the national government is secured with relative ease, probably through electoral means. Only scattered resistance is offered from the left, and other protest groups tend to fall into line in support of the new party which promises reform and renewal of the American dream. In a burst of patriotism and relief at the prospect of return to order and prosperity, a mood of sacrifice and submission develops.

From this point, consolidation begins. Profit-maximizing needs of the economic system require order and management of workers, plus extensive use of government as purchaser, subsidizer, and regulator—as well as procuror and defender of markets abroad. This process is masked, and fundamentalist support mobilized, by a scapegoating campaign. The ills of the nation are blamed on the plots and activities of certain intellectuals, left groups, minorities, and other unorthodox persons. Foreign intervention and attempted subversion through these agencies is also charged, and severe danger from them envisioned. Investigations reveal the "truth" of these allegations in several cases. Trade unions, already weakened by indecisive leaders and the appeal of populism, are further neutralized in this way and become insignificant.

The left responds with scattered strikes and acts of terrorism, which feed the general public hysteria and lead to further surveillance and repression. Juries and courts legitimize severe repression and extensive controls over the society "for its own defense," and the general public is successfully mobilized behind the new government's policies at home. A variety of international threats to American well-being and national honor and prestige are soon discovered, necessitating substantial military buildup and further sacrifice of civil rights and standard of

living by the citizenry. Extensive government management of the
society assures profitability for major industries, and other problems
are "solved" through repression or obfuscated through focusing attention elsewhere. Without bothering to draw the line precisely, at some
point in this process a threshold is crossed which marks the beginning
of modern American fascism.

No doubt this scenario seems farfetched, even hysterical; certainly it
is not the balanced evidential analysis that attaches demonstrable facts
to incremental projections of the status quo and proclaims a discovery.
The latter method is of course that preferred by our present ideology
and consciousness, and well suited to the description of conditions and
events of the recent past. This is exactly my point: to see where we are
going requires that we look *forward*, not merely projecting the present
but also the trends and problems evident in that present. It is not easy
to envision fascism in the United States, nor have I suggested that it is
inevitable. But I do argue that the odds are stronger for this form of
fundamental change, not necessarily by the route imagined above, than
for any other specifically portrayable new system.

There are other possibilities, as I indicated earlier, which can occur
without basic consciousness change. Each of these, however, is
probably only a temporary stage (unless conditions and problems
change dramatically, which they show no prospect of doing) on the
road to fascism. The first is what I have termed superorganized state
capitalism. It differs from fascism chiefly in the fact that civil liberties
are for the most part preserved, and life is freer for individuals in that
respect. But economic exigencies and social conflicts require a highly
organized, bureaucratized social system with surveillance and control
over practically all aspects of life in order that the disintegrated social
fabric not visibly collapse. Big capital and government are fully merged,
with the fact that control lies in the "private" economy-grounded
ruling class—the only real distinguishing feature from state socialism,
where control lies in the hands of a party or state bureaucracy nomi-
nally responsible to the people. Through this system, a declining but
definably better quality of life than that likely under fascism can be
maintained for a while, until conditions build to the point where the
fascism scenario takes over.

The other major possibility is sheer chaos. This assumes splits within
the ruling class such as to prevent any one group or coalition from

becoming dominant over the state. Both government and economy show incapacity to cope with growing problems, and the society degenerates into clashing groups and local entities, each seeking to preserve as much as possible for itself. Because each group sees only its own remedies as the appropriate ones, and the country is very large, no coherent system is possible. Many current images of the desirability of each group "doing its own thing" (minorities, women, community control advocates, or various others) lead in exactly this direction. The great danger is, of course, that they will founder against the rocks of power—the eventual alliance between big capital and protest movements that spells fascism. As fascism knocks on the door, it will no doubt interrupt still another academic debate among such groups about a new and effortless way in which liberating fundamental change will automatically occur.

Neither fascism nor its two possible way stations are attractive to contemplate. I set them forth in this blunt fashion not from an effort to frighten the reader into attention (experimental evidence demonstrates that threat-generated motivation is weak and ineffective in any event), but simply to stress the point that *within our present consciousness* these are the only major alternatives which present conditions and problems offer us. The motivations and basic character of our political economy preclude solutions of the problems that are rending and disintegrating our society. But if our present consciousness holds us within the range of assumptions and solutions compatible with that social order, then we have no prospects but devolution into fascism or its way stations. And many of us will support them, because we can conceive of no alternatives. How and why does our existing consciousness do this? Why, for example, is reform not capable of averting these alternatives and enabling us to achieve something better? I shall take up the latter issue in the next chapter, as one extended example of how our consciousness achieves its effects, and then move on to the exploration of consciousness as such in Part 2.

CHAPTER FOUR

The Limits of Reform

I have already argued that reform tactics and goals are, by their very nature, unequal to the problems we face and incompetent to avert the alternatives that lie ahead. This chapter documents that subthesis, constituting in effect a short course on the character and dynamics (and limitations) of the American political system. My larger point, of course, is that reform itself is a trap, an energy-absorbing narcotic urged upon us by our ideology and consciousness. To make that point adequately, however, requires that we critically assess both the capabilities and the inherent limitations of reform in a balanced fashion.

By *reform*, I mean the correction or improvement of government personnel, procedures, or policies to bring them more in line with traditional political values as they are understood to apply to current circumstances. The *goals* of reform are shaped by such generally accepted values; the *tactics* of reform, accordingly, are limited to the use of the orthodox political channels or, if necessary, the reinvigoration of such channels through use of several at once. The essence of reform, and what distinguishes it from revolution, is adherence to both established procedures and traditional values.

It would be absurd not to recognize that there are many changes that can be accomplished through informed use of the orthodox political channels of the American system. Many of these are identifiable as significant reforms. Some of them are, in terms of our earlier definitions, examples of top-down marginal change. Ralph Nader's combined research, litigation, and lobbying strategy has succeeded in writing a number of consumer-protection provisions into law and spurring the ecology movement. John Gardner's Common Cause lobbying and litigation have modified both law and practice with respect to campaign financing. Some other reforms involve somewhat more originating thrust from the bottom up, followed by effective top-down action, to bring about a series of marginal changes. The social welfare legislation of the New Deal is one example, and the series of statutes and other federal government actions as a result of the civil rights movement is another. All of these changes represent significant achievements, particularly for those people most intimately affected.

But it is essential to notice *what* sorts of things can be accomplished through these routes, what the *pattern* of results of such efforts are over time, and what the *range* of solutions that are possible is at any time. The Nader and Common Cause achievements are very much changes at the margins. They *are* visible, and certainly inconvenient to and opposed by powerful vested interests. But they are *not* vital to the nature or operating characteristics of the structure of power or to the basic pattern of burdens and benefits accomplished by public policy. Their importance lies less in what they actually bring about in tangible terms, than in what they symbolize to the public at large—by means of the news media—about the capacity of "citizens' groups" to win battles against vested interests. If such efforts were applied more broadly, people can think comfortingly, there is no area of politics or public policy that could not be reformed.

But that is just the point: they *cannot* be applied more broadly, because of the concentration of research and lobbying energy, public attention, and legislators', courts', and lawyers' time required to nail down *one* change. Even if "citizens" were mobilized in infinite numbers and possessed unlimited energy and resources, the time and dockets of legislators and courts are finite. More important, if more than occasional victories were won, corporations and other vested interests would be forced to mount a systematic campaign to defend their practices and prerogatives—and the trend of policy would soon head in their direction again. It is only because the Nader and Common Cause achievements are one-shot changes at the margins that they are possible at all. And ironically, though perhaps not coincidentally, just such changes are instrumental in regularly renewing our faith in reform.

The *pattern* of results offers further insight into the affirmative capabilities of reform within the American system. By this I mean the tangible consequences of apparently successful reform movements, viewed comprehensively and from an ample time perspective. The New Deal period, for example, appears to be an era of significant reform and redirection of policy and practice to benefit the ordinary citizen. But an overall assessment of the period suggests that it was the time when business moved into the final stage of "partnership" with government. No significant redistribution of wealth or income occurred as a result of this package of reforms; the data show instead a widening gap in subsequent decades. To be sure, much vital social legislation—the basic framework of our welfare state—was enacted. But it took a massive popular upsurge amid desperate circumstances to accomplish what most industrial nations already had in the way of social insurance, and the United States still trails most other such nations in basic social services and human welfare programs.

Once again, the changes wrought by reform appear more symbolic than real. Or, perhaps equally accurately, reform political changes are readily absorbed and adapted into the powerful mechanism of the ongoing private economy and its associated social pyramid. We are all inextricably enmeshed in the latter system, which functions as a vast and implacable upward-redistributing machine. Not only is it flexible and powerful enough to absorb and convert to its own benefit all such comparatively minor political innovations, but by the end of World War II it also had essentially captured the political machinery itself, and integrated that as well.

How shall we assess the civil rights movement and its policy accomplishments? Certainly the legal rights of blacks and other minorities have been distinctly advanced, although much self-congratulation seems somewhat hollow in light of such questions as why it was necessary or took so long. Nevertheless, there was much apparent change from the situation that had existed. There has been much less change, of course, in the *actual circumstances* of minorities. An ambivalent and fluctuating kind of support flowing from Washington has made the civil rights policy package a symbol of first hope and then increased frustration for blacks. Simultaneously, it has signalled the fulfillment of an obligation to some whites, but deep fears and threat to many others. In another ten years, I suspect that we shall recognize the civil rights movement as having assuaged guilt and changed opportunities for some, while setting off bitter and enduring conflicts for many. But the most significant realization may be that its ostensible goals of true equality simply could not be achieved within our current economic system, with its dearth of available resources and jobs, and in a society emphasizing competitiveness, individualism, and the quest for status—part of the very definition of which is skin color. What was attempted, in other words, was beyond the capacity of the political system to deliver. As long as basic values (not just racism) and the existing economic and social systems remain fixed, the goal of full equality cannot be realized.

In the case of both the New Deal and the civil rights periods, moreover, what reforms were accomplished were not achieved solely by the orthodox methods urged by the principles of reform. In the New Deal, hundreds of thousands of determined men and women defied injunctions, fought scabs, police, and National Guard, and seized entire plants in a series of small-scale insurrections. Dozens died, hundreds were hurt, and millions of dollars in property destroyed, before even the reforms we have described could be achieved. The civil rights movement similarly defied legal limits and prohibitions with marches and sit-ins. The whole nonviolent movement succeeded, in so far as it did, because it deliberately teetered on the edge of provoking mass white violence in front of the television cameras—and adamant white officials gave in rather than be exposed as denying the most basic of their country's values.

Thus those who insist that change is possible through exclusive use of orthodox and legal channels simply do not know their history. And some conventional wisdom of political science must be revised as well. One interpretation, for example, holds that the source of change is to be found in the wise decisions of an elite subculture of governing activists, who spark popular attention and acquiescence by government action to cope with problems. Another sees change emanating from decisions taken within the dominant political party, with popular approval normally following and the minority party becoming the vehicle of opposition. In both of our illustrations, it appears that the actions of people *outside* of these orthodox channels were the cause of what change did occur—regardless of what party was in power or what it decided, or what dominant elites happened to think wise.

We come now to the question of the *range* of what can be accomplished through reform, which is what this chapter is really about. The vital point is that certain limits on what can be done are structural, built into our political system by its very nature, its most fundamental features. Our laws, institutions, and practices are not neutral, but deliberately constructed so that in and of themselves (not counting the similarly-directed efforts of their incumbent officials, or those outside who support and direct them), they will protect property and preserve the status quo. Thus, no matter how effectively citizens might mobilize, what they can accomplish is limited in the end by what their political system is capable of delivering.

This is a final and complete answer to those who continue to say that the reason why reform fails is that "the people" do not care enough, do not become involved in large or knowledgeable enough numbers, do not remain attentive enough after new laws are enacted, and so forth.* All of these charges may be accepted as true, though one might then ask whether the system was *designed* so as to serve the wants of masses of people only when they were mobilized at near-hysterical levels requiring sacrifice of vast amounts of time and income. Even if people conformed to these impossible standards, however, the point remains that there would still be limits to what could be accomplished—limits flowing not from the power or manipulations of opposing interests, which are normally more than ample to control, but from the very nature of the laws, institutions, and practices themselves.

But nevertheless reform remains the sincere hope of millions of concerned citizens. In the 1970s, its promise has gripped intellectuals, middle-class activists, students, and the "little man" alike. Reform's attraction is fed by a variety of authors whose trenchant criticisms of the American system and its policies are followed by exhortations to their readers to act—but in the most innocuous and traditional ways.

---

*Notice that I do not even consider the argument that reform fails because people want such different things that public officials must serve as brokers, accommodating these conflicting wants, and thus existing policies really represent the compromise product though they fully satisfy no single group. The whole pattern of policies and their consequences over the last century, and the related inequities of wealth and income distribution, stand as a denial of such an argument.

For example, in a major book portraying a gigantic new international corporate economy, dwarfing states and nations and penetrating the American government in octopus-like fashion, attorney Richard J. Barber concludes with a call for the reinvigoration of the antitrust laws.[1] And at the close of a solidly-documented survey of corporate exploitation of middle- and lower-class Americans in every aspect of their lives, but particularly through domination of their government, *A Populist Manifesto* calls for expansion and greater use of the voting franchise and new campaign disclosure laws.[2]

Thus there are two important "WHY?" issues before us in this chapter. First, we must be entirely clear as to why reform cannot solve our problems or avert the alternatives discussed in the last chapter—why our institutions preclude the necessary changes. This is what I have been calling a short course in American political institutions and dynamics. But second, we must also try to understand why it is that so many people, including so many active in and presumably knowledgeable about politics, nevertheless are so exclusively and completely committed to reform. This is an even shorter course in the effects of American political ideology and consciousness. It may serve as preparation for the more extended analysis of that crucial topic to follow in Part 2.

THE MULTIPLE DEFENSES OF THE STATUS QUO

Reform faces truly formidable odds—odds befitting a far better cause. Reform almost always involves the use of government as an instrument, if only because the impetus normally comes from those who hold few resources of power except ideas, hope, and numbers. Were reformers located at the centers of corporate or financial power, of course, their routes—and their chances of success—would be very different. But their situation obliges them to seek redress through political means, and immediately their troubles begin. Our formal structures and procedures, and the informal styles and practices that have grown up around them, are both strongly biased and readily manipulated to support the status quo. They were erected with deliberation and care to establish and defend a capitalist-liberal social order, and they have been perfected over the years so that they do their job relatively unobtrusively and yet very well. Moreover, there is a particular social pyramid behind this set of political structures and processes, one in which a relative few have enjoyed great benefits which they fully intend to preserve. And they have the power, the experience, the legitimacy, and the opportunity to do so through the apparently neutral vehicle of these same structures and processes.

Thus there is really an interwoven network of mutually reinforcing layers of defense of the status quo that confronts the would-be reformer. The outer layer consists of a set of structures and procedures which are biased toward capitalism-liberalism and defensively manipulable by those now at the top of the system of power created by capitalism-liberalism. Next comes that system itself, with its distribution of power and advantage, its imperatives, and its associated values and ideology. And there is also that particular social pyramid resulting from capitalism-liberalism, in which those who have benefitted over the years are determined and able to maintain their status by any means necessary, starting with political structures and processes.

The Law and the Legal System

But it is the structures and procedures—the outer layer—which concern us here. Some examples of the manner in which reform is defined, deflected, channeled, and absorbed may be in order. Let us consider the legal system, a characteristic recourse of the avid reformer. What is law? Can it be neutral and available, both as a basis of order and a tool of reform? The answer is of course negative, for three major reasons which go deep into the essence of law itself. First, the very idea of law, as a system of rules prescribing for the conduct of public and private affairs in a society, is inherently and necessarily conservatizing. Law does not drop from the sky, nor does it embody some detached or mystical higher reason. It comes from people, and it reflects their preferences. It is formulated by specific individuals or groups, and draws upon *their* past experience, current positions, and hopes for the future. It embodies *their* version of normative principles, defends *their* particular status and prerogatives, and solemnly asserts all of these as "law" for the guidance and control of others in the society. Believing in the rightness of their position and the society that gave rise to it, the lawmakers prescribe as acceptable methods of change only those means which they believe are compatible with the maintenance of the system.

All others are discouraged or outlawed. To do anything else would be to invite their own overthrow. The only wonder is that so many sincere people can nevertheless believe that because a particular change seems right it must be possible to accomplish through resort to the legal system.

Second, even if the law were in itself even-handed, unbiased, and merely a neutral set of mechanical arrangements for transacting public affairs, the social pyramid with which it is associated would prevent it from having such effects. How could the law be neutral in its consequences when the society with which it is linked is not neutral? It is a *particular* social order that our legal system enshrines and defends, not an ideal one. The reality of our social structure is a pyramid, as we have seen, in which burdens and benefits are distributed unequally. Not everybody is similarly affected by the application of law; some will be advantaged, some disadvantaged, by the most theoretically neutral actions—because of their pre-existing situations. And those at the top of the social pyramid are able to use their power to determine what the law shall be and how it will be applied. There is little or no uncertainty about the outcome—it will favor those who have, and restrain those who have not.

Third, the law is not self-executing. It can only be applied to specific situations by real people, who can only act in terms (again) of their own experience, biases, and preferences. Because of specialization and division of labor, moreover, this task falls into the hands of a small group of better-educated professionals, the lawyers. For the most part, this group is drawn from the upper echelons of the society to start with. Whatever one's origins, the experience of law school inculcates belief in the rightness, inevitability, and efficacy of the law. To be a success in the practice of law—to make money—one is drawn to apply this training to the service of the corporations, banks, and other sources of wealth whose interests require good legal services. Because lawyers have a monopoly on the capacity to provide necessary services to the society, they tend to use their unique skills to enhance their own status, mystify the general population, and play a special role in governing. The most successful and politically ambitious lawyers become judges. Appointed by other successful political figures, they apply the law in behalf of the values, interests, and preferences which their life experience has taught them are right and proper. In short, they make the instrument of the established social order work effectively in behalf of the status quo. Indeed, it would be strange if they could bring themselves to do otherwise.

We could go on, but perhaps the point has been made. The law and the legal system are, in various and essentially inevitable ways, instruments of social control, bent to the support of the existing social order. They cannot, by their very nature, serve as agencies of any but the most modest reform—except on rare occasions, and then only to the extent that other forces converge to push reality a little closer to the traditional values. That so many Americans see the law as the potential remedy for injustice or the route to reform can only be the mark of another massive triumph of the dominant ideology.

Consider the Constitution, at once the corner stone of the legal system and our principal focus of ideological glorification. Is it neutral? Does it erect a system open to the desires and participation of all on an equal basis? Does it facilitate reform? Patently not. And yet it remains the fundamental "given" which all accept, the source of legitimacy, and the image of wisdom and justice. It is somehow inappropriate to point out that in its own language it is severely biased towards those who hold property, that it locks the government in on the side of capitalism and makes it the servant of financiers, speculators, and entrepreneurs unwilling to undergo any risks they can avoid. Or that the social reality which lies behind it is unequal and exploitative, and that to uphold the Constitution in the abstract is to endorse that social order in the concrete. That some have found ways to use the Constitution to promote the goals of equality and justice is obvious; but the general, routine pattern of consequences of this Constitution is in exactly the opposite direction.

National Government Institutions

Let us examine another set of barriers to reform, the institutions of government erected by this Constitution and the rules under which they operate. The Congress perhaps best testifies to the success of the Framers' efforts to design political institutions that would effectively dilute and absorb mass-based thrusts toward change in the workings or results of the "private" economic order. Almost every characteristic of organization and operation of the two houses of Congress serves to further this basic purpose. For example, Senators and Representatives owe their positions to independently determined nominations and separate elections in distinct geographically defined units. In practical terms, this means that they will be selected by and respond to those interests which are at the top of the small-scale social pyramid in their state or district. The social reality of the 100-member Senate or the 435-member House of Representatives thus becomes almost exclusively upper-middle class lawyers and businessmen, concerned primarily with the furtherance of the economic interests in their localities. The political reality is that of institutionalized conflict among middle-level elites over who is to get what from the regulatory activities and the revenue-raising engine of government.

Is this too harsh? By no means; if anything, it is a testimony to the achievement of the Framers' frankly acknowledged intentions. Circumstances and Congress' own actions have contributed substantially to this cause also, however. In many states and districts, the dominance of one party or the traditions of the electorate assure an incumbent legislator of lengthy periods of service; thirty- and forty-year terms are not uncommon. Only about 150 seats in the House are truly competitive— i.e., likely to result in election of a nonincumbent candidate. The rest regularly return incumbents or their successors from the same political party. Thus, the degree of actual choice on the part of voters in any constituency, or the capacity of the electorate at large to effect drastic changes in the makeup of the House, even in years of great popular concern with issues, is greatly reduced. Not that choices between candidates selected by and responsive to quite similar sets of interests would necessarily be meaningful, but it is worth noting that not even such a choice occurs in most states or districts. Both House and Senate therefore endure essentially unchanged despite possibly deep currents of change in social conditions or popular needs in the country as a whole.

Because of shared class perspective, continuity of membership, and sense of concern for predictable transaction of business, the Congress has developed a set of rules that further assure protection for the status quo. Necessary division of labor by means of the committee system combines with the tradition of assigning chairmanships by means of seniority to place great discretionary power over wide areas of legislation in the hands of the Congress' oldest and generally most conservative members. To rise to such a position, one must come from a "safe" district, which frequently means a rural Southern or Midwestern area. Junior members have neither the time nor the information nor the parliamentary skills to challenge the oligarchies that reign in both houses. They are induced to "go along," to defer to their seniors, to serve their constituencies' special interests so that they can assure their re-election, and to generally play the traditional game of move-up that leads to power within their house. To step out of this pattern is to risk social disapproval, isolation, and enforced ineffectiveness—and quite possibly electoral suicide. Thus by deliberate intent, basic structure, social reality, and internal traditions, the Congress can be and do only certain things—and purposeful reform is not one of them.

The Presidency appears to offer much more hope as an instrument of reform. It is, after all, the key source of leadership and an office filled by election of all the people. But here again both structure and social reality dictate otherwise. The President and the upper echelons of the federal bureaucracy must and do represent the highest strata of wealth and power in the society, not necessarily in their personal origins but in their orientations and actions. It is the *national* social pyramid, rather than merely local ones, that finds expression in the executive branch. This is because no person can rise to the point of serious candidacy for the Presidency without undergoing intensive indoctrination in the priorities, style, and practices of American politics. No person can compete for nomination, or hope to conduct a visible campaign, without vast sums of money—which can only come from those who hold such wealth today. No President can conduct the affairs of state without coming to terms with the basic units of power in the economy—units whose needs and capabilities are such that he would risk the national welfare itself, to say nothing of his own capacity to accomplish other goals, by not engaging in some form of partnership operation.

The President must staff his cabinet and other key offices in the federal bureaucracy with knowledgeable and competent persons, most of whom he finds among his political supporters in the business world. Because of the importance of the financial policies to be set at this level, no action can be contemplated or taken except in the context of and amidst pressures from the world's leading monetary and banking centers. The middle and lower echelons of the federal bureaucracy are already populated by persons habituated to doing business on behalf of business. Close relationships between regulators and regulated naturally develop, until in time government agencies become lobbyists for the clientele whom they are supposedly regulating.

Nor is the President's range of alternatives and action anything near as wide as might at first appear. Most of the coming year's budget, for example, and that of years and years after that, is already committed through standing authorizations; the only question is how much additional moneys can be found to do a little more in one or another direction. When it is sought to reduce spending, the most vulnerable programs are the newer social services, which are not defended by powerful continuing interest groups. To rationalize government programs, or initiate significant changes of any kind, the Congress must be persuaded to concur—a process that involves great amounts of time and energy, to say nothing of political debts. Only one of two major items can be fought through this process in any Presidential term, except under the most unusual circumstances. But the President has little control over the uses of his time and leadership capabilities. Events of various kinds, from war and the threat of war to racial conflict at home, may completely reshape his agenda. The conduct of foreign policy, because of its potential life or death implications, frequently takes over the President's attention. Out of all these factors, and despite the best intentions, the American government is likely to produce exactly what it did yesterday and the day before, only perhaps a little bit more so. Reform via the Presidency is not likely to be sought in any fundamental way, and even less likely to be achieved.

And then there is the Supreme Court, the Framers' choice as the citadel of conservatism. To an extent, the Court can and has served as an agency of reform. But probably it was seen as such in the 1950s and early 1960s principally because the President and Congress were so totally inactive. (The limits to the Court's capacity to affect actual behavior, as opposed to merely enunciating rules of law, quickly became evident in this period as well.) What the Court does is very much the product of whom the President appoints to serve as judges, and special circumstances can converge to make a majority of the Justices appear more responsive to appeals for reform than other institutions at any given time. But historically, as the Framers assumed, the judges have lagged behind the other institutions.

By and large, however, the primary limits of the Court's capacities are set by the nature of law itself. Every limitation noted in our discussion of the law and the legal system applies to the Court. Moreover, and in the light of that discussion, there is great significance to the fact that many of the great social issues of American life are presented to the Supreme Court for decision as matters of law. What does it mean that we as a people permit many of our great questions of goals and purposes and moral commitments to be decided not by ourselves but by nine appointed members of a tiny elite? Nine men who apply the conservative, property-conscious rules of the law in ways consistent with their own experience and preferences to situations requiring frank value choices, and then hide their choice behind the rhetoric of the law and the symbolism of the Constitution? Clearly, it means at least that we have yielded up our own capacity to choose the directions the society will follow. It shows how fully we have been captured by the ideology of legalism and have permitted ourselves to be constrained by its special biases. And it implies that even the exhaustive effort to achieve reform through bringing cases before the Supreme Court offers only quite limited prospects. Without social support and enforcement by the other institutions, the most promising rules of law are meaningless. But rules of law themselves are only the most modest steps within a preconfined framework. That they appear large or desirable is indicative chiefly of the distance we have to go, and the unwillingness or incapacity of other institutions to take us there.

What we have seen is a set of structures openly designed to limit the capacity of those who seek to intervene in the workings of the private economic order, working just as they were intended. They are supported, moreover, by the social reality behind them, in which each major source of power in that private system is able to reach into the political process and assert its preferences in some effective manner. And yet, these very institutions enjoy strong support from the same people whose efforts at reform through them are regularly frustrated. Again and again, new generations of reformers exhaust themselves amidst the nooks and crannies of procedural limitations or outright resistance, only to insist at the end that reform can and must take place through these same institutions.

This is surely an important lesson in the strength of the grip that orthodox American ideology holds upon us. The Constitution and the institutions it erects are so bathed in legitimacy and symbolism that many people can conceive of no other routes toward their goals. The soothing rhetoric and appearance of decisive action that come from the President reassure us that our interests are being served, and the dignified deliberation of the Congress and the Court convey a sense of accommodation, security, and legality. The educational system, the media, and our anxiety to believe that what we have is right, all have combined to prevent us from seeing how institutions, Constitution, legal system and procedures make up an integrated barrier to all significant reform.

Informal Practices

Nor have we but begun to identify the ways in which the thrust toward reform is broken, channelled, and ultimately absorbed within the society. All that we have said so far pertains only to the *formal* structures and procedures of politics. Many of the most effective limits on the capacity to use government to effect change have not even been touched upon. For example, even if we assume both the desire and the capacity to act on the part of governmental institutions, the nature of our economic system would erect powerful barriers. It would deny both money and means, and ultimately even the will, to reform. The earning of profit is the fundamental purpose of the entire economic order, to say nothing of the source of new investment and jobs for the population. Resistance to taxation on the part of major units of economic power is thus strong and constant, and the support of hard-pressed individuals is not hard to develop. Property rights are readily defensible in court, and the only means that government has to redress inequalities inevitably conflict with such enforceable private rights. Policy makers must see that intrusion upon profits can only be limited, and thus that revenues will always be much less than needed to meet problems. They must realize that the boundaries of the legal system prevent all sweeping change in the current pattern of distribution of burdens and benefits, and thus that only slow and incremental changes can be wrought in situations of long-accumulated explosiveness. Moreover, resistance is bitter and determined at every step of the way. At some point, these understood if not explicitly discussed limitations begin to sap even the will to act. What can be done is so trivial as

to be provocative rather than ameliorative. In this context, the temptation is to resort to symbolic reassurances, or to content oneself with
private gratifications while insisting that the principle of self-help is best
after all.

Some other informal limitations on the possibility of reform also
deserve mention. Many of these flow from the social reality of those
who would most benefit from reform. For the most part, such persons
are relatively poor, economically insecure (at least to the extent of
having to work each day to earn their living), and divided from each
other by their ethnic, racial, religious, educational or occupational
backgrounds. They do not have time to bring their weight to bear in
politics, they do not have the money to hire others to work in their
behalf, and good leadership is hard to find. Internal conflicts obscure
shared needs and goals. In fact, what divides them from others in
essentially like circumstances may be more important to them than
anything else. The apparent hopelessness of gaining the material or
spiritual goals they seek may lead them to vent their frustrations upon
each other.

All of these characteristics are deliberately used from time to time
by those who wish to frustrate reform. Many local elections, for
example, are held only during daylight hours, when most lower class
persons are at work. Playing off black against white is an old and almost
unfailingly effective practice, as are the deliberate provocation of
religious or ethnic conflicts or geographic or class tensions or differences. When a group or community does appear to have organized
itself under competent leadership and shows signs of making itself felt
in politics, other tactics may be invoked. One is cooptation, in which
indigenous leaders are encouraged to believe that they will be able to
gain more for their followers by entering the established political game
and playing under its rules. They are appointed to various official
positions, given programs to administer, brought into the circle of
leadership, etc. Soon, such leaders develop greater loyalties to their new
status and positions or to their fellow politicians than to their followers. They begin explaining to the latter why their goals are too
extreme or premature, or why they should support the dominant
political party, and the movement has been effectively blunted. If
cooptation fails, there is always outright repression, for which police,
courts, and ultimately the army are legitimately available. And the

support of the general public is almost always again available for such action as government officials deem necessary and appropriate. After-the-fact justifications are normally accepted, just because government officials are viewed as being right in situations of uncertainty.

Elections tend to embody many informal reform-blunting processes. Participation by all in this periodic ritual is strongly urged, for then later it will be possible to argue that officials represent all, were chosen by the people and are therefore legitimately empowered to act, and that all have a stake in their government. Candidates were chosen, of course, by those with the most time, money, power, and interest in the outcome. Their differences can only be marginal, for no sources of the money needed to campaign are likely to seek fundamental change in the system that sustains them. Nor can such candidates, if elected, be anything but either the captives or the willing agents of the powerful social and economic forces that pressure government to act as it does. The range of what they can do is firmly fixed by all the forces we have noted. Nevertheless, vast amounts of energy and time are regularly invested by reformers in the process of seeking to elect one or another person whose rhetoric or "principles" are marginally better than another candidate. Such candidates, and surely their supporters, are often quite sincere. And in specific instances, it *can* make a difference who holds office. But the net effect of all these efforts is not—*cannot be*—anything but newly banked support for the status quo. If they are successful in electing their candidate, they will no doubt feel gratified at the proof that the system works; it will be some time later before they realize that the "triumph" was ephemeral and meaningless. If they are not successful, they will have wasted time and effort, but probably will still feel better for having tried. Either way, elections have once again proven functional—useful diversions which contribute to the defense of things as they are.

The true hopelessness of reform only becomes visible when all of these factors are seen together as a deep network of blatant and subtle defense of the status quo. Structures and procedures, some formal and some informal, are supplemented first by the character and imperatives of the capitalist-liberal system and its associated values and ideology and then by the social reality that is linked to both. Any thrust toward fundamental change, in those few instances where there is capacity to generate it, is either denied or broken down into a set of marginal change questions. These questions are channeled and shaped into smaller and smaller versions, then submitted to the automatic workings of accepted procedures—in which the result, if any, has been endorsed in advance through the operation of legitimacy and ideology. Simultaneously, change-oriented energy has been absorbed, the public has been symbolically reassured, leaders have been coopted, a few instances of repression have occurred, and the essential outlines of the status quo are exactly as they were before the process started. Only the reformers learn no lessons: at the close of the process, their calls for the same tactics to right the same wrongs are just as loud and as fervent as ever.

THE PART PLAYED BY BASIC POLITICAL VALUES

One of the further ironies of reform is that the very values that it seeks to restore or modernize—the basic motivations of reform itself—are often at least contributing sources of the problems reform seeks to solve. The traditional methods thus could be as workable as our assumptions and rhetoric proclaim, and activists could achieve all their goals—and nothing would be different, if all they sought were the effectuation of the traditional values. No problems would be solved, and none of our current needs would be served, in any basic way. Only a series of band-aids would have been attached to the most superficial symptoms, while the reformers retired amid self-congratulation and satisfaction. Let us see why this is so.

One of the most basic of American values is that of individualism. Not only is the individual the focus of political thinking, but the highest good is to be found in the self-seeking of each individual. Self-interest and self-help are held to be sufficient sources of "social" progress, and a proper basis for organization of the society and economy themselves. When such commitments are raised to the level of basic operating principles in a context of drastic inequalities, they effectively deny equally basic human needs for sympathy, cooperation, and the development of community. We must compete, rather than aid each other in the struggle for self-development. We must act in ways that cut ourselves off from others, and we must judge those who do less well as inferior. Society cannot be a community of shared risks and opportunities where mutual assistance spurs the human progress of all.

It can only be a hierarchical pyramid of advantages and disadvantages, in which the isolation of all is justified as necessary to our nature and to social progress.

Moreover, the goals of individual self-seeking are—according to our traditional values—materialist in character. Whether the individual is worthy, whether he has achieved or not, is measured in terms of the extent of his acquisition of wealth and other material rewards. Next to individualism, property reigns as the dominant American value. Seeking after property, guarding and holding it, using it to acquire more property—these are the basic motivations and purposes of individuals and the dynamic forces of the society. Thus the inequalities that are evident in our society are necessary, and must be protected, even furthered, as part of our commitment to these traditional values. It is good to gain property, and so those who have the tools to do so are encouraged to gain as much as they can. Those who do not have such tools are by necessary implication consigned to the left behind. It is bad to take property away from those who have gained it through hard work and personal competence (or through previous advantages and outright looting). Thus the existing pattern of wealth and property distribution must be maintained. It cannot be significantly altered without abandoning our commitment to property as a basic value.

The value that does the most to support individualism, materialism, and property as basic operative principles in American social life is legalism. This implies commitment not only to established laws, rules and procedures, but also the particular network of courts and lawyers to go with them, with all the special-interest effects that we noted in our discussion of law and the legal system. Our reverence for legalism and the central role we grant the law mean that the existing social order first gains legitimate and significant rigidity, and then is placed in control of the process of change—so that all changes can be channelled into those forms that can be best accommodated and absorbed by that same social order. Along the way, the management of the society and of change is conducted by a small and self-interested group amidst the highest aura of legitimacy. Attempted deviations from the prescribed methods and behaviors are readily and legitimately crushed.

Taken together, these traditional values give a particular—and severely limited—definition to freedom, equality, and democracy. The latter can only be understood in ways that are consistent with the former—with individualism, materialism, property, and legalism, the central values of capitalism. To endorse and seek to effectuate American values is to affirm *capitalist* freedom, equality, and democracy. It is to affirm the rigidities and inequalities inherent in individualism, materialism, property, and legalism, and in effect to embrace the social order as it now stands. *Reform in principle is rigidity in practice.* There is no way to escape this: one cannot fundamentally change something by emphasizing the very values that built it in the first place. What we have today in the way of a society and a set of problems is only marginally a corruption of basic American values. For the most part, it is the logical flowering and fruition of them, the contemporary real-world manifestation of the life they promise. To seek "change" with the traditional values is not to seek change at all. It is sheer illusion. If this life and these problems are not acceptable to us, we must seek change at the only place where it can begin—with new values and new consciousness.

But we are neither ready nor yet forced to do so. The strength of our present consciousness still holds us to the hope of reform or to the avoidance of confrontation with reality.

IDEOLOGY, CONSCIOUSNESS, AND THE POWER OF REFORM

The vital question is, of course, why reform continues to be such a focus—and why people fail to see *either* that its methods are unequal to its goals *or* that its goals are unequal to our current problems. The answer lies in the compelling character of our political consciousness. When we think about change, all we can think *about* is the use of the standard machinery of the existing political system. All else is darkness, either an unthinkable void or so full of uncertainty and fear that we are both unable and unwilling to try to penetrate it.

The Exclusivity of the Urge to Reform

How does our political consciousness achieve this remarkable triumph? Both negative and positive approaches are involved, each in powerful but varied forms. First, our present consciousness operates to deny that there are real alternatives to reform. Next, it insists that the traditional values are right, inevitable, and capable of providing every desired satisfaction in life. Some examples may be in order.

Alternatives to reform are denied or negated in a variety of ways. One set has its roots in our conceptual capacities and habits. We learn to think about change exclusively in terms of elections, lobbying, and Presidential leadership of the Congress, and we are taught to view this range of action as the entire political arena. This narrow focus blinds us to the realities of power distribution, the effects of ideology, the impact of economic forces, and the wide variety of other factors that affect who gets what out of government. We lose even the feeling of a *need* to conceptualize nontraditional processes of change, let alone the capacity to do so. It is only when some spontaneous event occurs that we suddenly become aware of such possibilities. Thus, many were surprised at the results achieved by the civil rights and antiwar demonstrations of the mid and late 1960s. Still others then acted as if this tactic was always and equally applicable in all situations. Very few people had thought beforehand of what to do and why, or what the limits of the tactic were in the total context of power and interest in the society. Still fewer, even of those most dedicated to fundamental change, have even yet seen the need to think comprehensively about a total process leading to the acquisition of state power by a new social grouping with wholly different priorities and purposes in mind.

The other side of this inability to conceptualize the process of change is the demand for a complete blueprint of the entire process, from start to finish. Show me, the challenge goes. Tell me each step in the process. Who does what with what results? etc., from now until the new society, guaranteed to be better, is brought into being. No such blueprint can be provided, of course, and no ironclad guarantees can be made—which immediately sends the challenger back to renewed commitment to traditional reform. The blueprint demand grows out of our faith and hope in reform, as well as out of our liberal rationality's insistence upon plans, timetables, and cost estimates. The very act of making such a demand forecloses recognition that fundamental change can only come about through consciousness change. It is a demand made very much within *this* consciousness for description of an event that can only occur through a *new* consciousness. The only way in which it can be met is to take the challenger patiently through the stages of developing that new consciousness, by which point his need for a blueprint would be replaced by a conception of the outlines of a process with many crossroads but nevertheless clear potential. Justification of that new society must also follow a similar route. It can be made up only in part from those values and personal relationships that are part of this consciousness and this society, and depends in essential ways upon the qualitatively different capabilities and potential that are realizable only under a new consciousness and a new society.

The inability to conceptualize a nontraditional process of change and the opposite demand for a comprehensive blueprint are supplemented in our present consciousness with a special fear of violence. This combination then forms another major bulwark against any but traditional methods of reform. The violence that we fear and reject is nonofficial violence, meaning any act defined by incumbent officials as unlawful. We do not fear or reject violence in the form of routinized brutalization of ghetto populations or of assembly-line workers, or in the form of police repression, but only that of people who are driven to respond to such conditions by nontraditional means such as demonstrations or strikes. This is a strange phenomenon in a country with such continuing experience with violence, and another testimony to the power of ideology and consciousness. The mere fact of nonofficial violence awakens disapproval and rejection in us, quite apart from any perhaps justifiable surrounding circumstances. Violence becomes an independent touchstone of judgment, to be condemned regardless of conditions and provocations. Behind this lies fear of the unknown, no doubt, or of chaos or change itself—as well as conviction that what we have is right or inevitable or at least the best possible under all the circumstances.

Another way in which our present consciousness leads us away from all but reform methods is found in our special attachment to revered symbols. The concepts of democracy, freedom, the Constitution, the majesty of the Presidency, the sanctity of the law, patriotism, nationalism, etc., all are fully integrated with "goodness" in our minds. Not only do such stereotypes and symbols provide us with reassurance, satisfaction, and diversion, but they themselves may become our focus. That is, the symbolic gratification takes precedence over the events or processes that are being described or interpreted. It no longer matters what is actually being done; all that counts is that there be an opportunity for the manipulation of the familiar and welcome symbols. This may be another version of our preference for activity as such rather than concern for the consequences of such action. To many Americans, it is more important to play the game than to worry about who won and who lost. We concentrate on the procedures by which the game is played, the style and the rhetoric, and we pay relatively little attention to the final result. Both symbolism and this activity-focus lead us toward the traditional game of politics and away from the question of who wins and loses, or what tangible results emerge from this process. Only the latter, of course, raise issues such as the efficacy of reform or suggest that some better routes must be found if results are really desired.

Finally, our present consciousness negates alternatives to reform through a series of blocks against all serious analysis or even consideration of political conditions, goals, and aspirations. A deep sense of inevitability about all things American pervades our thinking, linking up with a sense of how fortunate we are to enjoy such a standard of living and relative individual freedom. The United States has emerged as the world's greatest power under our present system. Therefore, we shall no doubt muddle through somehow and enjoy continued affluence and prestige despite apparent difficulties.

Inevitability and fatalism permit individualistic, self-indulgent orientation. Problems are too complex to be affected by any one individual, so why bother. Better to seize what pleasures one can find in the immediate present. Moreover, intellectuals are untrustworthy and impractical, prone to dangerous ideas and abstract theorizing. Anti-intellectualism runs deep in the American consciousness, insulating many people against serious confrontation with different concepts and ideas. It is fed by the vocationalism of schools and colleges, reinforced by the media, and confirmed by the refusal of many intellectuals to take themselves seriously.

Spurred by anti-intellectualism, self-indulgence, and fatalism, there develops a kind of massive hopelessness about the mere possibility of change. Isn't our situation the inevitable product of human nature itself? There has never been a really human, egalitarian society, has there? There has never been a period of fundamental change in an advanced industrial society, has there? Then why should anybody think or act seriously in hopes of achieving either now? Better to settle back and seek only the pleasures that can be obtained for oneself right now, and let others watch out for themselves.

And then there is the positive side, the affirmation that our consciousness attaches to the idea of reform. In part, this consists of insistence that the political and economic order is self-restoring. Whenever it develops problems, inadequacies, or other imperfections, certain natural, built-in correctives begin to go to work to restore the proper balance again. In this respect, it works self-correctingly just as the free economic market does when faced with changing supply and demand situations. If the power of business is too great, labor will organize to counteract it and balance will be restored. That the "free market" is neither free nor known to operate in this self-correcting manner is no obstacle to this assumption. Neither is the fact that combinations of the most powerful can work to the detriment of all others, or that any particular loss of balance may be permanently disabling to the prospect of restoring the previous situation. Such caveats do not withstand consciousness-generated faith in the natural workings of a self-correcting system.

In larger part, the affirmative side consists of massive endorsement of the traditional values. Because these values are so right and good and peculiarly appropriate for the United States and its people, they must be restored in all their fullness. This is the essence of reform: the affirmation and achievement of the traditional values in the context of the present. Thus, the validity of these values and the exclusive utility and importance of the process of reform are really two sides of the same principle. To accept and revere these values is to accept and seek reform—and nothing else. Once the premise is accepted—that the traditional values are right and good and sufficient—no other commitment but reform can consistently follow. Thus, the more powerfully the present consciousness confirms and endorses these values, the more it also compels people to think and see only in terms of reform.

And, just as we recognize that its triumph is indeed complete, so must we acknowledge that consciousness change is the key to political change. We *must* understand how we think, what it does to the lives we lead, how it shapes the alternatives we face—and how we can learn to think differently.

NOTES

1. Richard J. Barber, *The American Corporation: Its Money, Its Power, Its Politics* (New York: E. P. Dutton & Co., Inc., 1970).
2. Jack Newfield and Jeff Greenfield, *A Populist Manifesto: Call for a New Majority* (New York: Warner Paperback Library, 1972).

PART

Consciousness Change: Seeing Differently

CHAPTER FIVE

Ideology and Consciousness:
The Culture Trap

What are the essential characteristics of the ideology and consciousness that so effectively combine to contain thrusts toward change? This chapter explores their substance, from the perspective of their function as means of social control.

All existing industrialized societies operate through multiple systems of social control, involving various degrees of coercion, the dominant ideology, and the underlying consciousness. The more powerful and less recognized the ideology and consciousness, of course, the less likely will be direct challenges that oblige the society to maintain itself through outright coercion. The latter may have to be employed from time to time, nevertheless, to repress outbreaks developing out of intolerable conditions or provoked by particularly inept elite uses of power. A sketch of the relationship, sources, and manifestations of coercion, ideology, and consciousness may serve to frame our analysis of the latter two in terms of their mutual social control function.

Let us envision coercion, ideology, and consciousness as levels or styles of social control that can be located on a continuum of increasing subtlety and self-administration. *Coercion,* though sometimes not always perceived as such (as in the case of the economic market, for example), is normally visible and externally imposed. *Ideology* is first communicated to people, then internalized by them, and finally drawn upon by leaders to explain or justify their actions or marshal support for their policies. It is enforced by the actions of others, but it has many of its effects because we respond "voluntarily" as it prescribes; thus it is a mix of about equal parts externally and internally imposed. *Consciousness,* however, involves still more fully *self*-administered limitations on our range of thought and action. Acquired more or less implicitly from our culture and social institutions, and operating at a deeper and earlier stage of mental activity, its continuing effects are usually unrecognized. But paramount among such effects are the plausibility and power it confers upon ideology.

Table 5-1 represents this continuum, and connects the styles of social control with illustrative social institutions and processes from which they emanate and examples of ways in which they manifest

TABLE 5-1   Styles of social control, their sources and manifestations

Sources: Social institutions and processes	Manifestations	Levels or styles of social control	
1. Police, armies	Injury and death	Physical coercion	*Most exter-*
2. Courts, legislatures	Laws, prisons, fines	Physical coercion and threats thereof	*nally im-posed,*
3. Economic market	Inducements: goods, income, profits	Economic coercion	*visible, etc.*
Family, schools, media, leaders' rhetoric, etc. (Chiefly Explicit)	Democratic mythology — Anticommunism The Work Ethic	Ideology	
Family, schools, forms of social organization, interpersonal relationships (Chiefly Implicit)	Language, logic, concepts, symbols, culture, values, ways of knowing and thinking, etc.	Consciousness	*Most subtle, most self-administered, etc.*

themselves in our lives. Neither divisions nor categories are really so sharply marked off from each other or exclusive, of course, but the basic relationships are captured by this representation. Ideology, for example, is manifested in such principles of belief as the work ethic and democratic mythology, both of which are explicitly communicated by family, schools, and media. The culture- and consciousness-teaching agents turn out to be many of the same institutions, but now operating at an often subverbal level—communicating by what they assume, how they act, and what they exclude as "wrong" or "impossible." Their success is manifested in values, language, concepts, symbols, and ways of thinking generally.

By contrast, the actions of coercive institutions on behalf of established rules are deliberately visible—and often quite tangible. The purpose of such social control is to apply physical inducements or restraints if necessary, in order that the prescribed routines of the society continue. But no society can function long, and certainly not stably, where it depends primarily on outright coercion. These are institutions and processes of last resort, and their regular application may best be understood as acts by rulers who have failed to manage the society in other ways. Where numbers of people have rejected the dominant ideology that legitimates coercive tactics, and have the motivation and self-confidence to act to change their social and political systems, neither courts nor armies can in the long run preserve a social order.

Because outright coercion is not independently capable of social control, we shall concentrate here exclusively on the other levels. But ideology is relatively visible, and frequently rejected by those who allow themselves reality-testing opportunities—so our consideration can be relatively brief. It is our consciousness, at once all-encapsulating and the vital key to change, on which we shall focus our primary efforts.

IDEOLOGY: SUBSTANCE AND ROOTS

American ideology sets forth some basic premises and goals, and prescribes the routes by which the latter are to be achieved. We shall briefly sketch the substance of orthodox ideology in four categories, emphasizing the roots of beliefs in basic societal values. Thus, we shall describe the ideology's view of what *people* are or should be like, what *society* is or should be like, what *government* is or should be like, and what the *results* would be if all the "should be's" came to pass. Few persons would hold such a detailed and coherent version of the ideology, of course. Most hold only isolated scraps, and there are variations between the beliefs held by persons at different class levels or regions of the country. But we shall set forth the dominant or mainstream version from which all variants take off.

What People Are or Should Be Like

The individual is the primary focus, the beginning point around which all political thought is built. Each person has wants and needs that he or she must seek to fulfill, and this ceaseless striving gives rise to the dynamics of life and politics. People are naturally competitive, and by striving against each other will improve themselves as well as better achieve their goals. Learning self-reliance and building character are major grounds for this emphasis on individualism.

What is it that people are or should be striving *for*? The wants and needs that motivate people most strongly are for status and recognition. Often they take the form of materialism—money, property, etc. The desire for property is "sewn in the nature of man," and one's success in amassing material wealth can be employed as a rough measure of one's talent, self-discipline, and character. Respect for the property of others, and a high regard for those who have achieved success in such terms, naturally follow. But it is also possible for people to denigrate materialism and seek satisfaction from other forms of competition. The point is that their status depends on demonstrating in one or another way that they are better than others.

People also wish to take part in their government, and it is their right as free persons to do so. All are equal in the sense of having a single vote. They are capable of exercising their political rights and casting their votes rationally, and majorities should control.

People are also equal in their entitlement to take part in the struggle to acquire material wants. But they are clearly *not* equal in talents and capabilities, either to be a wise leader or to succeed in amassing wealth. And some groups of people, such as nonwhite races, some foreigners, and most women, are by background and nature less competent than white male Americans in either of these arenas. In such cases, they must be provided for in other ways, with decisions made for them and under different standards.

What Society Is and Should Be Like

Because the paramount goal of individuals is fulfillment of their material wants, the best society is one organized to maximize their chances to do so freely and efficiently. The device which best makes this possible is the free and competitive market. All persons or firms can offer their products and services and seek the highest possible prices. Simultaneously they can seek to acquire the goods and services they want and need at the lowest possible prices. Acting freely, they make contracts to buy and sell. Those who are most efficient make the highest net profits, and all receive what they deserve. The society as a whole benefits from the automatic balancing of supply and demand achieved by this voluntary system, and because competition to provide the best products leads toward ever-improving quality and a rising standard of living.

In a larger sense, the market principle is applicable to all aspects of society, not just economic production and exchange. It permits all manner of tastes to be served, all types of preferences—religious, political, aesthetic—to find outlets and satisfaction. Wherever there is demand, there will be supply. Wherever there is an attractive or useful product or service (or art form or political candidate), there will be those who wish to buy. The free and competitive market harmonizes the great diversity of wants and needs within the society with a minimum of coercion. The result is a maximum of freedom for all.

What Government Is and Should Be Like

Government is basically the referee, and the policeman where necessary. All the primary forces of the society are at work, and it will be best if they are left completely free to harmonize diversities and permit individual achievement. But occasionally conflicts develop, or some participants in the private striving process take advantage of others, or the whole system must take action with respect to the outside world, and so government must act. Several principles guiding such action may be identified.

Government should of course observe the limits set by the natural rights of individuals. Its role is to enforce contracts, not to interfere with them; where one person or firm is entitled to collect debts from another, for example, it should be able to call on government to enforce collection. Property cannot be taken without just compensation and, given the variety and extensiveness of private property-holding, this means that much government action is either subject to challenge or costly, and perhaps both. These are necessary and proper limits to government's capacity to act.

In order that the prospects of arbitrary government action be reduced as much as possible, an elaborate set of procedures is established. These procedures provide explicitly for the ways in which decisions shall be made, who shall make them, and what limits must be observed. Because of this elaborate network of procedure, things work almost mechanically. If everybody does his part, as everybody has an interest in doing, the result (the government decision) will be fair and just for all. These procedures, of course, are neutral. That is, everybody has an equal chance to be heard and there is nothing pressing the decision in one direction or another except the particular merits of the case itself. (This principle reaches further, to link up with the social base of interest-group conflict, but this has already been described earlier under the title of democratic pluralism and need not be repeated here.)

Given the importance of contracts and property rights in the private sphere, and of procedures and rules in the governmental arena, it is only proper that the law play a special role in this system. By setting principles down in precise fashion, and settling disputes in courts, fairness and consistency will be promoted, individual rights secured, and government arbitrariness effectively prevented. Moreover, the disruptive potential of conflicts will be muted and business can go on undisturbed. There is therefore very heavy emphasis on what the law says, on obedience to the law once it is enunciated by legislatures and courts, and on the need for legal determinations of all individual claims and conflicts. Again, as with procedures generally, the law is mechanical—automatic, neutral—and no personal preferences are involved when it acts to the advantage of some and disadvantage of others.

Although the great majority of issues or problems are best resolved through private activity, or through the impersonal, objective application of law and procedure, some situations may require purposeful government action. Regulation of economic activity, subsidies for particular purposes, assistance to particular groups and classes of people, are all justifiable if it can be shown that serious problems or deprivations would otherwise occur. But such actions should be understood as exceptions to the still-valid general principle of laissez faire.

Another area in which government action is proper, even rigorous action, is with respect to the outside world. Because business needs hold a high place among American priorities, it follows that government should aggressively support and further such interests overseas. Moreover, a powerful military capability and an alert stance against communist subversion or outright aggression are necessary to the very security of the United States and its way of life. Communism represents the most profound threat of all those things most treasured by American ideology, such as property, individualism, political freedoms, and religion. Thus, anti-communism joins nationalism as a vigorous supporting factor behind an active governmental role in international affairs.

What the Results Will Then Be

If these principles are followed, the results will be equality, freedom, and progress. Equality is assured by the continuing opportunity to participate in government, and by government assistance to those who are not as well prepared to compete as others. Freedom is built into the protection of the economic market and the analogue to that free and competitive market in the larger society. Progress is inevitable, where the competition between imaginative suppliers for the informed buyers' dollar is real. The more intense the competition, the better the products and the faster the rise in the general standard of living of the society. Moreover, the quality of personal development on the part of individuals will inevitably be advanced by such competition.

In bold relief, we have portrayed liberal democracy as it is understood in the United States. It is *liberal* because of the primacy of the individual and his self-seeking, and the protections surrounding the market's provisions of opportunities to do so. It is *democratic,* at least under dominant interpretations, because of the assured opportunities for individual and group participation and the assumed fairness of decisional procedures. Because it is *ideology*, however, there is no necessary reason why it should be true. It is what many people believe, and what leaders also either believe or find it convenient to use as self-justification for what they want to do for other reasons. It is normally effective for just such purposes, moreover, which is what gives it its great importance in the analysis of political change.

But belief in, and acceptance of actions justified in terms of, these principles is not the only reason why ideology is so important. It also—just because it is so dominant in the United States—fixes the frame of reference and many of the terms of political argument and action. For example, where exceptions to the ideology's characterization of life are visible, the issue may be limited to how to correct them. In other words, the principles may be accepted as unquestionably valid and all effort directed at conforming reality to them. In this way, the ideology short-circuits re-examination of more basic questions—such as the validity of the principles themselves. Or, to take another example, challenges may be raised to the definitions or relationship of certain values contained in the ideology, such as equality versus property, while all the other principles are accepted as valid. Or, finally, the ideology may be used so exclusively as a target of criticism that there is no time or energy left for consideration of what to substitute for it—and, once again, it has effectively set the terms of argument and held the day. Even those who try to contend against it are in many respects helpless to escape it.

In summary, the dominant ideology is resilient and pervasive, however superficial it may be by contrast with political consciousness. It is effectively promulgated by family, schools, media, and experience. Always available in the minds of citizens, it can be drawn upon by leaders as a means of social control. We are all more or less tied in to this system of belief and subject to its attractions. When leaders or would-be leaders manipulate the proper symbols, we snap to attention and "understand" events as intended. Almost anything can be (and is) legitimated under these circumstances, unless people have a clear objective basis for reality-testing readily at hand. Moreover, even those who seek to escape and challenge it are often powerless to do so. Instead, as we have just seen, they often end up actually reinforcing the dominant ideology. This is not just because of the strength of the ideology itself, of course, but also due to the preparation and support provided by the underlying political consciousness.

CONSCIOUSNESS: CHARACTER AND MANIFESTATIONS

Consciousness in the general sense is the way of thinking characteristic of a particular culture. It embodies the basic values of the society at a much deeper level than ideology's explicit teachings, by taking them as "givens" and shaping basic thought patterns accordingly. Quite naturally, therefore, consciousness articulates with ideology, making the latter appear more believable and inevitable. In seeking to understand the character and political significance of the American consciousness, we face two major obstacles. One stems from the elusive nature of consciousness itself. It is not easy to describe or analyze a way of thinking and knowing; the discussion readily becomes so loose that multiple understandings (or misunderstandings) are likely. We may do best to talk about consciousness in separate components, i.e., in its several dimensions: its nature, sources, and effects, for example, as well as how it works and how it contrasts with other ways of thinking that exist in the world. To fully understand the character and limits of our own way of thinking, however, implies that we have gained some distance and detachment from it. In effect, recognizing it for what it is and does may be the first step in the process by which one extracts oneself from it.

The other obstacle to understanding consciousness today is that referred to earlier: the mis- and overuse of the term, and its resulting trivialization. *Consciousness* is often used interchangeably with *ideology*, for example, so that when one rejects some version of orthodox American ideology, it may be said that one has experienced a "consciousness change." Another superficial use of the term occurs when all that is involved is growing awareness of institutionalized discrimination or systematic exploitation; in such cases, the phrase "consciousness raising" is often applied, particularly by minority or feminist groups. Or some limited insight into one fragment of the character or workings of consciousness may be celebrated in the form of knowing references to "consciousness" in general.

Understanding consciousness is a process of self-sensitization to the workings of one's mind, and of steadily expanding awareness of what factors have shaped its conceptual capabilities. For most of us, our consciousness is all-encompassing, an utterly comprehensive world in which we are necessarily dependent; to become independent and autonomous, we must at least reach the point of self-consciousness about how we think. This section attempts description of the several aspects of consciousness, in no particular order because all flow into and merge with each other. I hope it will be clear that the subject under analysis is something deeper, more fundamental, and potentially more encapsulating than most current usages of "consciousness" might suggest.

The Nature of Consciousness: A Preliminary Example

Consciousness is preverbal, at times preconceptual, in character. As we experience the first stirrings of feeling or thought in our minds, consciousness begins its work also: it offers a particular set of concepts or words with which those feelings or thoughts may be expressed—and no others. Certain thoughts simply cannot be framed, for there are no receptacles available to contain them. Some things are taken as so self-evident that thinking begins with them as *premises* instead of potential questions. What does it mean to be *an individual*, for example? The first conceptualization is likely to be that of distinction, of isolation, of the separation of oneself from all others. This may then be followed by thoughts of independence, of specific wants and needs distinct from (though perhaps similar to) those of other individuals, and of a general situation in which many people are striving to satisfy their respective wants and needs. It may even appear that this is a description of human nature—universal characteristics of all people, an important part of the essence of what it means to be human.

Each of these responses to the question, however, is particular to our consciousness. *None* of these is the only possible way of conceiving of *an individual*. To some societies, perhaps to some Americans, to be an individual is not to be distinct from, but rather integrally a part of, other people. Wants and needs could have entirely different dimensions, satisfiable only through noncompetitive relationships with others. Our understanding of "human nature" can quickly be shown to be little more than a projection of those characteristics of people which our culture emphasizes and our economic system requires.

But nevertheless most Americans understand themselves as individuals in at least the first sense. We live our lives in the context of such assumptions, perhaps connected also with a culturally received understanding of what it means to be a "good" person. In other words, our most basic personal identities are shaped by particular consciousness-dictated understanding of who and what we are. What we do, how we live, what are right and wrong things in our world, are all bound together and integrated with our consciousness. Small wonder then that it is both difficult to identify consciousness as a separate containing force and painful to undergo consciousness change—the most basic self-conceptions, identities, and life-adjustments are at stake.

The Coherence Between Consciousness and Particular Cultures and Social Systems

It is no accident that the characteristics of our consciousness coalesced into the integrated package now under analysis. They did not independently converge by a variety of evolutionary trails to make up a merely coincidental set of values, language, logic, and ways of thinking. There is an underlying coherence to them, an organizing principle that relates them consistently to each other and to the culture and social order of which they are a part. Consciousness is *specific* to the *particular* social order in which it exists. It embodies the normative principles or culture on which the social order rests, and the way of thinking that is generated flows from and supports those normative principles. The components of consciousness are extensions of those normative principles and of the social formations of that particular social order. They are not generally applicable, but instead limited in use to the kinds of communication and understanding that are appropriate to that social order.

The world has known a number of different bases of social ordering, and anthropologists are still reporting new ones. The one in which we live is a special variant of capitalist-liberal society, which replaced feudalism in Europe in the seventeenth century and took over the American continent soon after. The normative principles on which it rests are those of individualism, self-servingness, material measures of success, progress through maximizing individual self-servingness, and so forth. Because consciousness must provide ways of thinking that are consistent with these principles or the social order will not survive, it becomes in effect the *completion* of the objective conditions and normative principles of that social order, forming a *coherent whole* with them.

Our consciousness is a special—exaggerated in some ways, unique in others—version of capitalist-liberal consciousness. History and social circumstances have not generated the challenges to capitalism-liberalism, either as a social system or as a dominant consciousness, in the United States that they did in Western Europe. Favored by economic opportunity and uncontested, the American version has come to emphasize individualism more exclusively. It also has come to appear so self-validating and compelling that even many intellectuals find it difficult to understand what another culture's way of thinking might be like or how it might justify a social order quite different from ours. Certain unique features of the American consciousness are also evident, as a result of the same historical and social factors. To at least some degree, it is more imbued with racism, messianism, moral and cultural arrogance, and religiosity than the Western European variants.

How Consciousness Is Absorbed

We learn to think only through social institutions and experience, not through self-development independent of the world around us. Social institutions such as the family and the school provide the earliest cues to the definitions of words, the meanings of symbols, what is good and what is bad, and how to interpret observations about the world. Later these institutions are supplemented by others, such as churches, communications media, business and government organizations, unions, etc. All of these provide the individual with further cues to how to think about the world, to an extent explicitly, but perhaps more powerfully by nonverbal communication. All of them exist in capitalist-liberal society and *assume* its continued existence as a matter of course. Their priorities and practices, their entire frame of reference, are *consistent* with (and *only* with, in many cases) capitalist-liberal normative principles and social formations. And so everything we can learn or experience from them must be also. The sources of our consciousness lie in the social institutions compatible with capitalism-liberalism, and we can only emerge thinking in ways consistent with that system. In short, *we* assume what *they* assume, across time.

At all times, therefore, the basic social institutions and processes of the society are routinely banking unconscious support for the existing social order. Every major social formation in the society reflects this social order, and teaches thought patterns and behavior consistent with it. The nuclear family is a clear example. It expresses possessive individualism in the most profound manner. From this basis emerges a whole set of ideologies rationalizing female subserviency. Thus, given this definition of the family—and taking it for granted that this is not only the natural form of human relationship but also the basic building block of a society—it is little wonder that Americans unconsciously see their very personalities as deeply invested in the capitalist-liberal social order.

Other social formations similarly if less fundamentally reinforce the status quo and transmit its associated consciousness. This is as true of some of those which appear to have been formed to challenge that order, as it is of some others which are its primary beneficiaries. Trade unions, for example, are as much sources of linkage to the capitalist-liberal system and carriers of its consciousness as are corporations. They assume the continuity of the larger system, and the legitimacy of its basic operating principles (i.e., competition, private property, profit), seeking only a somewhat larger share of the returns from one specific enterprise for the members of that particular union. They emphasize the particularity of the employer-employee relationship and teach that solution to workers' needs are to be found there rather than (for example) in association with all other workers as a unified class, or in taking control of the mechanism of government or ownership of the means of production generally.

The educational system is of course one of the most visible and deliberate transmitters of the capitalist-liberal consciousness. Compulsory public education at the elementary and secondary levels assures that every member of the society is exposed to twelve years of systematic indoctrination in the inevitability and rightness of our method of thinking. The expansion of colleges and universities has led to broadened opportunities for more subtle inculcation of thought patterns and attitudes that are equally supportive. Students learn to accept and to perform—for the purpose of receiving grades or other certification—rather than to think and to know for themselves. The universities also produce the society's official versions of truth, and certify such knowledge to all other areas of the society for appropriate action. When is a person's behavior "deviant," for example, and when should that person receive what sort of rehabilitative treatment to enable him to be "normal" again? Taking the existing social order as fixed or desirable, the psychiatrist, criminologist, and social worker will combine their skills and status to prescribe how that person's "problem" shall be understood and (in effect) what shall be done to him to make him conform to what the social order can tolerate.

From all of these social formations and their routine activities, people learn to see their world in ways that embrace and support it. They also learn to see and deal with each other in similar ways. Thus, personal interrelationships tend to become objectivized. Other people are tangible objects out there, to be treated as one would other material elements. Some are to be manipulated for personal gain, others collected for enjoyment as property. There is very little understanding of, or time for, the "unproductive" aspects of human existence or capability. Intuitive, experiential, or mystical dimensions of life are not just deemphasized—they are effectively denied within this political consciousness.

The general result of this process of social transmission and enforcement of the single dominant consciousness is of course a highly supportive situation within the society. The capitalist-liberal system is not only legitimate and highly desirable, it is inevitable—God-given and immutable. In a practical society where no alternatives are visible, no other conclusion is likely.

Consciousness as Ways of Thinking and Knowing

What are the sources of knowledge? How do we know when we have found truth? To analyze a situation or find a solution to a problem or achieve a goal, we must start with something we can rely upon as true. The American answer involves *empiricism*—the belief that the world has only tangible reality, that things exist out there and their nature and characteristics may be discovered as facts in themselves. There are such things as cause-and-effect relationships; to demonstrate which, all component elements must be concretely identified and a step-by-step showing of one acting upon another must be accomplished. If we cannot find "hard (tangible) evidence" about conditions or how things work, then they may not be real, or at least we cannot take them seriously as subjects for thought and action.

In effect, empiricism reduces complex social reality—that interpenetrated mixture of subjective, objective, and historical dimensions—to material "things" that can be touched, measured, and used under the methods currently known to us.

Moreover, empiricism mandates compartmentalization of thinking and rigid separation of areas of knowledge from each other. In order to conduct analyses that will be able to specify in sufficient detail the conditions that exist or the steps by which social result is produced, the scope of investigation must be sharply narrowed. Subject areas must be separated out, for development of special expertise, and subareas within them examined in depth. Thus, parts are sliced away from the whole, from the larger context in which alone they have meaning. All the interdependencies and intricate interrelationships of a complex world are denied or ignored as one small component is subjected to the microscope and interpreted as a world in itself. Further, this world is stopped in time, viewed as a snapshot. Small wonder then that empiricism maintains that each problem is distinct, that economics is here and politics is over there, and that there are no one or two underlying causes or dynamics which give coherence to the larger world. Empiricism by its very nature cannot look at that larger world, much less seek to understand it as a totality.

Associated with empiricism are *positivism* and *pragmatism,* which in their politically relevant forms combine with empiricism to establish a particular sort of rationality peculiarly appropriate to capitalist-liberal society. Positivism insists that laws or rules of human behavior or of the operation of societies be induced from the visible or provable only. Things are only what they can be shown to be, and societal affairs are conditioned only by identifiable forces whose consequences are demonstrable. Change must then occur through formal means, resting on an ordering of priorities and goals and the availability of the means of enforcement. Pragmatism holds that one must start from the demonstrated "is" of the present and undertake only those improvements that can work under those conditions. "Realism" requires that we attempt what, only under our existing understanding, appears to be within the range of the attainable. In effect, the future is thus limited to an incremental change amounting to a modest projection of the present—one which unfailingly preserves all the basic structures and principles underlying that present system.

This combination produces a rationality that accepts as real only that which has demonstrable material existence, considers as relevant social forces only those things whose tangible form and consequences can be identified, and envisions no more than what can be projected from the immediate present. Missing, or sharply reduced, are most of the intangible aspects of human thought and emotion. Ethics and morality become what people actually *do*. There is little or no place for profound faith or the mystical depths of human spirit and imagination and interpersonal relationships. Not included is any sense of the *potential* that people and societies may have to become something fundamentally different from what they are, to skip stages or shift directions under certain circumstances or with particular purposeful actions. Little or no attention is paid to historical trends or the emergence of new social forces and relationships. No sense of dialetic, of inherent tensions giving rise to new possibilities, is to be found. Nor is there any intimation of intervention by outside and potentially cataclysmic events or forces. In short, the world runs only as it now runs, subject only to the visible and material factors that now operate step by step to bring about tomorrow.

This rationality yields a world that is immensely predictable, unidimensional—or, in a word, flat. As such, it is peculiarly appropriate to capitalist-liberal society. The only things that matter are those immediate material units and factors that are relevant to profit now. What can be appropriated and used today is what is worth considering, and is the only thing that can be considered where criteria of cost and efficiency control all investment of time and energy. There is neither time for, nor profit in, the other levels and types of understanding. In time, we have come not only to disdain such other types of thinking in favor of our empirical-pragmatic version, but to lose the very capacity to use our minds in this fashion. We have only *one* way to think, which happens to be specially congenial to the capitalist-liberal social order. Other ways are almost by definition ineffective, obscure, "mystical," or impractical. And so we are led back into the capitalist-liberal paradigm again, either proposing to change that system in mechanical, materialist, pragmatic ways or abandoning the project in hopelessness or withdrawal.

A final characteristic of our method of thinking, one perhaps more closely linked to liberalism than to capitalism, has to do with the "tolerance" of diversity. Proceeding from the analogy of the competitive market, which dominates so much of our thinking, we insist that all ideas and principles are entitled to be heard. But often implied in that principle, and frequently raised to the level of a basic premise in its own right, is the pervasive view that no ideas or principles are any more valid or true than others. Just as there is diversity of interest among social groupings, the argument goes, so might there be a set of ideas and principles perceived as valid by each. In other words, truth as such does not exist—it is all relative, depending on your point of view or personal values and interests. Thus, tolerance must be extended to all, and the marketplace of ideas is just like the economic market. No moral judgments about particular capitalist products are in order, for there are always buyers whose preferences and wants should be honored. Similarly, neither moral nor other bases of judgment are appropriate in the realm of ideas, for all may be true for somebody and there is no truth in any other sense.

There are at least two important fallacies here. One is the obvious one that the market in political ideas is not free at all, no more than is the economic market which serves as the model. Decades of socialization and legitimacy, to say nothing of the surrounding political consciousness, support only the dominant belief system of the society. Thus, the whole analogy is a facade that serves only to cloak perpetuation of a single set of ideas.

The other is the principle that truth does not really exist, that it is always relative, that no one can be right for other than himself. Let us grant immediately that this is a deep-seated tenet of liberalism, and that there are surely areas of personal preference where it is justified. We must nevertheless face the fact that such principled skepticism, where applied across the board to matters of social existence and human progress, is destructive of man's capacity to control and improve his future. It isolates those who are already powerless, when their only chance is to be united. It provides a "legitimate" ground on which to mobilize support against those who claim to have a morally and socially justifiable alternative to the status quo. Of course, many ideas and associated movements are false and misled. They should be challenged on the *merits* of their claims, however, and not on the grounds that people believe strongly in them. For it is possible that some ideas might be correct. If we knew the nature of true knowledge, its sources and character, we might well be able to use it as a basis for establishing principles of social order defensible as universally valid. To deny this is to cling to liberal consciousness. At the very least, we ought to acknowledge that such conviction is essential to change. Leaders and movements paralyzed by skepticism and divided by doubt have defeated themselves before they start.

Consciousness and Limits to the Range of the Possible: An Example

What is already in our minds as a "given" when we start thinking about a subject or a problem? Essentially, the parameters of our thought are those established by the capitalist-liberal social order that surrounds us. We assume, usually unconsciously, that this social order and its basic priorities and practices are fixed. For purposes of our analysis, it is sensible for us to look only at those things which are changeable. What can be modified, of course, may be only the most limited aspects of a problem, perhaps only its superficial symptoms. In all probability, its causes lie deeper and are entangled among those priorities and practices which are basic to capitalism-liberalism. Thus, our reflections and actions respecting the problem *must* have the effect of *preserving* its basic causes—and thus making sure that it will continue in worsening form—while we apply limited remedies to its surface manifestations. This is the cause of the "band-aid" approach to problem solving with which we are all familiar.

But sometimes this myopic approach can result in either total misdefinition of the problem or seriously misguided efforts at solution. The ecology-environmental crisis is an illustration. We noted earlier that projections of the exhaustion of resources and the destruction of the world's ecosystem have led to a vigorous movement for Zero Population Growth. Consider what this "remedy" *assumes* however. It assumes (and not incidentally deflects all attention away from) the continuity of the American capitalist political economy. Included is continuity in the extraction of resources from Third World countries, which leads to the sight of 6 percent of the world's people using 40 percent of its resources. Also included are projections continuing our rising rate of exhaustion of energy, pollution of air and water, and various other forms of industrial and automative destruction of the environment.

At no point does ecological-environmental concern address the characteristics of the capitalist system as such. It never notices, for example, that maximizing profit *requires* dumping of untreated wastes, burning off various by-products, selling vast numbers of automobiles, utilizing existing sources of fuel or existing plants until maximum returns from investments are realized, etc. Instead, we hear only that "people pollute" and "we should be more careful." And, perhaps more destructive, we are told that limiting population growth is the only real answer. This really means that the world's people should adapt themselves so that the capitalist economic system can go on and its owners continue to profit. It is essentially a return to Malthusianism. The Zero Population Growth movement must be acknowledged to be either one of the most revealing examples of the narrowness of the American frame of reference, or one of the great triumphs of the managers of the American mind.

In summary, we had best note that these characteristics of the American political consciousness are only illustrative. They are by no means comprehensive, for a much more elaborate discussion would be necessary to encompass all aspects of that political consciousness in adequate detail. We have suggested only that significant shaping effects are created by the social sources of consciousness, and that the latter manifests itself (for example) in our language and symbols, our methods of thinking, and the frame of reference with which we view our surroundings. Ideology, however potent, is only the superficial first line of defense thrown up by the capitalist-liberal social order. Underlying that, and providing the most basic tools and methods of thinking itself, is a consciousness that is part and parcel of—an inextricable component of—the capitalist-liberal system. We too are this part of the whole represented by that social order, and we can think only in ways ultimately consistent with it, if not actually supportive of it. To challenge it would acquire vast exertion of imagination and intellectual determination, qualities not often conveyed by this consciousness. Thus, even those who are unsatisfied with their lot in the society see no alternatives to it, and end up either paralyzed with hopelessness or withdrawn into one or another version of self-indulgence. We learn to want what is available, and little else—at least little else which we can actively conceptualize or define. Those problems that are visible become the fault of inevitable forces or of the *un*wisdom of people, never of the capitalist-liberal system itself.

Some Contrasts: Radical and Minority "Consciousness"

This analysis suggests that there is a great gap between (1) merely rejecting the dominant ideology and/or condemning certain observable conditions and their roots in the capitalist-liberal system, and (2) experiencing transformation into a fundamentally new consciousness or way of thinking. In the American context, however, the term *radical* is indiscriminately employed for both. Most radicals, of course, never get beyond the first stage. They continue to think with the same essential consciousness, and thus to criticize, mobilize opposition, and act in ways that are at best unlikely to do more than marginally alter the existing system. Their analyses often employ empirical methods and data to effectively disprove the claims of dominant ideology. But they cannot offer alternatives except in terms of different ordering of the same components, using many of the same techniques as before, though now with somewhat different purposes. Their actions—because conceived within the existing consciousness—*cannot* lead to a qualitatively different society. Working with the same tools as capitalism-liberalism, they can at best create modestly different versions of the *same* society—and at worst repeat its failings or develop new corruptions worse than the present forms.

This is why so many of the organizations set up by radicals really *assume* the continuity of the capitalist-liberal system and seek only to extract modest concessions from it on behalf of particular groups. At issue here is the key question of whether a step-by-step process of "radicalization" can lead to a change in ways of thinking or consciousness sufficient to enable people to think in terms of fundamentally new kinds of societies and ways of getting there. I argued before that no such linear process exists—that cumulative marginal change could never add up to fundamental change, to a qualitatively different society. The same point applies to radicalism: while many of their criticisms are valid and their goals distinct improvements on the present society, the scope of what they can accomplish in such ways is very limited. In our terms, it would probably not be much more than the temporary delay or marginal amelioration of fascism. To work with the conceptual tools of capitalism-liberalism is to remain within the range of the possible set by that consciousness. The evolving social and economic conditions at work to convert the capitalist-liberal system to fascism or its way stations would then have the same effect upon "radicalized" versions. The cliché that yesterday's radicals are today's conservatives does not mean that *they* have changed, or that the *times* have changed so much as to make them *appear* conservative; it means that there *never was* any really fundamental difference between such radicals and the dominant consciousness of their society.

Minority consciousness may represent another situation entirely, however. Although most American minorities—blacks, Chicanos, Indians—have undergone intensive assimilation into the capitalist-liberal consciousness, in some respects there remain indigenous cultures and ways of thinking. These may not be appropriate to the reconstruction of a late twentieth-century industrial society. But they certainly can show the inquisitive subject of capitalist-liberal society what different values, concepts, logic, and ways of thinking would look like. They may help to provide perspective on, and ultimately detachment from, the dominant consciousness. Indeed, their example might serve as a crucial first step for those until now unable to see, let alone break free of, the confining power of capitalist-liberal consciousness.

I do not for a moment suggest that any minority consciousness as it stands offers a complete alternative to Americans, nor that minority leadership of social movements is indicated by virtue of the distinctiveness of such consciousness. Only guilt-grounded romanticism would so argue. What *is* important is that interested dominant-consciousness Americans may come to understand the particularity and limits of their way of thinking through serious study of indigenous minority world views. They are, for the most part, all we have within our society in the way of truly distinctive consciousness. That we must soon have more, or pass mindlessly on to fascism, is the major thesis of this essay. Let us move now to the question of how an escape from the grasp of our consciousness may occur.

CHAPTER SIX

Consciousness Change:
Problem and Process

The problem of (constructive) fundamental political change can be reduced in the first instance to the problem of consciousness change. There are crucial issues and problems remaining, of course, even if the great problem of consciousness change is solved. But unless that key threshold is crossed, no constructive fundamental change is possible at all. It is no exaggeration to say that this threshold is the barrier which has marked the furthest progress of fundamental change possibilities in the United States. Most change-seekers, unperceptive about the limiting effects of the dominant consciousness, have not even reached this point. And those few advocates of change who have understood the nature and consequences of capitalist-liberal consciousness have had great difficulty in conceiving of ways in which the grip of that consciousness could be broken and something else developed. They either assume it *will* happen because it *must*, or suggest a multitude of "possibilities" not critically connected to existing or prospective social conditions or processes.

But recognition of the depth and importance of the problem means only that it deserves the most careful analysis, not that it is impossible. We have explored the character, sources, and workings of our capitalist-liberal consciousness in sufficient detail to be able to say what must happen in order for consciousness change to occur—or at least to ask the right questions about consciousness change for others to answer. In this chapter, we shall first identify some of the problems involved in consciousness change, and try to develop a general image of what the process would be like. Then we shall face the issue of what sort(s) of new consciousness are necessary or desirable, and look critically at some models of the process of achieving such change—both for *some* people, and for *many* people (i.e., enough to bring about fundamental change).

THE PROBLEM OF CONSCIOUSNESS CHANGE

Two premises must necessarily underlie our effort to grapple with the problem of consciousness change. One is conceptual, the other social. First, there is a dilemma stemming from the fact that we have available only the language and concepts of our *present* consciousness, but we must try to understand a process that culminates in *another* consciousness. At least part of that process will only be intelligible in the concepts and way of thinking of that new consciousness—it will not "make sense" in our present terms. Thus there is an inevitable limit to how fully we can describe what must occur—and this essay is marked in another way as only a preliminary framework.

The second is a different sort of dilemma. Consciousness change depends in the first instance upon the enabling effects of large-scale social conditions. There *must* be a convergence of social and economic forces appropriate to detach at least some appreciable number of people from their normal encapsulation within the dominant consciousness. But the same powerful factors that can cause first a few and then more people to become open to the possibility of consciousness change also have the effect of pressing the society toward those forms of social and political change that are most likely within the *existing* consciousness. In our case, that is once again fascism and its way stations. Thus, every social pressure that contributes to the opportunity and possibility of constructive consciousness change is simultaneously propelling the society toward its practical opposite, fascism. Not incidentally, this is why the knowledgeable and purposeful intervention of determined men and women, at an appropriate stage in the process of social disintegration, can be decisive in shaping the outcome. But at any point in the fragile social dynamic and consciousness change, the entire process may be terminated by the finality of the fall into fascism.

What Consciousness Change Would NOT Be

Consistent with our first premise, we can talk most clearly and concretely about what sorts of things would *not* constitute consciousness change. Our present language and way of thinking are certainly adequate to describe a number of currently imaginable processes that are inconsistent with, or would inevitably fall short of, real consciousness change. By citing a few examples, we may be able to imply or infer certain not entirely expressible characteristics of the process.

First, to be of the depth and scope of consciousness as we have been talking about it, the change could not be instantaneous, effortless, or automatic. It could not be instantaneous, either for one person or for many, because consciousness is rooted in multiple linkages accumulated over an entire lifetime. It is connected to relationships with one's family and friends, to one's schooling, job—to a variety of social institutions, as well as to language, logic, and aspirations. Many of these connections are not consciously perceived, and most of them go deep into one's personality structure. Nothing so deeply rooted can possibly be completely transformed overnight. The closest one might come to instantaneous consciousness change is a moment of revelation—a moment of intense awareness that there is such a thing and that some part of it is taking place in one's mind at that moment. Such a moment of awareness is sometimes mistaken for the completed fact of consciousness change, of course, and many who proudly assert their crossing of the consciousness threshold have merely progressed to this point. Often, they have stopped right there, and by their aggressive self-labelling become living examples of the trivialization of the concept of consciousness change. Even the attainment of this moment of awareness, however, is not an instantaneous product, but rather the cumulation of a process of convergence of social forces operating to detach one to some extent from the dominant consciousness. There is no way in which true consciousness change can be a matter of instantaneous achievement.

Nor can such change be effortless, for quite similar reasons. Consciousness is so deeply rooted as to be bound up with our social and personal identities. Who we are in the eyes of others, and in our own eyes, is partly a result of our mutual absorption of the dominant consciousness. To be a college professor in the United States today, for example, is to live in a role made up of the expectations of students, colleagues, administrators, and the larger society—all of whom see and think in accordance with the dominant consciousness. All of us internalize whatever roles we live, becoming the role required of such a person. And in our personal lives, we learn to relate to other people and to "be a person" in the same ways—ways communicated to us through our existing consciousness. As (or if) we begin to be shaken loose from that consciousness, our very identities as people become threatened. We no longer are sure we know who we are. It is bound to be painful, as family or friends drop off and we seek new social support or experiences. And one cannot help but be conscious that something fundamental is happening to one's life adaptation. In trying to understand what is happening, the human mind is taking the first steps in the effort to gain control over the process—or at least to gain insight into it and some measure of ability to adapt to it. Some part of consciousness change, in other words, is *conscious*; how much, and to what extent the entire change can be accomplished deliberately and consciously, are open questions to which we shall return. But no experience that is both painful and conscious can, by any strength of the imagination, be viewed as effortless.

Deterministic images of consciousness change must also be dismissed. There can be no automatic change as a result of particular social conditions (e.g., a massive depression or ecological catastrophe). This is because all the existing social institutions and associations that individuals have, operate to hold them to their existing consciousness. In times of great stress, many if not most people tend to cling even more strongly to established values and institutions, in hopes of somehow weathering the storm. Consciousness does not change because it would be rational or appropriate for it to do so, in the abstract sense. The human search for security is more likely to take the form of resistance to change and reassertion of traditional values and practices. The social order may change, but many individuals within it remain the same or move only to acceptance of the necessity of whatever changes do transpire. In our case, of course, we are again talking about fascism and its way stations. But even where individuals do begin to experience the beginnings of consciousness change as a result of converging social conditions, there are many alternatives open. It is simply not the case that only one alternative consciousness awaits them; deterministic advocates of socialism, anarchism, tribalism, etc., should suspect this, if only from listening to each other.

Second, consciousness change cannot be an individualized act or process in our ordinary sense of that term. One cannot experience consciousness change by oneself or in isolation, with the possible exception of unusual cases involving extraordinary intellectual capability and effort. We have already noted at length that powerful social forces and conditions are prerequisites, necessary preconditions for detaching people from their unexamined encapsulation within a dominant consciousness. It also seems clear that, just as the source of our present consciousness lies in our surrounding social institutions and the cues and support we normally receive from social relationships generally, so must consciousness change and a new consciousness have similar social origins and support. This does not imply total reconstruction of all institutions and relationships, of course, for that would make consciousness change dependent on prior fundamental change—truly a cart-before-the-horse situation. But it does suggest that the presence of others who are undergoing the same experience is vital. And it implies that new relationships between people—incipient new social institutions—must develop to give support and momentum to the process of mutual-and-individual consciousness change. In effect, we are starting to see expanding need for a *conscious* process of change.

Another reason stems from the fact that individualism is such a general characteristic of capitalist-liberal society and its consciousness: to change from such a way of thinking must imply leaving its most basic unit behind. We could not, for example, envision a new set of social relationships in which individuals were contractually assured of expanded rights as against each other and their government, in the manner of our current Constitution. That would be the creation of our *present* consciousness, rather than of a new one. Perhaps it is clear why this is so, but if not, the reader should re-examine his or her understanding of the nature of consciousness. To think in terms of contractually-assured rights for individuals, even the most attractive and satisfying economic and social rights, is to set the individual off from others, to assume competition, and to build in the most basic capitalist-liberal ways of thinking. Sooner or later, such a scheme can only take on the other components of the capitalist-liberal consciousness as well. To live in another consciousness must mean at the least to reconstruct the essential nature of relationships between people and the way that people conceive of themselves and of each other. Starting with isolated individuals and assuring them of rights as against each other is the exact opposite—a tiny projection of what we already have in capitalist-liberal society.

The unit which we use as the basis of our thinking carries profound importance. In our current consciousness, the individual not only serves as this unit, but also unites ideology and consciousness, making the latter an even more effective support for the former. First we think naturally in terms of the individual, and then ideology tells us that individualism is the way to be a good person.

But what if we took another unit as the basis of thinking? For example, we might think in terms of the group or the community, an integrated unit made up of several persons. Or another consciousness might begin thinking only in terms of tribes or nations, taking them as organic units with existences prior to and separate from those of the persons who were their members at any given time. Still another unit for thinking might be the entire world or all humanity. With such a basis of thought, it would be very difficult to settle for political systems or programs that did not take into account the welfare and other needs of the entire world population, and organize and plan accordingly. Where individuals or tribes or groups are the unit of thinking, either no organization or only small-scale organizations seem necessary. Clearly, the choice of the unit of thinking is in part an *ethical* choice, and one which carries implications concerning one's basic attitudes and relationships to other human beings. Can a unit of thinking that involves *less* than all humanity be justified, for example?

Third, most forms of social protest, however militant in character, are neither indicative nor productive of consciousness change. In fact, they often serve to reinforce the existing consciousness. This is because most protest actions aim only at the achievement of a specific goal that is visible and available within the framework of the capitalist-liberal system as it stands. Militant strikes for higher wages or better working conditions, protests against food prices or the denial of governmental services, or demonstrations against racism or sexism in housing or employment—all such actions normally assume continuity of the basic features of the larger system and ask only for specific changes favoring the protesting group. Some other protest actions are less specific, and draw their support from generalized dissatisfaction with social conditions. Ghetto riots, student outbreaks, and other spontaneous actions—as well as much of the support for populist or anti-establishment political candidates—are expressions of such unfocused resentment.

In both cases, however, the protest actions or movements are operating entirely within the capitalist-liberal consciousness. Their demands are for some or more of the things that are already available, and for the most part satisfiable by delivery of such things. If or when the latter occurs, the existing conciousness is in effect validated and reinforced. Where protest goals are not achieved, or the protest merely expresses generalized resentment, those engaged in the protest may retreat into frustrated apathy—which has much the same effect. Only when people begin to see systemic causes for their circumstances, and to connect these with their own values and ways of thinking—and therefore to make demands that go beyond the existing system—can social protest become a part of the consciousness change process.

What Consciousness Change WOULD Be

We have begun to develop some insight into the character of consciousness change by saying what it would *not* be. To an extent, we can now say that it *would* be the reverse of all that we have just identified. That is, it would be a continuing, painful, social process in which large-scale social forces enabled individuals to break out of the grip of the dominant consciousness and, at least in part consciously, re-shape themselves and each other into new people with new ways of seeing and understanding the world and its potential. But it would also be more. Perhaps we can gain insight into these additional dimensions by building on the base of what we have already seen.

The nature of the necessary part played by large-scale social forces in enabling or inducing consciousness change should probably be the first to be expanded or elaborated in this fashion. Not all of the workings of various large-scale social forces are likely to inspire or permit more than the usual handful to break away from the dominant consciousness, nor would the direction of such changes always be the same. In other words, it is probably only *particular* conditions, converging in a *par-*

ticular way, that have the effect of nudging *certain* people in *specific* directions. When a country enters a major world war, for example, a surge of nationalism and patriotism usually sweeps the society, effectively blocking rather than spurring consciousness change. Only in the case of disastrous defeat does the prospect of consciousness change gain a boost from such social forces. Clearly, it is those large-scale forces which have the effect of eroding the legitimacy of major social institutions that are relevant to the possibility of consciousness change. If visible social or economic problems cannot be solved by such established institutions, or if the country's leaders appear consistently inept or corrupt, then the possibility of consciousness change for some becomes real.

In all probability, those who are least firmly attached to the existing order and least fully absorbed into its associated consciousness will be the first to experience the reactions that may lead to consciousness change. Those strata or groups least integrated into our society are, of course, minorities, young people, and lower-class persons—not necessarily in that order. In the early stages of the detaching effects of large-scale social forces, conscious awareness and response is likely to be limited to the more intellectually inclined individuals in such categories. (This does not necessarily mean those in college or with college degrees; the incidence of true intellectuality is probably only slightly higher among college populations than the others named.) The point is that certain types of individuals from specific sectors of the population are likely to be the most responsive, in consciousness change terms, to the kinds of large-scale social forces that we are experiencing in the United States at this time. Others in the same categories, however, may well experience the sort of malaise and unfocused dissatisfaction that lead to fundamentalist solution-seeking. Quite opposite responses thus may emerge from the same social strata, and some individuals may even flip from one extreme to the other in very short periods of time.

We may also expand upon the image of consciousness change as a social process. Let us look first at what is implied by *social* here, and then at the meaning of *process* for our purposes. We have already said that our consciousness is derived in the most basic ways from the social institutions, expectations, and practices with which we are surrounded. It then follows that new institutions, expectations, and practices will be necessary to help us move towards a new consciousness. We cannot achieve such change by ourselves because we are not in complete control of our consciousness. It is partly a product of how others see us, think about us, and act towards us. But it is possible to be relatively more self-conscious about the nature and workings of our consciousness, and thereby to make important personal contributions to, first, awareness of the limitations of one's present consciousness and, then, development of a new one. Thus, change in one's own consciousness becomes a mutual effort, in which the self and others play continuing and necessary parts. Moreover, as one becomes more aware of the nature and limiting effects of one's present consciousness, and begins to take part with others in the process of self-reconstruction, one begins also to have a consciousness-changing impact on those others. The mutuality is complete: we spur our own self-development by contributing to others' consciousness change, and simultaneously they contribute to our progress by viewing and acting toward us in new ways.

The development of such new social relationships, within which the individual can achieve self-reconstruction, implies certain requirements. It must be a voluntary act on the part of the individual involved, a self-conscious act together with the relevant others. One's defenses must be down, for example, or at least not actively maintained. It is hard to imagine this process succeeding where imposed from above, or even where a respected "teacher" sought to provide guidance to willing "students." It must be an active process, not a passive one. The insight and change which one seeks must come from within, as unrealized human capabilities are released. What is to be learned is about oneself and one's capacities to think and feel and relate to other people, and these things can only be learned by doing and experiencing, not by memorizing instruction books provided by others.

Another requirement would be that of complete commitment on the part of participating individuals to the reconstruction of self-and-others in this manner. No part-time association can possible provide the sort of support and communication necessary for this process to succeed. I am not suggesting such high-intensity but transitory methods as encounter groups, but a continuing relationship in which the primary commitment of all is to the achievement of consciousness change for the self and others. A final requirement would be that such loose association(s) of like-intentioned and committed people remain part of and act upon the contemporary world. The new social relationships can grow only through some shared efforts and experiences on the part of such people in the direction of modifying the present world. Not only will they then come to understand more clearly—and attract others to the vision of—how different the future society might be, but they will thereby speed their own process of consciousness change and development of new human relationships. In other words, only through acting to create the social institutions that make possible a new consciousness and quality of human relationships can individuals achieve for themselves such consciousness and relationships.

Much of what is implied in the use of "process" here has already been touched upon, but three major dimensions may be noted in summary fashion. One is that of continuity. Consciousness change is not the equivalent of stepping from one room into another. It cannot be complete until the new society with which it is to be coherent has come into being. Until that time, consciousness must remain in motion, constantly transforming as social conditions change and people come closer to understanding and acting in ways more and more fully expressive of human capabilities. Thus, consciousness change is not just a process in the sense that it cannot occur overnight, but also in the sense that process is its essence—it never ends.

A second dimension of the meaning of process is that of action. Those who seek consciousness change are most likely to achieve it through acting upon the world in a purposeful manner to shape it into the social forms and practices that can aid their progress. However slight their impact may be, the act of attempting such change has the effect of moving their process of consciousness change forward, concretizing or expanding new dimensions of their new consciousness. The third dimension of process involved is that of developing a sense of groupness or community among the participants. This takes time and shared experiences, for individualism is deeply grounded. As people struggle together, however, sharing many bitter defeats and a few successes, at the same time as they seek to build new relationships and ways of understanding their worlds and each other, they may overcome their isolation. What they seek, in other words, is to be found only through the process of seeking it.

To summarize what consciousness change *would* be, we might say that it involves not just change in values, relationships, or ways of thinking, but change in our personal *identities*. This may be an appropriately inclusive way of putting it: what would be different would be the kind of people we are, and necessarily that would imply changes in the other dimensions as well. On a relatively superficial level, it has long been recognized that changing economic and social conditions would make possible changes in our values. In a much-cited passage, John Maynard Keynes declared in 1930:[1]

> When the accumulation of wealth is no longer of high social importance, there will be great changes in the code of morals. We shall be able to rid ourselves of many of the pseudo-moral principles which have hag-ridden us for two hundred years, by which we have exalted some of the most distasteful of human qualities into the position of the highest virtues. We shall be able to assess the money-motive at its true value. . . . All kinds of social customs and economic practices, affecting the distribution of wealth and of economic rewards and penalities, which we now maintain at all costs, however distasteful and unjust they may be in themselves, because they are tremendously useful in promoting the accumulation of capital, we shall then be free, at last, to discard.
>
> . . . We shall once more value ends above means and prefer the good to the useful.

A change in values, of course, is only one dimension of what is involved in consciousness change. To live by truly different values means to *think* differently, to experience a wholly different kind of social order, and to *be* different kinds of people. D. H. Lawrence, though typically overindividualistic, has captured more of the essence of consciousness change than Keynes:[2]

> To open out a new wide area of consciousness means to slough the old consciousness. The old consciousness has become a tight-fitting prison to us, in which we are going rotten.
>
> You can't have a new, easy skin before you have sloughed the old, tight skin. . . .
>
> The two processes go on, of course, simultaneously. The slow forming of the new skin underneath is the slow sloughing of the old

skin. And sometimes this immortal serpent feels very happy, feeling a new golden glow of a strangely-patterned skin envelop him; and sometimes he feels very sick, as if his very entrails were being torn out of him, as he wrenches once more at his old skin, to get out of it.

Out! Out! he cries, in all kinds of euphemisms.

He's got to have his new skin on him before ever he can get out.

And he's got to get out before his new skin can ever be his own skin.

So there he is, a torn, divided monster. . . .

It needs a real desperate recklessness to burst your old skin at last. You simply don't care what happens to you, if you rip yourself in two, so long as you do get out.

It also needs a real belief in the new skin. Otherwise you are likely never to make the effort. Then you gradually sicken and go rotten and die in the old skin.

Consciousness change goes beyond this individualistic imagery to incorporate a social process leading to transformation of the social order itself. It peels off layer after layer of the way we are accustomed to think and feel—until the basic unit, the purposes, criteria, and manner of thinking themselves become different. A whole new *dimension* (not just *range*) of the possible, in terms of interpersonal relationships, must result. And all of this can take place only in the process of building something wholly new, of constructing the very institutions that will ultimately be coherent with the consciousness that is developing—and which will in turn make that consciousness possible for others.

Even this limited insight into the nature of consciousness change, however, raises some vital questions. To what extent is such reconstruction of the human mind possible? If we adhere to the assumptions about human nature that are common to the capitalist-liberal mind, we would say that the kinds of changes discussed here are impossible. Man is aggressive, competitive, self-interested, irrational at times, and prone to repeated self-destructive conflicts. Our understanding of history tells us this is true throughout centuries—that it is "human nature." But is it? Perhaps man has had to be this way, and the capitalist-liberal mind has had to see him this way, because of surrounding economic and social conditions—scarcity, inability to control nature, and a happy ignorance of the means of total self-destruction, for example. Under other conditions, faced with the certainty of extinction, might the "nature" of man become something different? Is man, the most adaptive and intelligent of nature's creatures, unable to transcend his own characteristics in order to evolve into a higher level of society and avoid extinction as a species? Anthropologists tell us that there are societies where people are not aggressive, competitive, or self-aggrandizing, but rather communitarian, cooperative, and contented. These reflections suggest that to write off the possibility of consciousness change as inconsistent with "human nature," or otherwise illusory, is to yield uncritically to the grip of capitalist-liberal consciousness. The history of the future is yet to be told, and there is no necessary reason to think that it will be just like the history of the past.

Consciousness Change to What?

So far, we have said little about the *nature* of the (or *a*) new consciousness. Consistent with our recognition of the impossibility of detailing the substance of a new consciousness when we possess only the language and perspectives of the present one, this is both necessary and appropriate. We cannot demand a blueprint of the future society, for its character and goals can only emerge from the process of bringing it about. We are necessarily limited in the extent to which we can see into the future, and we know that it would do us little good to seek to construct images of the future society until we develop the way of thinking that is appropriate to the qualitatively different social forms and human relationships that must mark that society. If we are afraid that it may not be better than what we now experience, we should remember that we cannot hold on to what we have—that in our present consciousness we face only fascism or its way stations.

It may appear that we are confronted by an insistent but impossible choice, between unknowable alternatives to an unacceptable future. But I do not think our situation is that desperate. There are criteria for judgment and choice. Moreover, they can be applied to the process of consciousness change, and the efforts toward social and political change which are part of it, as they are manifested in this world. And, because this process is itself the kernel from which the new society will and must grow, it is precisely the point at which our evaluative criteria and judgments are most appropriately applied. The process by which change is sought is all we have to go by; if it does not appear to contain the seeds of a better future when judged with appropriate standards, we may as well abandon hope for that particular version of a new society.

We must not judge the process of change by the standards of this consciousness, however, but rather in its own terms and by its capacity to become a decent and humane future society. However repugnant the taking of human life, for example, the fact that large-scale violence might be involved in a process of change would not *by itself* disqualify a particular version of a justifiable future and how to get there. There is much violence and injustice in our society now, and no doubt even more in the offing; we would have to calculate the relative amounts of human suffering likely under alternative futures to reach an adequate judgment. But we are surely justified in rejecting a process of change that amounts to no more than the substitution of a new set of rulers for the present ones, or one in which ultimate human relationships are the same as they now are. In other words, what we seek are means to peer into the process of change and discern the elements of a future society within it—and to accept (for the moment) or reject out of hand what we see.

At least two criteria appear to meet these general considerations, and to offer opportunity for choice among alternative versions of the future. One is the nature of the human relationships between the people who seek a particular kind of change. To what extent are they justifiable as movement toward the kinds of relationships we seek in our future? Granting that the change-seekers are, like us, children of this society and its consciousness, we still may ask what they can show in the way of creating new and more fulfilling relationships among themselves. If they have not done so, why should we have hopes for the society they would create? If the only way they can act to overthrow this society is exactly like those who rule it now, the chances are that they will build a new society much like the present one. The new society must begin to grow *now,* in the process of creation, not after some new social grouping acquires power.

The other criterion has to do with the nature of the incipient social institutions reflected in the organization or life-relationships of the people who seek a particular kind of change. This is critically important because such a social institution or practice both reflects and creates the new consciousness that is part of this particular version of a new society and related process of change. The social forms and way of thinking of the change-seekers are a foreshadowing of their future society. If certain change-seekers form themselves into a hierarchical and centrally-dominated organization, for example, what is implied as to the future society they would create? With the most sincere intentions to do otherwise, such people might nevertheless be led by the consciousness generated thereby towards a centrally-controlled future society—perhaps one that preserved much of what we now have. Inherent in the organization or set of life-relationships of the change-seekers, in other words, lies the image of the consciousness and society that they are likely to create. We have no warrant to believe that they would be desirous or capable of self-reversal after acquiring power.

In raising questions about routes toward change, we must not fall into the trap of applying unreasonable or merely this-consciousness standards. Neither revolution nor fundamental political change is likely to be achieved without violating some of the niceties of human relationships, nor without organizing as required to apply disciplined force. To avoid commitment on the grounds of minor imperfections or continued questions about change-seekers' alternatives is to invite paralysis—and fascism. We *must* choose. But we must choose wisely, for there may be no second chance. We do not *want* a blueprint, but the very opposite— an openness in which change and development is the only certainty. And we have a right to insist that the process of change itself contain the seeds of a better world, and that the consciousness revealed by that process offers hope of continuous progress toward something better than we now know. These are not the *only* criteria of choice, of course, for we must also ask questions about the practical prospects of various alternatives (as we shall do in the next chapter), but they are the basic moral and ethical grounds that we have to distinguish between one consciousness-process and another.

THE PROCESS OF CONSCIOUSNESS CHANGE: SOME MODELS

We now have some idea of what consciousness change would involve, and can turn to the question of how those conditions might actually be fulfilled in the real world of the near future. For consciousness change to occur (and with it the possibility of fundamental political change), all of the opportunity-generating social conditions must be fused into the specific social process that spells consciousness change. In what ways can we imagine this happening? Can we also envision ways in which not just a few, but *many* people, would undergo such a process? The latter question—how (or if) consciousness change spreads from the very few to the many—may lead most directly to insight into the probability and desirability of various kinds of change.

In this effort, we first add an additional assumption to the two premises already stated, and then critically examine three models of the way in which consciousness change might take place. The additional premise is that cultural change—a questioning and reshaping of traditional societal values—is already under way at some deep and relatively unconscious level as a result of the large-scale forces earlier assumed to be at work, detaching at least some people from the dominant consciousness. Cultural change is closely related to consciousness change, of course, but not coextensive. Consciousness change is the more comprehensive process, inclusive of cultural change and marking the culmination of cultural and other forms of change in the transformation of personal identity and ways of thinking. We have seen that consciousness change cannot come about automatically as a result of cultural change. The question thus becomes *how* underlying cultural change is translated into politically consequential consciousness change, first for some people and then for the many, and what particular processes *do* to the society involved.

The models of consciousness-change processes are intended to establish types or categories for later use in analysing various prescriptions for change. We shall assess the strengths, weaknesses, and associated characteristics of each process in turn. We must be able to recognize the implications of various possible consciousness-change processes—the relationship between characteristics of the processes and the nature of the consciousness (and new society) likely to be generated through that process.

The three types of consciousness-change processes include one more-or-less anarchist version and two more-or-less Marxist versions. The first is a small-group, bottom-up, and essentially spontaneous process that is assumed to be capable of multiplying into a mass consciousness change without benefit of organization. The second is more of a top-down process, in which a small vanguard and their supporters first seize state power and then employ it to reconstruct the consciousness of the masses. The third is something of a combination of the first two, in which largely spontaneous mass upsurges (strikes supported by broad segments of the working-class population) are helped by a knowledgeable vanguard to experience enough consciousness change to result in mass seizure of state power and subsequent completion of the task of societal and consciousness reconstruction. There are many other possible consciousness change processes, but these represent three basic types that will provide a set of tools for analysis.

Two cautions should be borne in mind as we explore these models. One is that we are critically examining them only in terms of their viability and implications as abstract types of *consciousness*-change process. Any specific prescription for fundamental *political* change would have to be examined concretely and in several additional dimensions, such as its practical possibility and the implications of its other (nonconsciousness change) characteristics, as we shall do in later chapters. All we are asking here is what is implied in the three different types of abstractly viewed consciousness-change process that we are imagining. The other caution is that we are still continuously threatened by application of *this*-consciousness concepts and criteria. We must try not to be bound by what we now understand as power, for example, or by static images of what is or is not possible. To talk of consciousness change is necessarily to suspend disbelief in some respects. How far it really profits one to depart from presently enforceable social "reality" is of course one of the crucial questions with which we must deal at some point.

The Small-Group Process

This version sees loose and shifting groups of people coming together on an ad hoc basis—at work, in schools, in their neighborhoods—to aid each other more or less consciously toward consciousness change. Social and political action may be undertaken at some point, but it does not constitute a generative purpose of such groupings. It is more likely to be forced upon them by the inevitably repressive response of the existing society to the kinds of lives and aspirations that they are starting to live.

Little contact among such groups occurs at first, in part because of lack of awareness of each other but also in part because of the absorption with the process. Another reason, however, is continuing fear of the effects of organization as such. Any hierarchical structure, or even nonhierarchical organizations of any scale, would necessarily contain and preserve so much of this consciousness that they would have to be rejected. This raises the key issue, of course: how likely is this form of consciousness change to spread from the few to the many? It *must* do so, or the few pioneers will soon turn inwards or withdraw, and in either case their political change potential will be lost. But such prospects appear to depend upon continued natural development of increasing numbers of small groups, rather than on any deliberate proselytizing by those already moving self-consciously toward consciousness change and more and more purposeful political action. An extended period of generative social conditions thus appears to be a necessary part of this image of the consciousness change process.

There is also a further problem. Will the consciousness emerging from this process contain some sense of how to cope with the problem of organization, for example with the task of managing an industrial society in the interdependent world? Can it handle the problem of acquiring power (if only to dismantle the state) or of defending a new society against reaction? There is an aura of automaticity, or perhaps a gap to be filled primarily with faith, in this version of the process of consciousness change. To assume that humanity can now abandon industrialization and technology appears to consign much of the world's population to starvation and suffering. It sounds like an exaggerated individualism possible only for those already well off. But wise and shared use of existing and new resources, in the construction of a better society and world, would appear to require coming to terms with the problem of organization in some fashion, or at some stage.

The Vanguard-Reconstruction Process

By contrast, this version sees state power as the necessary and appropriate vehicle for deliberately reconstructing the consciousness of the many. Only the vanguard and its immediate allies need to experience consciousness change prior to the actual seizure of state power and beginning of the combined task of social and consciousness reconstruction. This is usually accomplished through an intensive educational process within the tightly-structured organization that is to be the vehicle of mobilizing support and seizing power. Through propaganda and example, new members will be drawn into the organization and "developed" in terms of consciousness change and political sophistication. After power is acquired, educational programs will be integrated with changed social institutions to enable the masses of people to undergo the appropriate consciousness change.

No necessary implications should be drawn from the fact that the vanguard organization is prepared to re-educate the masses. Rather than placidly awaiting the perhaps illusory spontaneous transformation envisioned in the small-group process, it is acting to bring about desirable results while there is still time to do so. To an extent, only the capitalist-liberal mind would understand such a process of first indoctrination and then systematic re-education as "forcing others to be free." The fact is that almost exactly the same kind of indoctrination process now takes place in capitalist-liberal society, only it is so thorough and pervasive that we do not even recognize it as such. In other words, we are all and always essentially indoctrinated into *some* consciousness. Why should not the vanguard organization feel it their duty to inculcate a *better*, more humane, and justifiable consciousness?

Clearly, the better question is one addressed to the *nature* of that consciousness itself: what is there in its character, and in the quality of the social order it implies, that is attractive? Does the process, by which some consciousness and new society is growing and seeking to replace the existing one, meet the two criteria set forth in the last section? Or is this vanguard organization and the associated process really another reflection of the existing consciousness, merely seeking to replace one set of rulers with another?

Much human suffering has been caused by those who asserted that they offered a route to freedom and fulfillment, and claimed therefore the moral right to enforce it upon others. We may feel that a truly liberating and justifiable new consciousness and society would *have* to be self-generated, rather than imposed in any way from outside and above. But we must take account of the fact that existing social institutions are devoted to the cause of preventing just such an occurrence. It may be necessary, as a prerequisite to any widespread consciousness change, that the obstacle represented by such social institutions be removed and destroyed. Of course, this is the dilemma posed by all vanguard-dominated consciousness-change processes: can a desirable, liberating new consciousness and society emerge from a process in which a highly disciplined force first overthrows the existing social order and then institutes programs to reconstruct both consciousness and society from above? (Perhaps the dilemma is not a real one; there are certainly very serious questions to be raised about the practical possibility of this kind of vanguard-organized seizure of state power. But they must await more detailed analysis in the next chapter.)

The Mass-Upsurge Process

This version is not just a combination of the first two, although it does involve spontaneous mass action, a role for a vanguard, and later use of state power. It is a more comprehensive and context-sensitive image, with multiple stages and roles for various actors on the stage of history. Assumed are the kinds of social and economic conditions that trigger strikes, demonstrations, or other mass social action. The task of the vanguard is to convert the single-issue or economic demands of the already activated masses to far broader political purposes. The text for this process is Rosa Luxemburg's concept of the "mass strike," in which the spontaneous outpouring of people in support of originally economic demands is gradually focused on the larger problem of state power. Steps include the mobilization of supporting groups around the original demands, and the recognition that the power of the state (in the form of courts or National Guard, for example) is the real obstacle to attainment of the legitimate goals of the people conceived as a whole rather than as separate segments with purely selfish interests.

When, perhaps after a series of such strikes, broad alliances of major groupings of people have been forged and at least the leading layers of such groups have begun to undergo significant consciousness change, the question of state power is ready to be posed. Legitimacy is low and declining, and the next outbreak may cause the state to topple and the vanguard to take power in the name of the allied masses. From this point, appropriate programs of social reconstruction and consciousness re-education can be undertaken—not so much vanguard-imposed as self-administered by the newly augmented leadership echelons in their own interest.

This version captures some of the spontaneity envisioned in the small-group process, holding that the releasing of potential, and the growth of community that transpires in the repeated struggles of the mass strikes, will accomplish substantial steps in the consciousness-change process. The task of the vanguard is more to provide the means to accomplish what indigenous mass leaders have come to want, than to seize power to remake their minds for them. The crucial juncture, of course, is the shift from mere (capitalist-liberal, this-consciousness) economic demands to broader political goals. Historically, strikes in the American context have been limited in their goals, however militant in character. The exceptions are few, and even those general strikes that have occurred have dwindled after a few days because of failure to translate demands into goals for an entirely different social order. But this is precisely the task that this version assigns to the change-seekers. Whether they will have the legitimacy in the eyes of the masses at such times, or whether indigenous mass leadership will revert to goals conceived in the capitalist-liberal framework (or its fascist successor), are questions to be determined in the future.

Some Remaining Questions

We now have before us three broad categories: a bottom-up, wholly spontaneous process, a top-down vanguard-accomplished version, and an attempt to integrate the two. Each involves certain weaknesses as to the means of carrying the new consciousness to others, and as to the potential character of that new consciousness. The small-group process appears likely to have difficulty coping with issues of organization and requires time for the spontaneous development of the additional groups necessary to result in a mass consciousness change. The vanguard-reconstruction process must transcend its own highly organized origins to create and justify a liberating consciousness and society. The mass-upsurge process requires such a delicate combination of particular actions and responses that its viability may be illusory.

The issues raised in this quick survey of types of consciousness-change processes may be cast in terms of three broad questions. One is simply how much time remains before the slide into fascism picks up speed and forecloses any form of liberating consciousness change or societal reconstruction. If one assumes that there is ample time remaining—that the crisis point is still decades rather than years away—there may be relatively more confidence played in the small-group process. But if the crisis point is closer—if our earlier analysis, that much change is already occurring in a subterranean level, is correct—then we have much less time, perhaps only five or ten years. In such an event, we would have little choice but to take the latter two versions very seriously indeed.

The second question is closely related: what sorts of social and economic conditions are to be assumed for the immediate future? If we see a depression ahead, or even a continued and deepened inflation-recession period, the possibility of speeded-up mass protest becomes more likely. If chaos ensues, or if mass strike upsurges really do develop, the latter two routes again appear more likely. The small-group process is always possible too, of course, but it is less likely to result in the organized unit capable of resisting the prospect of fascism than either of the other two. If conditions do not change drastically, however, neither of the latter two will get the boost they need. Liberating consciousness change will then depend entirely on the small-group process, and the risk of a slow slide into fascism, developing gradually out of the apparently innocuous acts of incumbent officials and the needs of the system, will be much greater.

The final question is an extension of our earlier emphases. What are the goals involved in each version of the consciousness change process? We know that the future society is encapsulated in the characteristics of the process by which consciousness is to change. How well do we like the kind of society that each process tells us is in the offing? Somehow, the new society must grow amidst the old. Some people must, perhaps by means of a dramatic intellectual effort, wrench themselves out of the existing consciousness and learn to live psychically in the growing new world while they remain physically locked into the present one. And the manner in which they comport themselves, and act to bring the potential of that new society before us for judgment and action, will determine whether we can join them or not.

It will not tell us whether they can succeed, however. For answers to that question, we must turn to more careful examination of the other aspects of the process of change. Consciousness change, if begun, only makes possible the achievement of fundamental political change. A number of other issues must be posed and solved before we can assess relative prospects of success of various prescriptions for change.

NOTES

1. John Maynard Keynes, "Economic Possibilities for Our Grandchildren" (1930), cited in C. B. Macpherson, *The Real World of Democracy* (London: Oxford University Press, 1966), p. 63.
2. D. H. Lawrence, *Studies in Classic American Literature* (New York: Thomas Seltzer, Inc., 1923), Viking Press Re-Issue, 1964, pp. 52-53.

CHAPTER SEVEN

Connections to the Structure of Power and the Process of Change in the Total System

We have explored consciousness and consciousness change in detail because the latter is the essential prerequisite to political change—the missing ingredient in all American thought and action with respect to change. But consciousness change is only the first step in a total process, merely that which enables one to see and undertake a whole series of further steps. Consciousness change cannot progress beyond its early beginnings without appropriate action to reshape one's social surroundings toward the new society with which it is potentially coherent. By itself, it is *only* potential, an insight and capability that must be developed and applied in concrete social situations in order to be fully realized.

There is no way that consciousness change can be accomplished, let alone suffice for political change purposes, without change in the objective structures of the total system. Because there can be no separation of the subjective from the objective, neither can there be real detachment of the legitimacy (subjective side) of the structure of authority from the power components that give it objective reality. In other words, consciousness change cannot really occur, *nor would it have the slightest political consequences*, without being deliberately applied to the task of reconstructing the social order.

We are thus led insistently back toward the other half of the structure of authority—the objective structure of power and interest that is now dominant in the United States. It must be changed, through appropriate social action reflecting the new consciousness (or subjectivity), in order that the new society may move from conceptual existence in the minds of some to tangible social reality in the lives of all. Nor can this (once again, and for obvious reasons) be an automatic process. Only deliberate and appropriate social action can change social institutions in ways that will enable the new consciousness to further develop and the whole system to move toward the new society. People must act in their total social context, to shape the world of today towards the possible world of tomorrow. And we must assume that the existing structure of power will resist its replacement with all the means at its disposal—up to and including desperate massive violence.

The new consciousness, growing amidst the old, must understand, and act successfully to change, the other half of itself—the objective structure of power and interest that makes up the other half of the total system in which it is enmeshed. If it does not, it will expire for lack of social support and ultimate stagnation. The American structure of power, however, is no paper tiger. As we noted earlier, it has vast resources of power and legitimacy, ranging from millions of men in a newly-organized and well-paid professional military, to broad and deep support from a thoroughly indoctrinated population. It will not go away by itself, and it has a long history of successful deflection and absorption of thrusts toward change.

But this system is *not* immutable. The appropriate new consciousness, if applied creatively and decisively in the context of crisis-generating social forces, can transform this total system. History has not stopped; it is only the capitalist-liberal consciousness that is static. The world is full of powerful change-creating forces, swirling all about us and generating opportunity for the most fundamental social and political reconstruction—if we could only learn to see and use them. But we cannot see them from within the capitalist-liberal consciousness, which insistently tells us, first, that things are right as they are, and then, that they are inevitable and unchangeable in any event. To deny the possibility of fundamental change is to celebrate one's encapsulation in the capitalist-liberal consciousness. No one can *know* that fundamental change is impossible except through a way of knowing that so declares. With a different way of *knowing*, we might well *know* that it is both possible and potentially imminent.

The task of this chapter is to explore certain key aspects of social structure and processes in the United States that have acted as barriers to change, in both past and present. To accomplish this, we shall synthesize lessons of the past (such as the failure of fundamental change in previous crisis periods), some this-consciousness analysis of current power distribution and usage, and some sense of the potential of this crisis period to give birth to a new society, with respect to each of three questions or problems: the question of the *agency of change*; the issue of the *character of organization* appropriate to achieving change; and the problem of developing an adequate *scenario of a process of change* culminating in the transfer of state power.

Our goal is to identify what it is that makes them effective barriers, and to say what must be resolved or decided with respect to each, in order that we can see clearly *what tasks lie ahead of any new consciousness that seeks to transcend such barriers* and accomplish fundamental change. Knowing the nature of those tasks, we shall be able to ask appropriate questions of each of the contemporary prescriptions for change that we critically evaluate in Part 3.

THE QUESTION OF THE AGENCY OF CHANGE

By agency of change, we mean that sector of the population whose aspirations and action constitute the principal moving force for change. There are always many roles to be played by a wide variety of conditions, forces, and people in any process of change. But thrusts toward change do not emerge equally from all sectors of the society. Some people are rulers, some are relatively satisfied, some are ideologically quiescent or cowed by coercion. Only certain categories of people can or do assume the primary burden of pressing forward the cause of change. Identifying the groups or segments of the population who possess such potential, and understanding what factors make it possible for them to transcend their differences and constitute themselves into a socially effective force, are among the foremost tasks of a theory of political change. We cannot settle for images of a process of change which rest on mere faith that a social force will emerge from the undifferentiated mass of people at some appropriate time. *Which* people are most likely to shoulder the burden of change, and *why,* under our present circumstances? How can we locate the seeds of such potentiality, and what would enable them to flower?

The Concept of Class

The fundamental-change processes that are best known to capitalist-liberal societies were generated by a rising middle class of tradesmen, merchants, financiers, and professionals, collectively described later as the bourgeoisie. The latter were not a single-minded or clearly-defined group before *or* after the revolution-incorporating fundamental-change process for which they served as the driving force. They sought only conditions in which they could conduct and profit from the economic transactions that were newly possible. Feudal society offered no such opportunities for business, and their joint but unorganized—essentially self-seeking—activity simply reconstructed that social order into capitalist-liberal society. This reconstruction was then confirmed by armed struggle. Not necessarily deprived, the becoming-bourgeoisie were nevertheless a substantial sector of the population experiencing needs and desires that were realizable but not fulfilled under then-current conditions. And yet those very same conditions permitted them to accomplish the total reconstruction of the society by simply acting out their own economic self-interest.

But with the advent of industrialization and factory-production processes, suddenly most people found that they could earn their living only through selling their labor to those who owned the expensive machinery, for jobs and at rates convenient to the latter. And the property rights of the owners were defended by the power of the newly-centralized state. Thus, a new and dependent, hence exploited, grouping was created within West European and American societies. By the mid-nineteenth century, Karl Marx and others were referring to this relationship in terms of classes: the ruling or owning class, the bourgeoisie, and the proletariat or working class. The latter encompassed all those with productive skills, but who were morally and materially dispossessed, and constituted the primary force for change.

But Marx did not base his hopes for working-class-generated fundamental change solely on their real, relative, and increasing deprivation. He also saw this body of people as constituting the productive genius and potential for improving the lot of humanity as a whole. The working class contained within itself all those skills and capabilities that were socially necessary to permit greatly expanded material production and vast improvement in the quality of life for mankind. By taking power and reconstructing the society along rational, socialist lines, the working class could transform the social order into a new and higher form, ever closer to the realization of true human potential. The conditions of capitalist development made possible, for the first time in history, man's management of himself and nature in such a way as to achieve ultimate self-realization.

Thus Marx's identification of the working class as the agency of change was partly a categorization based simply on a relationship to the means of production, and partly an assessment of the potential of this class to represent humanity itself in a new form. The key to the awakening of this class and its purposeful action to bring about the new society was the development of class consciousness—the sense of shared deprivation, entitlement, and capability that could set the class in motion to change its world and itself. Before the development of this consciousness, the class was in Marx's terms only a class-in-itself: existing in fact, but with components divided against each other and paralyzed by bourgeois ideology—competitiveness, individualism, etc. With the development of awareness of what they shared, and what they could become through acquiring state power and reconstructing the society, the class would become a class-*for*-itself: self-conscious, purposeful as an entity transcending parochial interests, and capable of realizing its true potential and that of humanity as a whole. The instrument of awakening such class consciousness, of course, was a cadre of knowledgeable socialists, whose task it was to enable the working class to see its needs and necessary course of action more clearly.

Since Marx, the concept of class has been trivialized, mechanized, and romanticized. Its use in theories of change has been, if possible, even more variable. In one or another way, the defenders of bourgeois society and Marx's own followers have converted "class" into a flat, unidimensional concept devoid of the meaning it once had. Unsatisfied with the apparent unreality or emptiness of categorization based entirely on relationship to the means of production, and unreceptive to Marx's sense of potential, sociologists and others have sought other tangible (empirical) indicia of "class." They have turned to indicators such as income, education, and occupation, and built an image of society as a ladder consisting of stratum upon stratum of people with different levels of each. Such a concept leaves no room for dynamism in a class as a unit, but only mobility as individuals. Small wonder, then, that a shared class consciousness should appear unlikely, and that the concept of class conflict or class-based action of any kind should seem somehow unreal. Marx's self-labelled followers, however, have often gone in the opposite direction, with equally unproductive results. Instead of insisting that class could *only* have empirical meaning, they have transcended the need for any tangible evidence of its existence and viability at all. For the most part, they have treated "the working class" as an article of faith. Ignoring the crucial role of class consciousness in converting the class into a class-for-itself, they have insisted that the working class awaited only the right leadership and opportunity to seize power. Two results have then followed. Either such Marxists become totally detached from reality and end up in self-deluded isolation, or they see every minor movement and issue as the potential beginning of the surge to power and rush off to join it *on its own terms*. In so doing, of course, they assure that the necessary bridge from present to future consciousness will not be made, and effectively drain Marx's idea of class of its transforming (consciousness-connected) quality.

These three distinctive uses of the concept of class (there are others, but these are the major variants) may serve at least to focus some vital questions for our analysis. What ingredients are necessary to give reality or utility to the concept of class as an agency of change? Clearly, there must be an objectively identifiable social grouping similarly affected by some major dynamic of the existing social order, such as racism, wealth distribution, or ownership of the means of production. Shared values, attitudes, and aspirations must go along with shared characteristics of life situation. Then comes the key threshold: the development of class consciousness, not only in the sense that awareness of what is shared overcomes internal conflicts, this-society competitiveness, and individualism, but also in the sense of confidence in the necessity and capability of creating a new social order. At this stage, the class needs only the opportunity and the power resources (e.g., the capacity to halt the society's business, access to substantial means of violence, etc.) to pose the issue of transfer of power.

This brings us to the core of the issue regarding agencies of change in the United States today: Is there, in being *or* in potential, a "class" capable of serving as an agency of change? We shall critically examine several leading nominations. And then we shall turn to the question of other possible agencies, perhaps a new one more appropriately suited to our present social circumstances and to the kind of consciousness change process likely to culminate in an ultimately justifiable new society.

The Working Class

Marxists and some others turn automatically to the traditional working class. Some do so merely by rote, as we have seen, but others argue more persuasively that the working class is the *only* practical agency of change and that the combination of emerging social conditions and effective educational work by socialists can create the necessary sense of class consciousness. Two points are made with respect to the first half of this argument. One is that the working class is still the major locus of deprivation and discontent, as well as of the capacity to reconstruct the society. A lively controversy exists over the question of whether rising affluence in the United States has drained the working class of its revolutionary potential and converted it into a pale shadow of the satisfied middle class. The evidence makes clear that, in income and occupational terms, the working class is still economically marginal, living a life that is physically hard and psychologically destructive. But it is less clear whether the basic values and ideology of the working class are sufficiently distinctive from the dominant orthodoxies of the middle classes to serve as the soil of socialist consciousness. All recognize, of course, that the stake in society and the ideology of the middle classes cause them to identify with the interests of the ruling classes and serve as the major bulwark against fundamental change. But the controversy over the issue of a similar "conservatism" in the working class still endures.

The other point is incontrovertible, but little appreciated. The working class is the only social grouping in the United States with the capability to pose the issue of the transfer of power by simply stopping its normal work. If workers cease production, the most basic needs of the economy are immediately affected: profit is threatened, and mutual sustenance is cast in doubt. The state cannot long endure such a situation, and it is forced to try—by armed force if necessary—to force the workers back to their jobs and normal behavior. If they resist effectively, the great question of who shall rule is posed in the most basic way possible, and the future of the state is at stake. No other social grouping has the capacity to create this sort of situation; the working class thus has unique power resources, mobilizable easily through simple refusal to work.

The second half of the Marxist argument in behalf of the working class as the agency of change raises the question of whether and how mass-consciousness change can be brought about. There is little disagreement about the current lack of class consciousness among the working class, or about the extent of parochialism and self-interest that divides its members and prevents them from coherent and effective action in their own behalf. But the question of how this is to be done divides Marxists across a wide spectrum. Some argue that it is merely a matter of persuasion through propaganda and rational argument. while others say that dramatic events must first loosen the grip of capitalist ideology. Some say the message can be effectively brought from outside the working class by a self-nominated cadre, others that only indigenous leaders can serve the purpose. Still others believe that the key is to establish oneself as the major or hegemonic leftist political organization, to whom the working class will have to turn when they become ready to undertake serious political action. The important point for our purposes is that all brands of Marxists acknowledge the obstacle inherent in the lack of class consciousness on the part of the working class—an obstacle that must be overcome if the working class is to serve as the vehicle of change. Simultaneously, all Marxists appear to assume that the new consciousness must be one coherent only with a socialist state. Moreover, they assume that the appropriate socialist consciousness was sketched out in the mid-nineteenth century and need now only be inculcated by those knowledgeable enough to know its content. We shall have more to say about this in the next chapter.

The "New Working Class"

In recent years, a number of change-seekers have despaired of the prospects of "radicalizing" the working class, either because of its supposed affluence or its intransigent lack of class consciousness. Instead, they have located the potential for fundamental change among what they call the "new working class." This is the growing body of white collar and professional workers, particularly the younger members thereof, who may be middle class in socioeconomic terms but nevertheless conceive themselves to be deprived and feel frustrated in basic ways. This thesis gains support from the fact that the numbers of such workers are indeed growing, and the conditions of work in such jobs are not fulfilling in the sense of offering creative or self-developing opportunities. In several instances, younger echelons of government workers, teachers, and other professionals have shown militant opposition to established institutions and practices.

But there are at least two serious limitations to this thesis. One is that the middle-class individualism and material affluence of this sector of the population both limits their willingness to take the risks necessary to accomplish fundamental change and cuts them off from potentially vital allies among lower classes and minorities. Their orientations are likely to be toward reform—frequently the more exotic and less basically economic issues—rather than toward fundamental reconstruction of the system as a whole. They are neither comfortable with nor well received by working-class people, and little real communication occurs across this class boundary.

The other problem is that they have no power resources equivalent to the working class' capacity to shut down the society. When teachers go out on strike, for example, the schools are closed—but no fundamental interference with the operations of the society results. Similarly, the daily business of the society can go forward comfortably without the services of government lawyers, social workers, medical paraprofessionals, etc. The only ones who really suffer are the clients in each case—students, poor people, the sick—to whose welfare the new working class is supposedly dedicated. When postal workers or other key municipal workers strike, of course, the National Guard moves the mails or operates the bridges. Thus, the new working class has both class-grounded and power-resources difficulties standing in the way of assuming important stature as an agency of change.

The new working class thesis, moreover, treats the great issue of consciousness change in a manner that is at best unsystematic. On the one hand, the origin of the concept lies in recognition that this is a social grouping whose sense of frustration with their lives, despite material affluence, might permit the rise of new values. On the other, little or no attention is paid by the advocates of this thesis to the problem or process of consciousness change. They do not ask how individuals in this category are going to experience consciousness change, or what sort of new consciousness might or should develop in place of the existing one. The vital connection between consciousness change and reconstruction of the social order is left unexplored for the most part, with the exception of a few. The latter, no more productively than the advocates of the traditional working class, uncritically assume nineteenth-century socialism as the wave of the future. In both cases, of course, it may be that the problem of consciousness change has simply not been confronted in its true depth and scope.

Coalitions of Special-Focus Groups

If both the traditional and the new working classes lack the appropriate class consciousness to be an effective agency of change, what of the groups that are already organized and militantly seeking change? In some cases, these groups assert that they have already achieved important levels of consciousness change. This is certainly true, for example, of racial minorities, the womens' liberation movement, some local community organizations, etc. What are the chances of the equivalent of a "class" being formed through coalitions of such groups?

I would argue that the chances of a viable social force emerging from these disparate groups are very slim. They are organized around what divides them, rather than around the things that they share. The dominating purpose of their existence is to focus attention and power resources upon their supposedly unique entitlement to some additional share of what is available within the framework of the system as it is. This is not to say that their moral entitlement is not very strong, nor that their material needs are unimportant. It is simply to point out that their claims are being made in part *against* each other—often, in effect, cancelling each other out—instead of against an oppressive system that is the common source of many of their legitimate complaints.

Nor is it a sufficient answer to say that these groups are already organized and therefore must be taken as the beginning point from which further organization should proceed. In fact, that may be the best argument for seeking to transcend such parochialism. They have organized around single issues for the most part, issues which have only limited potential to reveal the comprehensive failures of the existing social order and to lead others to awareness of the need to replace it rather than repair it. If people take only one issue at a time, seeking to obtain remedies only for that problem, they will either spend a lifetime without ever approaching the threshold of consciousness change in the total sense, or they will end up settling for reforms. Moreover, the fact that these groups have organized around single issues in the present suggests that they have probably incorporated much of the present consciousness in their organizational forms and practices. When and if they do come together in attempted coalitions, suspicions go so deep that most of the energy expended is directed at the problem of transcending organizational or conceptual boundaries. Each organization or psychic identification, of course, is trying to preserve its distinctive identity as well as accomplish the goal of coalition *and* whatever larger purpose is involved. How much more direct it would be, and far more likely to result in a new consciousness, to eliminate the stage of separate identification, and move immediately to a focus on the problem that is shared by all—learning to transcend the divisions that might otherwise give rise to separate formations in the process of the struggle itself.

Parliamentary Parties

The other form of political organization already in existence that might conceivably play the part of the agency of change is the political party. Enough has already been said to suggest that this is the least hopeful of all so far examined. Not only is a political party understandable to most people in terms of the current consciousness only, but it must also undertake at least certain electoral rituals that can only be counterproductive. Assuming that a fundamental change-oriented group employs the political party form at all, it can only be for the purpose of educational and propaganda work, not with any hope or intention of playing by the existing rules or seeking to actually win the election. But even so, the image presented must be a this-consciousness image, and the fact of engaging in such rituals must slow the development of its members and inhibit others from joining with it and comprehending its real purposes. It can only serve as a limited or transitional tactic, not as the agency of change in the larger sense.

Non-Class Agencies of Change

This completes the roster of visible, existing, and familiar possible agencies of change. None of them seems immediately viable and ready for service; substantial barriers to such service appear in every case. To some, it may appear that these barriers are historically and contextually insuperable in the United States. and that there *is* little prospect of finding an effective agency of change in this country. But that may be only because we are looking for the wrong thing. The social and economic conditions of the nineteenth century created the concept and the potential reality of social class as an agency of change. If the social and economic conditions of the late twentieth century are significantly different, however, we are hardly well advised to search for the same sort of a vehicle of change. Perhaps there are rising or potential social formations that would be different, but play the same essential part in the process of change.

This is a possibility that is necessarily very difficult to explore. It would depend in part on the development of a new consciousness capable of discerning such potentiality and bringing it into existence. We can say only that in general such a new social formation would have to perform many of the functions previously assigned to the working class—mobilizing, developing the resources necessary to transfer power into hands able to reconstruct the society, etc. Such a new social formation might be less grounded in shared social-background characteristics than social classes of the past, and more based on shared subjective responses to world conditions. In other words, as world communications multiply and other interdependencies are felt more strongly, and more people (at least in the United States) come to have enough material assurances to feel secure against immediate starvation, specific features of one's social situation may become less confining in terms of one's world view and ideology. People may come to identify themselves more with non-tangible aspects of social life, transcending their own immediate surroundings and linking subjectively with groups, processes, and causes physically removed from themselves.

In this sort of situation, the crucial factor would not be social homogeneity but the new consciousness. The latter would serve as the principal defining factor in people's lives, and perhaps bring them together, at least initially, on grounds completely separate from the older ones of class. Once people were on the way to developing the new consciousness, their need for supportive social formations might lead to the development of multiple groups or layers with the capacity to develop the essential sense of shared purpose that could lead to fundamental change.

This is an entirely speculative foray, of course, but we must be open to the probability that each set of distinctive social conditions *precludes* certain previously familiar change processes but *permits* others not yet fully understood or describable. At some point. of course, the initial stage of almost entirely subjective development of a new agency of change would have to give way to a stage in which objective factors played a larger role. The subjective base of the structure of authority can only erode so far in an exclusively subjective manner. It requires enabling change in institutions and practices, for example, and it must face the prospect of reaction. The existing power structure will seek to prevent change, and the resultant rise of fascism will force mobilization of the means of violence if only in defense of the opportunity for change. But this may be a later stage, even less visible from this vantage point than the one we have been imagining.

THE QUESTION OF THE CHARACTER OF ORGANIZATION

What part is to be played by formal organization in a fundamental change process that is dependent upon consciousness change at an early stage? The issue reduces to a series of dilemmas. The basic question, of course, is whether there should be *any* such organization, and if so, what kind. If the answer to the first half of this question appears self-evident, the reader should take special note of the dilemmas as they are reviewed.

The first problem is one familiar to all—the fact that any formal organization quickly rigidifies, developing a life and needs of its own quite distinct from those people and purposes that brought it into being. The maintenance of the existence of the organization begins to become a priority independent of its program or goals, internal ideology and loyalties develop, and people begin to compete for status and control within its hierarchy. Two results often follow. The first is that ordinary participants become less consequential in shaping the organization's program or purposes than those who hold positions somewhere in the bureaucracy. Those with greater knowledge or commitment or insight into the organization's needs frequently take it upon themselves to influence or manipulate less involved participants. This may reach the point where the organization becomes much like the private property of its bureaucrats. We recognize this phenomenon under the label of "the iron law of oligarchy." What we do not always recall is that this phrase was coined over half a century ago by a frustrated member of a supposedly participatory social democratic organization committed to achieving fundamental change in Germany. Perhaps needless to add, the organization has endured to this day—as an instrument of liberal reform.

The second result is the rise of a kind of conflict syndrome, in which the self-distinguishing and self-justifying needs of the organization cause it to assert that its character and program are different and better from all its possible competitors. If they were not. of course, there would be no reason for its existence. But because they are, part of the reason for its existence must be the denigration of the other organizations or tendencies. Because it is better, it should challenge and replace the others, growing at their expense. This urge to conflict is particularly acute among leftist organizations, as a result of their shared belief in the principle of left hegemony. As noted earlier, this principle asserts that when the society begins to fall apart, the working class will turn to the organized left in search of leadership. It will not take time to review all the theory and analyses of each organization, but simply join the largest and apparently dominant such group. Thus each group has a stake in becoming the hegemonic organization *and* in preventing others from assuming or continuing in such a role. With this shared principle, continuing conflict is the only sure result; however self-destructive it may appear to an outside observer, those who believe in the principle of left hegemony cannot act otherwise.

In some ways, these two results can articulate with each other. An organization can escalate its rhetoric in order to justify and maintain itself in competition with others. And then in effect it becomes the exact opposite of what it ostensibly seeks: it serves to draw to itself those who agree with its change-seeking goals, but then it prevents them from acting in accordance with such goals lest that action endanger its continuity in the world as it is.

A second dilemma inheres in the fact that two of the major tasks of the fundamental-change organization impel it toward quite contradictory forms. To serve effectively as a spur to consciousness change, as well as to act in the most coherently disciplined manner at crucial moments, the organization should be small and intense. The level of interpersonal contact and mutual confidence must be very high. Communication must be regular and extensive, and members must be theoretically sophisticated. These needs suggest a cadre type of organization. But there are also needs for development of a mass base and broad power resources. Not only is the democratic participation of large segments of the population morally and politically desirable, but it is also vital to engage the maximum possible number of people in the society in the process of consciousness change and social action leading to the acquisition of state power. These needs, of course, lead in the direction of a mass political party.

This tension between types of needs can be stated another way. To defend the development of a new social order, and perhaps to achieve power in the first place, a powerful national organization seems essential. The American power structure will not evaporate, and in any event we have seen that the pressures that lead to fascist reaction are strong and growing. If only to defend itself, the new society will have to be prepared to cope with such threats—and it can do so only through a strong national organization. But it is exactly this kind of organization that poses the maximum threat to the equally necessary development of locally autonomous units which can create a new sense of community among Americans. Personal fulfillment and the experience of actually controlling the conditions of one's life are among the foremost goals of those committed to fundamental change. They are also essential components in the process of consciousness change. But submission to the centrally dominant discipline of a national organization capable of defending against fascism may be totally inconsistent with achieving such goals.

Let us now move from these relatively familiar, this-consciousness dilemmas to a larger and more comprehensive one that both incorporates them and focuses on the basic problem. The very fact of organization suggests hierarchy and permanency for a set of relationships that is consistent with the world as it is at the time of creation. In effect, organization implies the arrest of consciousness in its present state. The existing capitalist-liberal consciousness is encapsulated and preserved in the very social formation that purportedly seeks its replacement. What is needed is change—change *out* of the way of thinking that *is*, and *into* new relationships. How can this possibly be achieved within the stopped-in-time framework of an organization that was created under the old way of thinking and now seeks determinedly to maintain its existence exactly as it is?

There appear to be three possibilities. One is to create an organization today in the image of the society of tomorrow. This would be consistent with the need to have social institutions now that can help to generate the new consciousness. But it would require that at least some people be well along the path to self-conscious consciousness change, and competent to create such an organization. The social institutions that they need to progress along the road to consciousness change, however, are not necessarily formally organized ones. The chances would appear to be better that a formal organization would be created with the tools and assumptions and experience of this consciousness. Then it would begin to seek self-maintenance, and to arrest rather than spur the process of consciousness change. And soon, the change-seekers would find that they had lost their momentum and potential for transforming both themselves and their society.

The second possibility is the creation of a constantly self-renewing organization. This would assume regular and continuing reconstruction of program and structure and personnel, perhaps sporadic replacement of organizations themselves. It is different and better than merely multiplying organizations that are small but essentially permanent, for there would be no merit in *many* units stopped in time as opposed to one or two in a similar condition. Whether it is possible to actually create a self-renewing organization is a very difficult question; examples of such organizations are few and far between. Indeed, the very phrase "self-renewing organization" may be a contradiction in terms. But an even more crucial question would be whether such an organization, if brought into being, would be capable of performing the tasks that are normally thought to be the purpose of having a formal organization. So much energy might be expended in reconstructing the organization in various ways that little time would be left for undertaking its programs, and it would exhibit so little learning behavior and have so little experience with which to act that it would be ineffective for other reasons.

The third possibility may have more merit, even if it does appear to be an avoidance of the main issue. This would be to avoid all organizations until the process of consciousness change has begun for a sizeable number of people in informal ways. If that process can move some distance with only informal social supports, it might be possible at some later stage to create an organization or organizations that would more fully reflect that new consciousness. If so, at least some of the dangers foreseen above might be avoided. Of course, a potentially serious drawback is the fact that there may not be such time left before the society is faced with the issue of fascism versus some other form of social order.

The question we are dealing with is really that of understanding what the new consciousness requires to develop and transform itself into social action. We have seen that much of what might be undertaken in the way of formal organization-building would have the effect of limiting rather than spurring this process. Whatever organizational form and function emerges must be consistent with the essential goal of consciousness change and social action resulting from such new consciousness. These are the criteria that we shall apply to the critical evaluation of proposed and present organizations for achieving fundamental change.

SCENARIOS OF A PROCESS OF CHANGE
CULMINATING IN THE TRANSFER OF POWER

In focusing first on the nature of possible agencies of change and the parts that might be played by formal organizations in the process of change, we have started with concrete social units and problems that often derail fundamental change. The lack of a scenario of change is a similar social fact that has stood in the way of change. Without an awareness in people's heads of the ways in which we might get from here to there, and particularly the confidence that this *could* happen—

that a new social grouping with wholly different purposes might actually acquire power and reconstruct the social order—there can be no fundamental change. The development of such imagery and confidence, of course, is partly the product of events, partly due to effective demonstration of the possibility by informed leaders, and partly the result of the beginnings of consciousness change on the part of many people. We shall identify some of the sorts of things that must be included in some fashion in such a scenario, and suggest how ways of thinking might have to be altered by the new consciousness in order to develop the necessary awareness and confidence among numbers of people.

One of the first needs in developing a comprehensive scenario of change in the heads of people, who might then become the driving force in bringing it about, is an adequate sense of social context and process. People must learn to see themselves as linked to others and to social institutions and events in a total system-process, a multi-dimensional web moving through time. A scenario of change must then assign roles to various forces. In particular, people must know whether the sources of change are to be found inside or outside the system, and how they relate to each other to bring about change. For example, what role is to be played by economic and social forces and events generated out of existing or possible future conditions? *Must* there be a depression to bring about detachment from the existing consciousness and ideology, and is there independent evidence that there will be? Or, *could* the Third World develop the capacity to prevent American exploitation, and *would* that create intolerable economic and social strains inside the United States?

Unless these and similar questions are answered in such a way as to create a comprehensive scenario of what happens first and then how a subsequent stage emerges from that first one, and so forth, there is little chance that people can be drawn towards confidence that change can and will happen. I am not suggesting that any detailed blueprint can or should be prepared; later stages of the process can only be understood through the new consciousness. But there must be a communicable image of how it starts, enough of a scenario to focus peoples' attention on the necessity of transferring state power, and sufficient demonstration of the capability of governing to create confidence that life could be better under a new regime.

What we are talking about under the label of scenario is the rudiments of a theory of change, a basic description of how it might occur. In such a theory, however rough, there must be some provision for an agency of change, the role of organization, the nature and process of consciousness change, how power resources to do the job are to be mobilized, what part may be played by violence, what kinds of things will be done by the new regime once it acquires power, etc. All of these matters must be addressed in some fashion. Failure to do so implies that the prescription or group involved has not thought about them, and is relying on some faith or providential guidance to bring about the most difficult social transformation that the world has ever known. In either case, people are surely well advised to look elsewhere for leadership, and perhaps to make the best of their present circumstances. There has yet to be a transfer of state power from one social grouping and set of priorities to another in advanced industrial society, and to imagine that such a process could be either automatic or self-accomplishing is pure fantasy. It is a deadly serious business, demanding of the most serious and systematic thinking.

The part to be played by violence and by power resources generally is an important element in this scenario. Change-seekers must prepare people, particularly Americans, for the prospect of violence. It is part of our legalistic ideology that violence, by whomever perpetrated and regardless of the provocation, is wrong and should be punished. But we seldom see violence inherent in our institutions and practices, as provoked by systematic deprivation, or as routinely practiced by police and other law enforcement officials. We simplify complex situations by blaming those who engage in (nonofficial) violence and supporting their punishment. Americans must be brought past such one-sided and self-limiting attitudes. No fundamental-change process, in all likelihood, can long endure without at least the necessity of defending itself against reaction. And it may be necessary for state power to be acquired through the apparently unprovoked use of violence. Unless people are adapted to such facts, the fundamental change movement will crack and fall apart on this issue.

People must also come to understand where power is to be found, and how to mobilize and use it for constructive purposes. Power cannot be eliminated until the need for it is past. That condition cannot occur until those who would maintain or restore the existing society by force have been rendered incapable of doing so. The sorts of things that *can* and *cannot* stop the society must be understood clearly. To think, for example, that the shutting down of a few campuses would pose the issue of state power in a country as big as the United States, with as many institutions of higher education as lie scattered about the nation, managed by so many different public and private bodies, is to seriously delude oneself. Rather than any question of state power, it poses only questions of the rationality of those people or groups who would indulge in such thoughts.

Of particular importance to the development of confidence in the capacity of a new social grouping to reconstruct the society is the presentation of a program and its justification. In part, of course, this confidence is built out of the evident failure of current rulers to govern effectively. But it also depends on a showing of specific purposes and implementing means. Even if the later stages of development of the new consciousness ultimately invalidate specific programs, merely working out and presenting such a program and displaying the personnel and skills to carry it out may create a new level of confidence among people. The experience of running a city during a general strike, for example, can create such new confidence. Essentially, what is involved is the spread of understanding among the people at large that life can go on under another kind of government.

But perhaps the most important single element in developing a comprehensive scenario of how change might take place is the question of whether change is to be anticipated through linear processes or not. Here is where the new consciousness plays a key part. In the capitalist-liberal consciousness, change is understood only in terms of step-by-step extensions of the present. Everything that will be tomorrow is visibly present today, and specific increments that can be added by means of current techniques will move that tangible present to that equally knowable future. The development of more and more workers' control in the factory will inevitably result in broadened capabilities and aspirations for governing authority on the part of such workers, and they will ultimately come to demand control of the state. Or, steadily expanding demands for minority control of ghetto businesses will lead to demand for full control over the state. And so forth.

What the linear image of the process of change completely overlooks is the matter of consciousness change. It says in effect that everything into the future must take place just as things do now. Most important, it denies that any kind of change *not* fitting the criteria of the present (i.e., not amounting to an incremental, step-by-step addition to the world as it is) can occur.

With another way of thinking and knowing, it might be possible to see totally different types of processes of change. In particular, one might envision a process in which latent potentialities in the present were expanded and transformed into wholly new forms of social order. Pressures in the present would be, in effect, exploded through a kind of threshold into a future where the terms and causes of thought and action were totally different. In a new consciousness, that might be the usual nature of the process of change.

Notice, however, that assumptions about change which rely upon step-by-step processes are cast in the *current*, capitalist-liberal consciousness. They involve no reconstruction of consciousness, but only gradual expansion of what is—as if by such expansion of today's terms and conditions it might be possible to enter the world of a new consciousness. Everything we have seen about consciousness and consciousness change suggests that this view is mistaken. To change consciousness is to drop *all* of the present, or at least all that is really restrictive about the present way of thinking, and take on a wholly new way of thinking and knowing. Nothing in the step-by-step, linear process appears to permit or adapt to that necessity; instead, that process appears much more likely to hold onto the existing consciousness and doggedly project it into the future. Thus, it seems quite unlikely that the expansion of workers' control, or any other projection of present circumstances, will succeed in achieving a constructive (i.e., consciousness change based) version of fundamental change. If such routes *are* successful, which seems doubtful, they are much more likely to result in a mere exchange of one set of rulers for another within the same unsatisfactory consciousness.

SUMMARY: SEEING DIFFERENTLY

We are now beginning to think about *how to think about change*. We have seen that consciousness change is the essential precondition, without which no truly liberating or constructive political change can occur.

But consciousness change is not enough. It requires, both for its own further development and to make its appropriate contribution to necessary political change, that there be social action *consistent with* that developing new consciousness. Only that sort of social action intended to reconstruct the society in the direction of that social order with which the new consciousness is coherent is appropriate. But that type of action is essential. And it must be the sort of action that keeps open the possibility of continued consciousness change, rather than closing such chances in any way.

The agency of change must be one that incorporates and provides continuing opportunities for this consciousness change. No agency that does not reflect and expand this consciousness change can serve the cause adequately. This means, of course, that the agency of the future may be quite different from those of the past, for social conditions are different. Whatever the agency turns out to be in the way of actual social formation, we know that it must effectively translate the new consciousness into social action. If it does not, it is a barrier to change or at best a vehicle for exchanging one set of rulers for another.

The presence of formal organizations in the process of change raises several prospects of rigidity and prevention of continued consciousness change. Despite some obviously important needs that can only be served through the development of a powerful organization, the quality of the fundamental change process itself may be undermined by the effects of formal organizations. It may be that a necessary accommodation must be made in which organizations are avoided, at least until the process of consciousness change is well enough along to be able to shape a new type of organization.

It is essential also to develop a reasonably full scenario of a process of change that culminates in the transfer of power, in order to prepare people for the actual process that ensues and to give them confidence that it is possible. But any such scenario must be one that allows for new and different—wholly inconceivable within the present consciousness—types of change. There must be enough of a plan, in other words, to show that the enterprise is not hopeless; but it must also be a plan that is transcendable as soon as the new consciousness is far enough along to enable us to see totally new possibilities.

Each of these factors must be present, or even favorable opportunities for change may be lost. The case of France in May, 1968 is a good illustration. The complete lack of any theory of how change might occur eliminated whatever chance of fundamental change may have been present at that time. There was little or no explicit recognition of the central role of consciousness change. What did occur was spontaneous and (potentially) dramatically enabling, but its significance was not understood. No agency of change could be seen that did not have its origins in the nineteenth century, and important possibilities may have been missed therefore. The Communist Party's control of the key trade union, the CGT, caused it to avoid commitment at crucial moments. By acting to maintain itself, and totally within the framework of expectation of capitalist-liberal French politics, the CGT assured that it would hold the workers to their usual level and kinds of political action—and possibly prevented their seizure of power. Finally, the fact that there was no scenario of power transfer in people's minds caused the movement to fall back at crucial moments. People were not accustomed to thinking in terms of taking control of the state, but only in terms of protesting unsatisfactory conditions. Thus, when the issue seemed about to be posed, they were afraid—or at best unable to imagine what they might do if they held state power.

Each of the criteria discussed above must be answered and dealt with in some way before a particular prescription or process of change can be deemed viable. We have developed the beginnings of demands that can legitimately be raised of any prescription or movement that calls for fundamental change in the United States today. Separately, these are questions that change-seekers have to answer. Together, they are the germ of a theory of change. We know that change, in order to be constructive, must have these characteristics. It is now time to turn to some actual prescriptions and see how they measure up to the standards we have developed. At the same time, of course, we shall be able to revise those very standards and further refine the theory inchoate in them by contrasting them with such prescriptions.

3

Political Change: Seeing and Becoming

CHAPTER EIGHT

Contemporary Prescriptions:
The Legacies of Marx

Karl Marx is probably the most comprehensive and creative theorist of social and political change that the modern world has yet produced. The scope and character of the questions he asked are a model for all those who seek to understand how the past becomes the future as a total social process. In this sense, we should all be Marxists. Those who are not, do not even know the questions, let alone the answers.

But Marx was also an advocate, and the world he sought would have meant the overthrow of existing elites and their frightened middle-class supporters all across Europe and North America. Thus there have been two related responses that have effectively foreclosed the use of Marx as a catalyst for thinking about change. One is the dedicated surge of intellectuals to the task of misrepresenting, denying, or otherwise discrediting the concepts, methods, and results of Marx's work. The other is the massive ideological insulation of national populations against his basic teachings. Americans have suffered more seriously than any other society from the combined effects of these two responses. As a result, we have lost contact with the intellectual tools and tradition that yielded him such insight. And we have switched off our minds at the very mention of his name outside of the context of anticommunism, anachronism, or other pejorative usage.

This situation leads to some ironic consequences. When some Americans *do* begin to search for deeper understanding of social and political processes than is provided by their self-congratulatory capitalist-liberal ideology, they often suddenly encounter Marx—usually in some fragmentary but nevertheless helpful form. Lacking the intellectual background to fully understand what they have seen, and having to turn almost exclusively to the "vulgar" sectarians of existing Marxist political organizations, they seize scraps and are satisfied with them. Their new "Marxism" has provided the "answers" to the problem of political change. And, not surprisingly, the avidity and simplicity with which they embrace this supposed alternative only widens the gap between them and the essence of Marx's thought and method.

Our task in this chapter is, first, to briefly set Marx within the context of evolving critical social theory, in effect trying to recapture certain intellectual scope and insights that have been, over time, denied to Americans. Then, we shall critically assess the Marxist method and principles in terms of their applicability to the United States today. Finally, we shall review the positions and practices of those who advocate what they call Marxist prescriptions for political change in this country. This is not, nor could it be, an attempt at exhaustive evaluation of either Marx or American Marxists. Instead, it is a preliminary assessment in the light of our developing theory of change, for the purpose of refining that theory as well as gaining certain insights into the strengths and weaknesses of contemporary Marxist prescriptions.

Karl Marx and the Evolution of Critical Social Theory

We cannot digress here to undertake a full analysis of the character or history of German critical philosophy or its spin-offs into social theory. But it is essential for Americans to realize that a quite different way of understanding social "reality," one that stands firmly opposed to the empirical-positivism of capitalist-liberal society, offers a tested set of tools and methods upon which to draw for greater insight into our society and its problems.

This tradition is distinguished, first, by concern for the nature of knowledge itself, for the way in which the human mind conceptualizes and understands the surrounding world. Where empiricism sees external objects as having an intrinsic objective reality that we can grasp through our senses, critical theory says that much of that "reality" is the product of our mental constructs, in turn produced by our social environment. Thus, to understand our world, we should not only collect sense data about its supposed reality, but also examine the nature, sources, and implications of the concepts through which we interpret it. Its "reality," in other words, is part *it* and part *us*.

Next, critical theory sees social events or problems only as related to all other events, conditions, and activities in a total web of interconnections that is evolving steadily through time from past to future. In more technical terms, it is holistic and processual. *Everything* is related to everything else in a dynamic and particular manner; the observer too is a part of this moving interrelatedness, seeing it only as it permits. Empiricism, on the other hand, separates relationships into smaller and smaller segments and holds them static, the better to measure and quantify them accurately. The observer is thought to be neutral and detached, analyzing this package of facts in a value-free manner from outside and above. For critical theory, this is not only impossible but undesirable, for reality is found only in the entirety of relationships in the moving context-process. And observers must recognize themselves as integral parts of that whole, able to see only those "facts" that their value-shaped concepts permit them to see, and able to judge only with societally-generated standards.

Critical theory earns its label because its basic purpose is to see a social order not in terms of what it *is,* but in terms of what it could be or might become. It looks *behind* the surface reality. Objects and relationships are understood in part by what they are *not*; the contrast helps to heighten the meaning of what they *are*. Further, because critical theory emphasizes the dynamic context-process in which these objects and relationships exist, it anticipates change and searches for understanding in terms of their potential, of what they can and may become. To use a famous illustration, what do we see when we behold an acorn? Empiricism sees nothing but an acorn. A critical view would see the potential of an oak tree, the acorn in the process of realization of its essence—*if* a particular combination of circumstances obtain in the interim.

Translated into social theory, the critical perspective looks for the potentiality in social situations and human relationships, for the combinations of total circumstances that might enable man to realize his essence and achieve a truly fulfilling, human social existence. Naturally, this stance implies criticism of existing social relationships and the development of various concepts and tools for that purpose. Equally naturally, it generates reaction from those with a stake in maintaining those same relationships, who insist upon those concepts and methods that tend to support and defend the present order.

Marx's writings represent an important stage in the development of critical theory. In effect, Marx brought together two major streams of thought. From German idealism he drew the vital first step—the concern for the nature of knowledge and how the human mind works to create concepts and then understand social reality. But instead of finding the answers to these questions wholly within the mind itself, or in some metaphysical source, Marx turned to the materialist tradition and found the route to answers within social institutions and relationships. In other words, Marx argued that man's consciousness was socially produced, that what he understood as knowledge was what he had learned to accept as such through his social environment. There *is* such a thing as *true* knowledge, Marx insisted. But its truth depended on its relationship to a particular social and human setting and consequences. The touchstone of truth is whether a social institution or action contributes to the ultimate realization of the essence of man, his human fulfillment. True knowledge is that which enables mankind to move in that direction, adapting social formations and practices to aid in coping with the demands of nature and human self-realization. All else is partially true and partially false, depending on the extent to which there lies concealed within it some adaptive movement in the right direction.

In his early work, Marx stressed the unrealized human potential in man. He saw human fulfillment blocked in a variety of ways. One was through the false consciousness and ideology that was generated by capitalist society, which articulated with the conditions of labor and commodity-orientation to warp people into creatures far short of their potential. Moreover, they were led to believe that this condition was natural, either inevitable for the sake of "progress" or rooted in characteristics of human nature.

But, Marx argued, capitalism itself made possible, for the first time in history, a level of productivity that could free man from these conditions. Man had now acquired the capability to intervene in the process of social evolution and shape it toward that kind of society in which he could realize his essence or potential. But he would have to do that deliberately, and against two major obstacles. One was the determination of existing ruling classes to hold on to what they had, and the other was man's own entrapment in capitalist consciousness. If these obstacles were not overcome, however, and if capitalism held on through force, it would be disastrous for mankind; evolution would in effect be halted, and humanity would degenerate into ultimate extinction.

Thus, in his later work Marx devoted himself to the search for regularities or laws of social evolution, the patterns and causes in history that led to social change. He sought to understand historical evolution well enough to know when and how man might intervene in order to remake his own history according to his needs. In effect, Marx was *applying* critical theory in its then-current form.

It was not long before the reaction set in. Because of his many writings and appealing style (particularly the *Communist Manifesto*), and because he was tirelessly active in social terms, Marx became a principal focus in a variety of conflicts in the mid- and late-nineteenth century. Like Thomas Jefferson in the American context, Marx's name was used and his principles invoked by a wide variety of change-seekers, many of whom had little real understanding of the depth or subtlety involved in his analysis. He was not only the target of other socialists and anarchists, but also of the intellectuals who sought to defend the status quo of various European societies. Out of this emerged a way of thinking called positivism, a perspective that, grounded in empiricism, provided a solid wall of defense for existing social systems.

Positivism draws its name from the determination to affirm things as they are. If critical theory was *negative* in character, emphasizing all the things that were not as they could be in the world, *positive* theory would emphasize their achievements, what they *were,* that was, presumably, good. Thus, the achievements of existing social and political institutions and the desirable qualities of life, here and now, would be kept in the forefront by positivism. For this task, empiricism serves as a vital base. It can see no further than what is today, and implies that such conditions are either inevitable or practically remediable only in certain limited ways—and it has no capacity to offer fundamental alternatives. The intellectual linkage of empiricism and positivism has long provided powerful support for the continuance of capitalist-liberal society.

Marx thus served as a major contributor to the development of critical theory, and as its symbol during a period of massive reaction. But history did not stop there, contrary to the impressions of *both* many Marxists *and* their enemies. Critical theory has evolved, mostly through the work of European intellectuals, and has influenced several disciplines in a variety of ways. And yet it has done so under the shadow of the towering figure of Marx, whose powerful impact still serves as the point of departure for many intellectuals and social movements. Let us try to see what this has meant as far as the American experience is concerned.

Empiricism and positivism have always been dominant, first in Britain and then in the United States, to such an extent that we have been virtually unaffected by the intellectual turmoil surrounding Marx's merging of the idealist and materialist traditions and the development of critical theory. From our capitalist-liberal convictions and consciousness, we find these ideas very difficult to understand, and we tend to dismiss them as confused or irrelevant. In part, this is because these ideas are ultimately very threatening. The only parts of Marx that are understandable to most Americans are the empirical investigations of capitalist economic activity. These only make sense in terms of Marx's concepts and larger methodology, of course, but we ignore these, slice the empirical sections out of context, and examine them as short-term predictions or dated descriptions. The American intellectual tradition, grounded as it is in unexamined liberalism to the point where it is not even aware of its narrowness, has been almost completely impervious to critical theory in any form.

The social manifestations of Marx on the American continent occurred through German immigrants in the latter part of the nineteenth century, and were reflected in small socialist parties at the turn of the century. Nativism combined with the powerful effects of American orthodoxy to generate severe repressive measures, both official and private, against all such "foreign" ideologies. A series of "red scares" swept the country in the early decades of the twentieth century, and deportations, prosecutions, and investigations succeeded in intimidating or eliminating the socialist movement as a serious force in American politics. The appeals of private property, religion, and nativism have been deeply sunk into the American character, and lie readily available to be called upon by dominant elites and their followers to still social deviance or protest. Post-World War II anticommunism is only a recent version of a recurring phenomenon, the effect of which has been to effectively build a wall of insulation between Marx's ideas or any sort of critical theory—and the American people.

In Europe, however, the story has been somewhat different. Critical theory has synthesized Marx with humanism, existentialism, and phenomenology. Although it has produced no new Marx, this tradition is not only alive but continues to develop past Marx into appropriately modern forms. Few scholars can be considered serious who have not come to terms with Marx and this tradition in some way.

Marxist social movements have played important parts in most of these countries at least since the turn of the century. Many of these, of course, represent pragmatic accommodations to perceived social reality rather than any consistent effort to act out Marx's principles. When state power was somewhat surprisingly acquired by a Marxist organization in Russia in 1917, social circumstances and the inclinations of the organization led to a rigid and bureaucratized effort to institute socialism. Once rigidified and managed with acute concern for self-preservation, both of its own leaders and of the national state in a hostile world, the Soviet Union drifted further and further from the underlying philosophical methods and goals that were Marx's.

Most other European countries have also had large socialist parties and movements. In some cases, these have divided into accommodationist and revolutionary factions. The former have taken part in parliamentary politics and gradually lost their fundamental-change orientations, to the point where they resemble left-liberal or welfare-state Americans. Relatively fewer and much smaller groups have retained the revolutionary purposes that were originally theirs, but they still can muster respectable numbers on occasion.

Thus what is familiar to Europeans, though in a wide variety of forms (some of which are surely inconsistent with Marx's principles), remains quite unfamiliar to Americans. Moreover, when we look for guidance, the salience of Marx himself may serve as a kind of trap. First, he can only be understood in his own terms, and not through the concepts and tools of our empirical-positivist intellectual tradition *or* our related capitalist-liberal social framework. To be unaware of this is to consign oneself in advance to flat, rote application of his principles as they were articulated in the mid-nineteenth century. Second, we may mistake Marx for the entire body of critical theory, and create for ourselves a hundred-year gap in the intellectual toolbox that we draw upon. Marx does not offer the last word from such a distance, and would be the first to insist upon that; the method that he bequeathed to critical theory, however, modernized and developed by his successors in that tradition, may contain much of value. Third, Marx can be a trap if we understand him chiefly through the self-serving interpretations of his self-labelled followers. The multiplicity of versions of "true Marxism" alone should warn us against this possibility. It is Marx himself, evolving through critical theory, to which we must turn if we seek guidance from this direction.

THE APPLICABILITY OF MARX TO
THE LATE TWENTIETH-CENTURY UNITED STATES

There are two steps to this preliminary assessment of the strengths and weaknesses of Marxism for the American context today. The first is to distinguish Marxism as a *method* from Marxism as a set of dogmas. Only the former is consistent with Marx's own approach and principles. The latter represent a variety of failures to understand Marx and to avoid the rigidification and accommodationism inherent in formal organizations. The second step is that of identifying those elements of Marxism so conceived, that *are* and those that *are not* applicable to our distinctive social conditions and historical situation.

Marx's method was essentially a way of looking at the world, of continually asking questions that would point the way to the kind of social action that would contribute to bringing about the new society. The basic elements of critical theory, as set forth earlier, served as cornerstones of his approach. But by applying those methods, Marx emerged with some insights that he considered revealing of some basic characteristics of capitalism. These he translated into "laws," simply meaning observed regularities in the past and thus probabilities or tendencies for the future. He was in part an anthropologist, and an empiricist in the sense that he sought over and over again to validate his theoretical insights and projections from the data that he could find available. But all of this took place amidst the context of his vastly-encompassing conceptualization of the unfolding of history as a total process. None of his findings were meant as static, good for all places and times. And everything came back eventually to the question of the nature of human consciousness, its social sources, and the necessity for people to shed the false consciousness of capitalist society. How this might occur was obviously specific to particular times, cultures, and social circumstances.

Thus it comes as something of a shock that so many self-proclaimed Marxists can blithely seize upon one or another context-connected finding or observation and raise it to the level of an eternal principle valid anywhere at all times. Or that they can make of Marxism a package of conclusions or a cookbook of instructions for making a revolution. But this is exactly what has happened. Either through lack of understanding of the philosophical roots of his method, or for organizational reasons to be explored shortly, most Marxists think and act as if by rote, from a sacred text. Where Marx saw social evolution opening up multiple possibilities—opportunities and dangers, depending on social conditions and the character of human intervention—they see only inevitabilities. Where Marx saw constant change and continuing need to adapt, they see one flat picture of the world and cling to a mechanistic formula for action in it. And where Marx set consciousness change at the center of his problem, they act exclusively in this world. Sometimes it is hard to see Marxists as other than the negation of their symbol—as everything that Marx himself condemned as static and system-supporting.

Even when Marxism is understood as method, however, there are important obstacles in the way of effective utilization in the late twentieth-century United States. Let us grant all the scope and depth of insight possible through critical theory as Marx developed it—the great value of holistic, context-process images of our social world, of exploring how we know what we know, and of recognizing that to conceptualize the future we must find ways of understanding potentiality, both in our own consciousness and beings and in the social setting in which we are located. All this granted, there are still limitations present which must be overcome. Nor should this be surprising, for even great intellectual creations require reconstruction to suffice as a comprehensive theory in a distinctive setting a century later.

One major problem with Marxism lies in the nature of the economic and social conditions he envisioned. His world was that of early capitalism, with the forms of industralization and resulting social class system that then existed. Millions of subsistence-level industrial workers, manufacturing basic products in a few major industries, gave visible reality to his conceptualization of the working class. Marx saw this class as the exclusive vehicle of change, and designed all his expectations around its prospective awakening. In the later stages of capitalism, the multiplication of productive industries, the rise of various service industries, the development of science and technology, etc., at least raise the possibility that a quite different class system now obtains. Certainly, the sheer size of population and the scale of organization are unprecedented. Many different kinds of work have emerged, and large numbers of people have been satisfied by an equally unprecedented level of material well-being. Reliance upon the traditional working class as the exclusive agent of change thus seems unnecessarily self-limiting, perhaps quite wrong.

A related problem has to do with the solution toward which all of Marx's efforts were bent. For Marx, socialism—a centrally planned and conducted state apparatus managing the productive activity of the society in response to basic policy decisions taken by the people, once they were competent within the new consciousness—was the only and necessary alternative. While not impractical, socialism today would appear to require at least as extensive, hierarchical, and centralized an organizational network as we now have, perhaps vastly greater. To the extent that present problems are attributable to the scale of such organization, socialism would be no better. Unless the organizations necessary to manage the society were uniquely well-constructed and operated, they would be obstacles to consciousness change rather than facilitators of it. The world that Marx envisioned not only had far fewer people in it, but it was simpler; today's prescriptions should take such factors into account.

Finally, there are problems flowing from Marx's assertions that true knowledge is to be found through theoretically directed social action to move the society toward its potential future, and his expectation that a small group of educators would have to act to bring consciousness change to the broad masses of people. Not only do such principles readily become a license for a *few* to do whatever they think best in the name of all that is moral and highest in man, but they build in a continuing elitist strain to social action and organization. Thus, they lead to both vanguardism and hierarchy, neither of which is particularly promising for a new consciousness or a new society. As the knowledgeable few set about to remake the world for the benefit of others, they may be inclined to take what looks like the easiest way—to simply seize state power and firmly re-educate the masses. Or they may be tempted to omit entirely the precondition of widespread consciousness change, even for their own group and followers.

These problems might not have been such in Marx's time, or when he was available to correct misapplications. But today, the exclusivity of the working class as the agent of change, of hierarchical socialism as the only alternative, and the tendency to vanguard self-assertiveness all represent serious weaknesses. Ironically, each flows from one of Marx's strongest points. He knew that there could be no change until a social unit capable of transforming the society became conscious of itself and of its capabilities. His choice of the working class surely made sense at the time. His unit of thinking—humanity as a whole—remains unchallengeable today. Other systems of thought that employ the individual or the nation or tribe as their unit of thinking have far greater trouble justifying themselves morally. But socialism is not the only way in which the interests of world humanity can be set at the center of political thought and action. Marx's recognition of the social basis of knowledge was one of his most important insights. Only a remarkable intellectual achievement could succeed in wrenching a few out of this consciousness, to the perception of new and better ways of thinking. But this is a principle that very readily leads to the assertiveness of self-nominated vanguards—who may or may not have possession of the kind of truth and insight and moral purpose that Marx intended. The opportunity for corruption is only too clear, as is the fact that it was put there by Marx himself; ironically, there was no other choice in his system of thought.

To an extent, this critique has been directed at characteristics of Marxism itself. But it also has proceeded from a sense of the social circumstances of the United States today. It is certainly possible to overestimate the "uniqueness" of the United States; a careful comparison would acknowledge that many features of the American economic and political systems have ample parallels elsewhere. But there are certain characteristics about the United States that simply must be dealt with in any application of a theory of change, whether it is Marxism or any other. For example, there must be recognition of the scope and power of the dominant American ideology and its supporting consciousness. No European country, and probably no other country in the world, has known such a comprehensive and widely shared national belief system—nor one with such firm commitment to individualism and private property. Similarly, the United States is distinctive in terms of the advanced level and character of its productive system, its geographic size and decentralization, the multiplicity of divisions and conflicts (racial primarily, but also ethnic and religious) within its working class, and in the fact that there has been no enduring anti-capitalist tradition. These two sets of reasons—the weaknesses of Marxism itself and the special American circumstances to which it is to be applied—raise serious obstacles for American Marxists. At best, Marxism would have to be carefully supplemented and adapted for effective application here. It is one thing to draw upon Marx himself for some key insights and approaches to the general problem of thinking about change. But it is quite another to pick up a body of eternal truths and advance upon a distinctive society with the intent of using them to transform it. In the next section, we shall see to what extent various American Marxists escape the latter characterization.

AMERICAN MARXISTS: SOME ILLUSTRATIVE CATEGORIES

Applications of Marxism in the American context occur in several distinct forms, representing a rough continuum from rigidity—both in adherence to sacred texts and in organizational forms—to flexibility and adaptiveness. We shall take up three categories spanning this continuum: one at the rigidity pole, one emerging from this group and developing organized but unprecedented types of action along Marxist lines, and one made up of the independents and scholars who engage in little or no organized activity. Together, our categories will encompass all major uses of Marx in the United States today.

Classical Marxist Organizations

This category includes those groups, such as the Communist Party and the Socialist Workers Party, with roots in the experience of the Russian Revolution and its aftermath *and* long histories on the American scene.

It also includes their young peoples' organizations, the Young Workers' Liberation League and the Young Socialist Alliance, because they are controlled by the same assumptions and principles, i.e., by their parent organizations. And it also includes a multitude of tiny sects which derive their principles from split-offs from the older groups or from more recent revolutionary successes in China or Cuba. For the most part, these are so inward-focused, isolated, and in such a constant state of upheaval in membership and program that they have no current or future prospects of impact.

As a group, these organizations are a series of case studies illustrating the problems of the organized left in the United States. To begin with, they exist in a special kind of isolation. This isolation arises, in part, out of the great distance between their analyses and prescriptions and the kinds of political discourse familiar to Americans, and in part, from the systematic repression radicals have experienced in the United States. Then each adds another kind of isolation from its existence as an organization, with an internal life and needs that further detach it from its surroundings.

But isolation is only the beginning, in effect a spur to some of the worst effects of organizational hardening of the arteries. Because these organizations have been in existence for some time in a hostile environment, they have made several kinds of adaptation that, taken together, almost totally remove them from any prospect of achieving Marx's goals. Concern for the preservation of the organization has been paramount, displacing thought and action directed at revolutionary goals. The rhetoric of revolution lingers, but the *practice* is exclusively that of preserving the organization into the long-term future. The organization and its leaders assume continuity in most other aspects of social life in the United States, and their efforts are directed at surviving within this system. Thus the Communist Party and the Socialist Workers Party often base their policies and actions on very conservative estimates of the American future—estimates involving less expectation of change than most businessmen would take for granted. Although paying continued lip service to the idea of capitalist deterioration, actions are based on the assumption that real change, if it comes at all, can only occur in a very long-term future. None of the classical Marxist organizations foresee major crises in the near future.

Consistently, these groups tend to be embarrassed by opportunities.

They are ready with numbers of reasons why any particular development must be treated cautiously and with due regard for the
preservation of the organization. Their history of frustration and defeat
combines with their lack of current theoretical analysis to cause them
to discount strikes, tensions, or other aspects of social crisis as potential
opportunities to do more than add a few members to the organization.
Consequently, they relate to such moments only in terms of their
organizational needs—recruitment, self-justification, distinction from
other organizations, etc. They do not see spontaneous outbreaks or
other developments as possible stages in a larger process leading to mass
revolutionary action.

The Communist Party in particular has failed to take advantage of
possible opportunities over the years, in part because it has been forced
to serve primarily as the American extension of Soviet foreign policy.
At times when it might have gained significant strength and perhaps
generated real impact, instructions from Moscow caused it to change
policies abruptly, to bloc with various other groups, and even to
support Democratic Party candidates in elections. Moreover, the high
visibility of the Communist Party, again produced by its ties with the
Soviet Union, has made it a convenient target for a variety of American
officials and would-be leaders. Not only can they score points on the
scoreboard of American politics by finding and prosecuting real or
supposed Communists, but the charge of Communist associations or
leanings is a convenient tool for discrediting enemies of all kinds.
Understandably, this has contributed to the sense of caution and lack
of aggressiveness on the part of the Party. Paradoxically, however, it has
also created certain kinds of opportunities: if some Americans should
decide upon the necessity of revolution at this time, they would
probably think first of the Communist Party as the major organization
committed to that end.

But the Communist Party has made little or no effort to take
advantage of any of its opportunities. Its ranks depleted by post-World
War II waves of red-baiting, it is an organization of the very young and
the very old. It lacks any theory except what is produced from Moscow
out of the official Soviet version of Marxism, tempered by the needs of
the Russian national state. It stands today as a bureaucratic shell,
functioning chiefly out of memory of times past when great prospects

seemed in the offing and heroic sacrifices were made in already-lost causes.

Another form of lost opportunities is evidenced by the Socialist Workers Party. Although talking officially about revolution and continuing to stress its Trotskyist origins, the practice of this organization is almost totally accommodationist. Its approach is to take up every issue of liberal politics as they arise, joining in the discussion on essentially the same terms as other electorally oriented groups. Through such participation, presumably, some in the general public will come to see the superior merits of socialist solutions to problems. Perhaps some may be led to join the organization. The brand of socialism involved, however, and the bases on which such new members would be drawn into the organization, would be only slightly different from left-liberal politics as already practiced in the United States.

The latter point underscores an element conspicuously lacking in all of these organizations. None appears to have any strong commitment to the idea of consciousness change, and no sense of why or how such change should come about. Whether through failure to see this crucial element in Marx, or because of their ongoing adaptation to the world of capitalist-liberal politics, the matter has been almost completely ignored—or trivialized in most superficial fashion. It amounts to another—and particularly telling—indication of the absence of a comprehensive theory of change. In some respects, these organizations have not even come to terms with Marx, let alone devised ways in which to bring his teachings to fruition in the United States.

This brief overview suggests that the classical Marxist organizations, particularly including the tiny sects, may have come to the point where they are at best non-Marxian, and perhaps even anti-Marxian, in character. By acting as if capitalist-liberal society were a permanent phenomenon, by making continuity of their organizations their first priority, and by adapting to the existing consciousness, they have departed significantly from their mentor's principles. Most destructive of all, however, they continue to employ revolutionary rhetorical appeals without the slightest capability of delivering on them. Those few who actively seek revolutionary change within a Marxist perspective and who turn to such organizations, may only be effectively withdrawn from any such struggle. Instead, they will be absorbed into a self-preservational activity of the supposedly revolutionary organizations, and never enter whatever real revolutionary process may exist or develop.

Nevertheless, these organizations continue to play a part in the process of change in the United States, if only a potential one. They are the leading carriers of the Marxist tradition and, if or when numbers of Americans turn in that direction for help in achieving fundamental change, they may be reinvigorated in numbers if not in capabilities. The Communist Party, with all its rigidities and other limitations, is still the largest entity in the United States that is apparently committed to the principle of fundamental change by revolutionary action if necessary. As such, it cannot help but remain a factor-though hardly one that has anything positive to teach us about the theory of change in the United States.

Post-New Left Marxist Formations and Applications

The amorphous, atheoretical movement of the 1960s known as the New Left has, for the most part, evaporated into liberal politics and lifestyles or withdrawn into a variety of individualist "solutions" to the problems that were felt rather than understood in that period. Its demise stands as an excellent illustration of what happens to people who, for whatever reason, fail to develop a comprehensive theoretical understanding or conceptual framework into which they can fit their experiences and render them personally meaningful. But some segments of the New Left *have* sought such deeper understanding, and in turn some of these have turned to Marx as a source. Younger and untied to the past, they have been freer to go directly to Marx rather than Marxists for their guidance. Consistent with the design of our continuum, they vary in the rigidity of both organization form and adherence to Marx's own principles (as opposed to idiosyncratic adaptations or modifications). We shall consider a relatively rigid illustration, the National Caucus of Labor Committees, and a much looser version, the collection of local groups and national celebrities that once went under the name of the New American Movement.

The National Caucus of Labor Committees (NCLC) was formed in 1968, as the New Left was beginning to break up. In contrast to other small socialist groups at that time, it has continued to grow into a centrally-managed organization with many local units across the country. It is more flexible and less centrally dominated than the older Marxist groups, and conceives itself as locked in struggle with them for hegemony among American leftist organizations. It is based on the most serious return to Marx himself, one that sinks Marx appropriately back into the German critical-philosophy tradition in order to understand him on his own terms. It draws heavily on a specialized interpretation of Marx's principles and methods by its founder, L. Marcus, whose writings transcend critical theory and other Marxists completely and amount to a major scholarly and revolutionary reinterpretation. All that is necessary and appropriate to informed action to bring about socialism is available from the proper (i.e., the NCLC's own intensely theoretical) interpretation of Marx himself. Thus the leap is made from Marx to the American present, and the NCLC uses the intervening past only for illustrations of the failures of previous socialist leaderships to follow Marx's real teachings.

The NCLC, comprehensively following Marx, sets the problem of consciousness change at the center of their intricate theory of political change. For the few intellectuals and potential mass leaders who make up the organization, the problem is dealt with by making the organization into an intensive self- and mutual-education effort. Extensive regular communication and repeated conferences of the entire membership serve the twin purposes of spurring the consciousness-change process and providing at least some opportunity for participation in governing the organization.

The problem of mass consciousness change is solved by a version of the mass strike route discussed earlier. The NCLC is of course committed to the traditional working class as the vehicle of change. But it conceptualizes this class in class-for-itself terms, i.e., as a class conscious of what is shared among its components and determined to seize power and reconstruct the society. The "class" has not yet reached this stage, to be sure, but that is exactly the task of the knowledgeable vanguard— to provide the guidance necessary to unite the unemployed, workers, minorities, etc., into one coherent fighting force conscious of its own strength.

Beyond the early stages of propagandizing and creating some illustrative organizational forms, however, there is little that even the best socialists can do. What dramatically escalates their opportunities is the breakdown of the economic system, which the NCLC (not surprisingly) sees as imminent. Inflation, fiscal crises, and a massive depression are anticipated in the immediate future, and with it the prospect of spontaneous mass strikes and other protest demonstrations. With effective and timely intervention, these mass strikes can be redirected from merely economic issues toward questions about who can and should manage the society, and toward what ends. The crisis will so undermine workers' commitments to the present consciousness that the spontaneous experiences and sudden awakening to a sense of power and purpose that occur during the mass strikes, effectively developed by the NCLC, will result in the beginnings of significant consciousness change. Socialism will then be possible. The state will serve as the vehicle of reconstructing both social institutions and people so as to move decisively toward the only viable future for humanity.

As may be obvious, the NCLC has captured some of the key strengths of Marx. But it also reflects some of his problems, and poses other dilemmas of its own making; as a result, it embodies a vast potential that may or may not be fulfilled. To begin with, it requires great intellect and total devotion to master Marx in his own terms. When a small number of young Americans set off on the road to consciousness change in this organized fashion, they can hardly help but soon feel distant from the great bulk of their fellow countrymen. A sense of achievement, of moral as well as intellectual superiority, can be a natural result. This can articulate with the vanguard-emphasis in Marx himself to cause the group to develop a self-confidence which may appear to be arrogance. It *may* be right on occasion but it *always* has ample intellectual agility to explain events in terms consistent with its theory. In any event, it assumes the right and responsibility to act in the name of the entire working class, or even of humanity itself, and demand that others follow for those reasons.

Convinced by its own analysis the NCLC does not doubt the immediacy or depth of the coming world depression and the prospect of prompt descent into fascism. It turns apocalyptic as well as vanguardist, and may run the risk of either adventurism or self-delusion. All those to the right are either fascists, incipient fascists, or their willing or unwilling collaborators. In either case, the NCLC is justified in taking whatever action appears both necessary within its theory and practically workable, on behalf of the cause of world humanity. This may take the form of destruction of other leftist organizations if they stand in the way or appear to be objectively collaborating with incipient fascists. The principle of left hegemony applies also, creating not only justification for, but the obligation to eliminate such obstacles to NCLC service as the leadership of the working class in the revolutionary movement.

Standing in sharp contrast to the well-organized and highly theoretical NCLC is a' loose collection of local organizations and itinerant celebrities who once used the title of the New American Movement. This association of ex-New Left and newly radicalized middle-class people sought a theoretical basis for understanding the American social order and how change might be accomplished, and found it in a sketchy Marxism linked to their own local organizing efforts. There is at present no real organization to this movement, and only the loosest shared tendencies and beliefs that can be analyzed. They are all, however, committed to some form of Marxist analysis, the goal of socialism, and the recognition that this will probably require revolution. For our purposes of critical evaluation, we may take a recent book by Michael Lerner, one of the prominent figures in the New American Movement, as expressing some of the central tendencies of this collection of groups and individuals. Entitled *The New Socialist Revolution: An Introduction to its Theory and Strategy,*[1] it is at least one of the few works that seek to deal comprehensively with the process of change in the United States from a generally Marxist perspective.

But it also seems clear that the veneer of Marxism is very thin indeed. Lerner's Marxism is neither philosophical nor theoretical. Rather, it is a gloss upon standard New Left rhetoric and existing practice which serves two primary purposes. First, it enables the blame for all that is deplorable about our current conditions to be placed on a single source, capitalism, and then it provides a basis for trying to incorporate the working class in the change-seeking movement. Its essence is a kind of something-for-everybody grab-bag. Not only does it accept as equally valid all the conflicting claims and programs of various change-seekers, but it also endorses a process of change in which all of these groups are invited to "do their own thing." Out of this, Lerner asserts, there will emerge a mass socialist party. Like the movement that inspired it, the book is a kind of case study of how Americans settle for the most superficial version of Marxism—but nevertheless believe themselves to have reached the heights of sophisticated analysis. It picks up key Marxist phrases that are profoundly meaningful in context, for example, drains them of their meaning, and then blithely applies them to the most trivial aspects of American politics, all the while acting as if some momentous insight has just been achieved.

Lerner's work emphasizes the necessity of consciousness change, and notes that the Charles Reich version is improbable and unsatisfactory. But it becomes apparent, when his meaning is explored, that he actually has very little more in mind than achieving understanding of capitalism and its workings as an unsatisfactory system. To begin with, Lerner argues that all necessary insight can be developed through empirical reasearch (p. xii). He stresses that "the claims made in this book are meant to be empirical, not empty and rhetorical"—as if the latter were the only alternative. At no point does he suggest other than empirical-descriptive insights as the content of the "new consciousness."

Lerner also stresses "class-wide solidarity." But he means only a grand coalition of everybody and every group seeking change. Repeatedly, he views each and every group or claim as equally justified and equally a contribution to the process of change. And yet it is this very multiplicity of conflicting claims that has kept the working class divided throughout American history. It has never been more seriously divided against itself than right now, but Lerner's Marxist prescription is for continued emphasis on what divides people rather than what unites them. The "class" that he talks about has no real existence in shared consciousness of its members; it is no more than a sociological abstraction.

In reviewing the contributions to change to be made by the various "constituency groups," Lerner sees the necessity for at least important segments of the working class to be in the lead. But he does not foresee either economic or social crisis, relying instead on less fundamental social forces to prepare workers for "radical consciousness." Nevertheless, a fifteen-year timetable for revolution is contemplated. Perhaps fortunately, however, there are already "millions of people in this country who increasingly realize that their only hope lies in socialist revolution." Where these people are, and how they have concealed their commitment so effectively, is left unexplained. But Lerner is confident that they will soon constitute themselves into a mass socialist party.

It seems clear that, again like the New American Movement from which it emerged, this book reflects a flat, empirical image of the process of change. Accepting every group and tactic just as they are, regardless of the many conflicts between them that promise only mutual cancellation, Lerner proceeds to endorse whatever these groups now happen to be doing, for various reasons, in search of change. He certainly deserves classification among the most flexible applications of Marxism that have ever been made. But the book should be popular on the left—because it is so completely within the existing consciousness, and because it so fully endorses every group and tactic now in vogue, *and* promises socialist revolution in fifteen years. Just as surely, however, it is likely to have little if any constructive impact.

Independent and Scholarly Marxism

Applications of Marx in the United States are, perhaps fortunately, not limited to organized groups. A variety of independents and scholars have employed Marxist frameworks to interpret and prescribe for American society, and thus served to carry this tradition forward into American discourse. To be sure, one of the problems of the New Left in the 1960s was that there was so little in the way of a viable Marxist tradition available as an alternative to atheoretical protest. But probably, given the disillusionments of the 1930s and the waves of red-baiting of the post-World War II years, the wonder is that there were *any* individuals willing to teach and write in a Marxist perspective.

In the United States, the scholarly side of the Marxist tradition has been preserved chiefly in the disciplines of history and economics. Historians such as Eugene Genovese and William A. Williams have interpreted the American past in Marxist terms, offering a view of our development that stands in contrast to the self-congratulatory official versions. Williams in particular has directly challenged American students to come to grips with Marx as analyst and humanist. Consistent with their disciplinary focus, however, none of these important contributions have sought to explore problems of change.

Marxist economists have repeatedly analyzed the workings of the American economic system through use of the technical tools of Marx's economics. Paul Baran and Paul Sweezy argued in their *Monopoly Capital* that the American economy generated too much surplus wealth, and that the country was therefore obliged to continually expand sales efforts, military waste, and imperialist activities.[2] A more current and more comprehensive description of the American system, from the perspective of "nondogmatic Marxism," is that of Howard Sherman in *Radical Political Economy: Socialism and Capitalism from a Marxist-Humanist Perspective.*[3] These and other similar works, however, are exclusively empirical descriptions of how things actually work in the United States economy. They quarrel with each other over technical aspects of the application of Marx's economic concepts (the law of value, for example, or the tendency of the rate of profit to fall), but they do not venture beyond economics. There is no consideration of any of the philosophical basis of Marx's thought, nor do these authors address the problem of change.

What the scholarly disciplines have managed to preserve, therefore, is a series of slices of Marx. Certain concepts with particular application to the specific field or subject area under analysis are revived and employed, but the totality and dynamic process of Marx are not carried forward. A somewhat more comprehensive job has been done by those who at some stage sought to employ Marx for purposes of political action. They were, of course, obliged to try to take Marx whole, in order to use him effectively. Foremost among such independent users of Marx (if not Marxists) are those who today are known collectively as the Old Left. Many were leftist activists in the 1930s, either members of or sympathizers with the Communist Party as a promising vehicle of fundamental change at the time. Despite their bitter disillusionment with the failures of the Soviet Union and its self-serving manipulation of the American branch of the Party, they have retained respect for the power of Marx's analytical framework. But, also because of their often disastrous experiences, they have cast their Marx into a firmly democratic mold, insisting on observance of the traditional civil liberties and incremental processes of change to socialism.

Michael Harrington may serve as a good illustration of the Old Left in modern form. He is the most comprehensive, modern, and salient American now writing within this general framework, though his personal experience does not reach as far back as most of the Old Left. In a series of books, culminating with his recent *Socialism,*[4] Harrington has sought to show the necessity of socialism and how it can be attained in the United States in the foreseeable future. *Socialism* undertakes a historical-analytical review of the substance of Marxism and its evolution in Europe and the United States. Not surprisingly, Marx emerges as first and foremost a democrat, willing to wait until the masses come to their senses and vote socialism into power. Nevertheless, the general historical effort is well done and useful to American readers.

When Harrington comes to the application of Marx to the United States and the problem of political change, however, the argument collapses. Totally ignoring the issue of consciousness change, Harrington operates entirely within the context of a linear process of incremental change from capitalism to socialism. No revolution is possible, he premises, and thus the question is entirely one of bringing workers and others to the realization that socialism is their only hope. How this is to be done is unspecified, but one gets a sense of the realism that animates Harrington from his repeated declaration that there has been and still is an "invisible mass movement" committed to socialism in the United States. Unfortunately, it has been obscured by its continued involvement and support for the Democratic Party. But, once awakened, it will move to convert capitalism into socialism by a gradual process of compensated acquisition of great wealth.

Harrington's prescriptions could as easily have been written by any liberal politician; it does not seem harsh to call him an establishment socialist. Indeed, this appears to be a role that Harrington has charted for himself. Reviewing Lerner's book in *The New York Times,* for example, he declared:[5]

> ... a basic lesson that every American radical has to learn is that the masses of any future socialist movement will come from the ranks of those who now consider themselves to be liberal, i.e., advocates of incremental reform but not of systemic change. Socialists are not liberals, but in America they must be loyal members of the liberal community.

In another telling passage, Harrington takes Lerner to task for parochialism. His allegations are that Lerner's evidential case does not accept enough of the empirical data produced by defenders of the status quo, and that Lerner insufficiently appreciates the winds of change that will flow through the universities "in about ten years, when the ex-New Left instructors of today are the department heads in the social sciences. . . . " This is surely the most modest and optimistic

incrementalism, if not outright liberalism: and incrementalism in
theory, of course, means perpetuity in practice. In any case, Karl Marx
might have difficulty in recognizing his teachings in this form.

Some Final Reflections

Marx has had a very hard time reaching the United States. Resistance,
intellectual and social and ideological, has been determined. Many have
seen only parts of his comprehensive theory, and others have fought
hard against seeing any. His followers have often been as effectively his
enemies as those who sought to discredit his work. Seen whole,
Marxism could have great value as a source of questions and insights
and comprehensive theory. But it must be updated, adapted, supplemented, and even corrected, something that few Americans appear
desirous or capable of doing.

In particular, we may ask why Marxists offer as their alternative only
statist socialism. At no point have any Marxists questioned the viability
or current applicability of the vast state apparatus necessarily involved
in modern socialism. Granted, it might not be greatly different from the
bureaucracies that have been proliferated in the last decades in order to
patch up the effects of capitalism. But that is just the point: another
intricate system of top-down management of a subordinate population
may not be much of an improvement over what we now have. At the
very least, we should seek assurance that a new consciousness is at
work, and that its use of the state will be significantly different. What
made sense to Marx when he wrote a century ago may no longer be
capable of serving the same purposes.

The problem of vanguardism is also unsatisfactorily dealt with by
Marxists—and by Marx himself. It is not enough to say that somebody
must be first to experience consciousness change, and that the same
somebodies must then educate the others. They must educate them to
be themselves, *what they can be,* and not necessarily what the educators want them to be. But there is an enduring temptation on the part
of vanguards to shortcut the delays and uncertainties and force the
process of change to its desirable end—with all the inevitable corruptions that then follow.

These are not the only problems in the path of applying Marx in the
United States today. There are more, some inherent in Marx himself

and some in the task of updating and adapting. But they should serve to establish the fact that the development of a critical theory appropriate to the American scene is one which involves selection and extraction from Marx and other sources, as well as the generation of new and specially designed criteria. Let us now see what may be contributed to this task from non-Marxist sources.

NOTES

1. Michael Lerner, *The New Socialist Revolution: An Introduction to Its Theory and Strategy* (New York: Delta Books, 1973).
2. Paul Baran and Paul Sweezy, *Monopoly Capital* (New York: Monthly Review Press, 1966).
3. Howard Sherman, *Radical Political Economy: Socialism and Capitalism from a Marxist-Humanist Perspective* (New York: Basic Books, Inc., 1972).
4. Michael Harrington, *Socialism* (New York: Saturday Review Press, 1972).
5. Michael Harrington, Book Review Section, *The New York Times*, April 22, 1973.

CHAPTER NINE

Contemporary Prescriptions:
A Search for Viable Alternatives

We have seen that Marx at least, if not Marxists, offers certain components of a method that might be adapted for use in building a comprehensive theory of change in the United States. Both as a way of thinking and as a strategy of action, Marxism has real strengths. But it also has significant limitations. The door is open, and the need is acute, for other sources to contribute to our developing theory. In particular, we need to incorporate creative ways of understanding, and of coping with problems, that are specific to the current American context.

This chapter, therefore, will critically examine several non-Marxist potential agencies of, or tendencies toward, fundamental change that are now active in the United States. Our purpose is again dual: to draw insights that may aid in refining our developing theory of change, and to evaluate the prospects and potential represented by these various movements and prescriptions. They are disparate, unconnected, and in their present form represent only slices of a total process of change. We shall not treat them only in their own terms, however, for that would be to repeat Lerner's mistake. Instead, we shall view them as potential parts of a larger whole, as the nuclei that might become absorbed and transformed into a larger way of understanding and acting that would be appropriate to fundamental change.

Some of these are relatively concrete and practical social movements, while others are more abstract or theoretical efforts at formulating prescriptions for change. We shall begin with the most familiar and visible agencies: minorities, women, and youth. Then we shall take up the closely related countercultural and anarchist movements or processes that are more or less broadly affecting so many Americans. Finally, we shall explore two major efforts at synthesis and prescription: Barrington Moore's humane application of every scrap of potential utility in the empirical tradition, and Herbert Marcuse's pathbreaking effort to bring an updated version of neo-Marxist critical theory to fruitful application in the United States. In each case, we shall seek to identify both strengths and weaknesses for thinking and acting in regard to fundamental change.

THE ACTIVE AGENCIES: MINORITIES, WOMEN, AND YOUTH

A cursory survey of active change-seeking forces in the United States would immediately identify these three categories of the American population as the prime movers. Most of the dynamics of American politics in the last decade are attributable to one or a combination of these movements. But to talk to fundamental change is to go beyond identifying or counting the dissatisfied, and to ask what it is that they may contribute to a process of change that would be capable of reconstructing the system and not just extracting more from it for a particular sector of the population. We need to know both what theory of change is present in each group (how consciousness change is viewed, what process of change is envisioned, what the new society looks like, etc.) and what social action potential for fundamental change they represent within the present social order. These kinds of questions must be addressed to each in turn.

Minorities

Each minority—blacks, Chicanos, Indians, Asians, and others—has its own history of exploitation by the dominant society. Their different experiences at the hands of that society and their own indigenous cultural distinctiveness lead them toward quite different types of claims against that society and equally different strategies for achieving their goals. Indeed, they often end up in conflict with each other over those tangible opportunities that the larger society does make available. But there are certain things which, as a category of change-seekers, they do appear to offer to the theory and practice of change.

Perhaps the most significant contribution that minorities make is in the area of demonstration of the meaning and importance of a different consciousness. The culturally distinctive values and world views of Indians and Chicanos particularly, and blacks to a lesser extent, provide an important object lesson for other Americans. Empathetic recognition of what it means to have such a different way of looking at and understanding the world can be the first step to a wholly new appreciation of the limitations of our present capitalist-liberal consciousness. None of these distinctive world views, to the extent that they exist as such at all, is competent to serve as a model for a currently applicable new consciousness. But they can and should serve as a route towards understanding of what is implied in consciousness, what is self-limiting about our present consciousness, and how deeply change would have to go to result in a different consciousness.

The status of minorities also carries some important empirical implications. Their situation, understood in all its depths of material deprivation and subjective despair, serves as a profoundly revealing demonstration of the extent and effects of the exploitation they have suffered. But it also strongly suggests that it is not only capitalism, but a culturally transmitted racism, that lies at the root of their problem. A fundamental-change movement, therefore, cannot merely assume that eradication of capitalism will automatically cure problems of race relations. Any new consciousness will have to take special care to solve the problem of transcending racism, not just for whites but for all races.

As they stand, of course, minority movements do not contain much else in the way of strengths. They are isolated and small in numbers, and the larger society is readily united by its antipathies toward them. There is very little prospect of success for minorities through direct social action, for achievement of their goals in this fashion depends first on the presence of legal rights, and then on the willingness of the larger society to allow courts or laws to overrule their commitment to the status quo and the protection of their own hard-won material rewards. There is very little real prospect for minorities to serve as the point of the lance in a fundamental-change process in this country. Not only are they parochial and divided among themselves, but their claims are highly divisive—rather than integrative—among change-seekers generally. So effective are race tensions in dividing the working class, and splitting off potential white allies, that the ruling class often finds it functional to endorse minority claims. Special programs requiring hiring of quotas of minorities, for example, effectively exacerbate tensions between whites and minorities. Where the issue can be converted from why there are so few jobs to whether blacks or whites should have such jobs, the minority movement has been used to defeat the larger purposes of uniting all change-seekers under one umbrella. Just to the extent that minorities succeed in uniting themselves around the fact of their distinctiveness, so do they cut themselves off from allies among other deprived peoples in the United States. And so the prospect of their serving as a major agent of fundamental change seems slight.

Women

In one sense, the women's movement has appeared to offer special prospects of spurring fundamental change. After all, women constitute more than a majority of the population, as contrasted with the tiny proportions represented by other change-seeking groups. But, of course, only a fraction of all women have identified with any part of the women's movement, and only a fraction of these seek reconstruction of the social and economic systems as part of the means to liberation of women. For most women, it is merely a matter of achieving parity with men in the supposed enjoyment of the rewards of the American system—jobs, legal rights, salaries, etc. These are not insignificant goals, and they will not be easily won, but they are certainly not goals that imply fundamental change. To the extent that these are the basic animating motives behind the women's movement (an issue not yet resolved, to be sure), that movement will barely reach the level of liberal reform.

But there are certain important insights to be derived from some segments of the women's movement. Once again, we find indications that it is not just capitalism that lies behind deprivation and exploitation, but a more complex set of culturally generated biases and assumptions. And it becomes clear that a new consciousness will have to find ways of surmounting this set of limitations also.

Even more crucial, however, is the insight beginning to emerge from some parts of the women's movement to the effect that consciousness change involves both personal identity change and the continued involvement of other people. For some time, women acted as if all that was necessary was to physically or psychically separate themselves from men and come to understand themselves as women. This meant some wrenching personal difficulties, as the ties of dependency were broken, and it often meant some very isolated political activities as well. The traditions and practices of male dominance clearly suffused supposedly fundamental change-seeking movements as well as the larger society from which they came.

But recently, some women have come to realize that liberation in the sense they seek it can only be achieved jointly with men, that freedom is indivisible. This is a late and far more promising stage, for it picks up our earlier insight, that consciousness change would be dependent on the provision by others of social surroundings that would confirm and support the growing new identity and consciousness. Neither men nor women can achieve such significant change by themselves, and each must depend on the other. And change in this kind of interpersonal relationships is vital to the development of that new consciousness; *no* patterns of dominance can survive into the future, if people are to be free and equal in fact and not merely in fiction.

The women's movement thus appears to be generating some valuable insights for the purposes of a theory of change. But it can hardly serve as a major agency of change: it is neither organized as such, or are its goals capable of sustaining such a movement. There is little or no theory present, and too great a potential for stopping short at the point of attaining parity with men in the present system. And there is little sign of coherent social action for the larger goals of fundamental change.

Youth

In the late 1960s, many thought that the American student movement had real purpose and staying power, and even that youth could be seen as the equivalent of a change-seeking social class capable of serving as the key to change in the society as a whole. Subsequent years have demonstrated that these hopes were far too optimistic. Significant underlying value change is certainly underway, but it has many possible directions to it, as will be examined in more detail in the next section. What the youth movement *had* going for it was the lack of attachment to existing institutions and practices. Historically, young people have maintained the lowest levels of respect and legitimacy for their elders and the hallowed traditions and procedures of their society. But this is a situation that, again, leads in many directions—by no means only towards constructive fundamental change.

It seems clear now that the protest movements of the late 1960s were specific to limited sectors of college-age youth, that they were motivated primarily by innocence and antiwar sentiment, and that they were sadly lacking in theoretical understanding or even intellectual receptivity. The rapid evaporation of the New Left testifies to the transitory nature of much of this protest activity. The sentiments and values that led to this wave of action may still remain amongst aging 30-year-olds, but they can be awakened again (if at all) only by a much more powerful and deep-running explanation-prescription. Moreover, youth are by their very situation a temporary force: not only are they isolated and inexperienced, but there are great gaps between them and the possibility of effective communication with needed allies in any process of change. The problem, if there is one here, does not really lie with the ineffectiveness of youth as an agent of change, but with the uncritical expectations or utopian hopes of those who thought they could serve as such.

Thus it appears that none of these three highly visible "agencies" of change can really serve effectively as such. Their theories of change are either nonexistent or intensely parochial. Their numbers and resources are limited, and their consciousness is more often that of the existing society than anything else. Their needs and demands, as they understand them, are conflicting, and potentially and mutually paralyzing. Only if they reach some shared version of a distinctive (non-parochial) consciousness can they merge themselves into an effective vehicle of change. And that consciousness is not yet visible in any of their present thought or action.

COUNTERCULTURAL AND ANARCHIST TENDENCIES

Something potentially promising *is* happening below the surface of politics, particularly to young people. It has been greatly exaggerated, celebrated, and contemplated—but nevertheless there is a core of reality to it, and in time there may be profound political implications. The term *counterculture* has been widely applied to describe the rise of new values, aesthetics, and lifestyles that has marked the last decade. No coherent social movement is involved, but rather a chiefly subjective process in which many people are affected, often in quite different ways. If there is a central political tendency at the moment, it is probably best understood as anarchism—and we shall analyze it as such. But there are other elements involved that also require comment.

To begin with, there are many things happening at the same time, and a large proportion of them are far from constructive. The malaise that grips the whole society focuses with particular intensity on young people, for they have no past to draw upon for perspective or purpose. For the most part, they see and experience a certain material abundance, but both jobs and fulfillment in jobs are hard to come by. Work is tedious, unchallenging, bureaucratized, and purposeless—and life in general is much the same. The scale of organization in the society, and the hypocrisy and corruption manifest throughout it, stand in sharp contrast to the ideals and mythology so mindlessly set out in schools and mass media. Nothing seems to work as it is supposed to, and nothing seems to have any meaning. This intensified malaise manifests itself in a wide variety of ways, from street and motorcycle gangs to drug usage to wild fads such as rock music festivals and fundamentalist religious revivals.

What may eventually prove constructive within this multi-effect package is—for at least some people—the reexamination of first principles about one's own life and purposes. In effect, liberalism is on trial in a way it has never been before. Materialism is being significantly reduced in importance as a dominating value. Young people seek only *enough*, rather than maximization of income or other tangible possessions. In many cases, they are quite ready to limit their consumption and work correspondingly less hard or only on a part-time basis. Increasingly, they see no point in formal political participation, and politics recedes further and further from the reality of their lives. Individualism itself, that core value of the American system, is being threatened. As yet, this has not gone further than reducing the emphasis on competitiveness and self-servingness, and a search for meaning and satisfaction through intense interpersonal relationships. The examination is underway, however, and if it reaches the point where people consciously recognize that they can be themselves only with and through others, the whole basis of the social order could be undermined.

But there are serious dangers inherent in the countercultural trend as well. The same forces that impel some to unconscious reexamination of materialism and individualism press others toward various types of fundamentalism, including both reemphasis on these same values (sometimes in new forms) and essentially counterrevolutionary reaction. Disdain for civil liberties and serious intellectual effort accompanies felt needs for order, regularity, and simple solutions. A kind of superindividualism emerges in some people, leading to withdrawal from social life or to exaggerated hedonism and self-gratification. Fads sweep other millions into repeated mass conformity, steadily rubbing out self-directed capabilities. Movements that promise to provide meaning and purpose—and that require complete dedication to and acting out of a set of "truths"—are able to draw many such people. The Jesus People's movement and other forms of religious revivalism have developed out of this deeply felt need for something to believe in and act for.

What all these trends reveal is a lively protofascist potential. Refusal to take complexity or established procedures seriously, the search for self-gratifying certainty, and the urge to find simple, action-oriented solutions, all add up to a readiness to support authoritarian rule. Millions of anomic individuals desperately seeking some sort of connection with meaning and purpose may well find it in the words and acts of an apparently benevolent leader—much as they found solace in the frenzied conformity of rock music festivals. Nothing else works, why not give him a chance? What difference does it make?

The anarchist trend of the consciously political aspects of the counterculture contains some of its most promising features. But it too involves some dangers. Anarchism consists of two strands—one highly individualist, the other communitarian. If sufficiently and properly pursued, they may end up as one and the same, a truly creative reconstruction of individualism. But as understood by most people today, they are opposed. Most Americans, unfortunately, have been attracted to the individualist version. The reason is obvious: it is not much more than capitalist-liberal ideology in a pure or exaggerated form. Thus, the danger in anarchism is that the average American may simply be re-emphasizing naked individualism—and effectively be held within the present consciousness despite the conviction that something very new has been found. This version of anarchism, clearly, offers little hope for constructive fundamental change. It is little more than very early liberalism, with an escapist, back-to-the-woods gloss.

The communitarian strand within anarchism, however, is a quite different tradition with a long and potentially rewarding history. It has important points of contact with the Marxist contribution to critical theory, and (most important) it gladly confronts the question of consciousness change. In essence, it is a call for a process of self- and mutual discovery and reeducation in what people could be, and then reconstruction of the society into the social institutions and practices that would make such lives possible. Of course this will require a different way of knowing, for the present one is obviously consistent only with dominance by certain key elements of capitalist-liberal society. Moreover, the very essence of that society has been encapsulated in its organizations—the state and its bureaucratic practices being the prime example. Such organizational forms thus are what should be most promptly eliminated and most determinedly avoided in the future.

The anarchist emphasis on community among people, newly freed from the hierarchical dominance of organizations, leads to commitment to socialism—but in a very different form from that of the Marxists. Anarchist socialism is libertarian or nonauthoritarian, as opposed to what they see as authoritarian or statist in Marx's version of socialism. It emphasizes workers' councils, self-management, decentralization, and only the most limited kinds of central tasks—which must then be democratically decided upon by the entire population. To the Marxist, of course, this anarchist vision is sheer utopianism: it fails to take into account the need for planned production and distribution to solve the problems of world humanity, and it has no capacity to defend itself against the inevitable reaction from the right that Marxists anticipate. But the two traditions argue about the proper nature of eventual socialism from essentially the same perspective. Both seek the kind of social institutions that would make for remarkably similar versions of the good society and human self-realization. The basic difference is that the anarchists see the necessity for a ground-up process of self- and mutual reconstruction, in which people must do spontaneously for themselves, without being subjected to the ministrations of others, while the Marxists believe that accommodation to reality requires that some lead and make possible the attainments of the many.

Perhaps the most promising aspect of the communitarian anarchist thrust is the renewal or reconstruction of the concept of individualism that seems to be necessarily involved. The individual in this scheme must come to conceive of himself/herself in terms of the community, the self as part of and completed by others. Not only is materialism sliced off, but so is competitiveness and self-seeking as an activity in opposition to others. Freedom is no longer an opportunity to amass material goods or gain other goals in conflict with others, but an opportunity for self-development through assumption of responsibility for oneself and others. Politics, presumably, would then become the mutual effort to contribute to group welfare, a means of meeting and knowing others and fulfilling their mutual needs.

At this point, neither the counterculture process nor the anarchist trend contained within it has developed into a significant political movement. Indeed, one of the major problems of each is that it is quite unconnected in any concrete sense with the problems of structure and process that now trouble the United States. But it may be simply too early for that. The absolutely necessary precondition, as we have argued, is a process of consciousness change. Despite the many dead-ends and dangers involved in the counterculture, the seeds of consciousness change are being sown within it. The anarchist trend is bringing a number of very important issues to the surface, and generating a pressure toward a particular redefinition of individualism that is potentially crucial for the future of fundamental change in the United States. If ways to emphasize these immensely positive contributions can be found, the limitations of the counterculture process may yet be transcended.

SYNTHESIS AND PRESCRIPTION IN THE EMPIRICAL TRADITION

We turn now to the examination of two major individual efforts to bring together analyses of our present circumstances and future prospects and work them into prescriptions for change. These too may have some important contributions to make to the developing theory of change, either through the insights generated or by means of the method employed. The first of these is a distinguished recent work by a major social thinker of the empirical tradition, Barrington Moore, entitled *Reflections on the Causes of Human Misery and upon Certain Proposals to Eliminate Them.*[1]

Moore is surely one of the foremost social analysts of our times. His *Social Origins of Dictatorship and Democracy*[2] is a monumental and largely successful effort to trace the causes of development of different forms of social order through time, a book that was both widely acclaimed and much used in a wide variety of college and university courses. His more recent work draws upon that and other experience and reflection to systematically and carefully examine the causes of present problems and the relative merits of various prescriptions for solving them. Moore is ever precise, methodically sifting evidence to test every step in the logical development of every argument. His value premises are those of the mature liberal intellectual, appalled at what human beings have done to each other over the centuries and soberly concerned for the future of mankind under today's conditions of social and moral crisis. In short, Moore represents all that is best in the Western scholarly tradition.

Reflections begins by noting that human misery has been and remains widespread, and that much of it is socially produced. Man is the cause of most of the misery of man. Moore operates with a kind of rough calculus of human misery, with which he can weigh the extent of deprivation and misery currently being suffered and compare it with what would be brought about by efforts to accomplish change and whatever new social arrangements might then result. Where a net reduction in the level of misery seems reasonably possible, Moore is ready to endorse a process of change—provided only that it continue also to seek minimization of misery.

This calculus and a sophisticated understanding of our current circumstances are then used as a base for critical evaluation of various contemporary proposals for change. Moore thoroughly and systematically exposes the weaknesses and dangers of every such analysis and prescription. Every error, every unsupported assumption, every leap of faith, and every utopian excess is mercilessly revealed. While sympathizing with the goals, Moore subjects each major version of radical change to the hard test of facts and logic—and finds that nothing offers much hope of reducing the level of human misery in the world. The tone and character of his measured assessment is well captured by this passage about socialism:[3]

> Marxism or centralized socialism has no answer to the question *quis custodiet.* The notion of transferring control over the means of production to the people or to society as a whole is an empty slogan. It says nothing about what people are to take charge of production. It gives no more than the faintest guidance about what policies they should follow. And it tells us nothing about how the leaders and policies can be changed by those human beings who are their victims. This failure to answer the query *quis custodiet,* I think is the fatal flaw at the heart of the whole socialist remedy for human ills.

Moore's own analysis is that most Americans simply do not want change, and are instead prepared to resist such efforts. He refers to the United States as "predatory democracy," where most people have enough to cause them to prefer the status quo to any risks of losing what they have. He foresees no economic problems of any magnitude, and no social crisis sufficient to cause real social breakdown. He acknowledges the possibility of fascism, both through abrupt change and by gradual development, but does not see it as imminent. Revolution too is possible but not likely under present conditions. Legitimacy is decaying, but there are still too many forces preventing change to expect any fundamental change to ensue.

Out of this analysis, Moore sees continued liberal reform as the only viable alternative. By steadily presenting rational analyses of problems and carefully worked-out proposals for their solution, people can be brought to see both the need and the means of coping with them. In this process, aid will be secured from the fact that recognition of abundance will cause change in some people's values—away from getting and spending to more humane concerns for others. All of this Moore sums up in the label "liberalism with a difference," which he puts forward as our best hope under all the circumstances.

Moore's case is flawlessly argued and totally convincing. The reader is captured by his urbane, humane, liberal, rational, empirical approach, and can hardly help but accept his conclusions. And yet, on another level, and just because the book is so vastly successful in its own terms, Moore's work demonstrates the complete failure of empiricism as a way of thinking about change. *Reflections* is at once the fulfillment and exhaustion of the empirical tradition. It reveals, as few other works could, how limited empirical thinking is, how it is unable to encompass the possible or potential within its world of "facts"—and how desperately necessary is a new way of thinking.

Given his way of knowing, Moore is restricted to calculations from objective facts only. He can only point out dangers in this or that situation or proposal. Based on analysis of the past, he must conclude that man is by nature aggressive and self-aggrandizing and that there can never be change in this basic fact; accordingly, all institutions and processes (and critical evaluations) must take this into account. All his analyses are cast in abstract societal-level terms, and in terms of material conditions of existence. At no point do changing meanings for individuals enter his calculations; they cannot, of course, for they are not objective "facts" that can be measured.

Reflections is an excellent book, perhaps the best of its kind now available, and one from which we can all learn. But what we learn most of all is that the empirical mode of thinking cannot provide us with the key to understanding change. It can help us to avoid many mistakes, and to find our way through many short-term problems. But it simply has no capacity to enable us to transcend our present social circumstances. To get out of our social crisis, we must first and foremost develop a way of thinking that has that capacity, and then see if it can lead us to the appropriate social action. This is, in part, what Herbert Marcuse has sought to do.

SYNTHESIS AND PRESCRIPTION IN THE CRITICAL THEORY TRADITION

Marcuse was educated and politically developed within the evolving tradition of German critical theory. Steeped in Hegel and Marx, he emigrated to the United States only in the late 1930s. From that time, he has waged a long struggle to bring aspects of critical theory into American intellectual discourse. Against towering odds established by the firm grip of empirical positivism, he has made significant headway. No other contemporary thinker has so profoundly affected the conceptual frameworks and basic substance of informed political dialogue in the United States in the last two decades.

In a series of books, Marcuse has expounded the nature of critical theory (*Reason and Revolution: Hegel and the Rise of Social Theory*[4]), employed it as a basis for a powerful critique of American society (*One-Dimensional Man*[5]), and then sought to develop from it an analysis and prescription for fundamental change in the United States (*Essay on Liberation*[6] and *Counterrevolution and Revolt*[7]). The latter two, published in 1969 and 1972 respectively, form the primary basis for this interpretation, but they can be understood fully only in the context of the others.

Marcuse is a true Marxist, or what today might better be called a neo-Marxist. That is, he employs Marx's concepts and method in a self-consciously adaptive manner, seeking a general critical theory that will facilitate understanding of the conditions, contradictions, and potential of the United States today. He regularly and specifically differentiates himself from rote or mechanical Marxists who merely apply the ritualistic slogans. The revolution that he looks for is totally different from that of orthodox Marxists:[8]

> It is precisely the unprecedented capacity of 20th century capitalism which will generate the revolution of the 20th century—a revolution, however, which will have a base, strategy, and direction quite different from its predecessors, especially the Russian Revolution.

Marcuse's method is that of the negation, of looking behind the reality to understand potentiality. It is in the combination of empiricism with the negative, with what it is not, that yields the necessary insight:[9]

> Negative thinking draws whatever force it may have from its empirical basis: the actual human condition in the given society, and the "given" possibilities to transcend this condition, to enlarge the realm of freedom. In this sense, negative thinking is by virtue of its own internal concepts "positive": oriented toward, and comprehending a future which is "contained" in the present.

The accomplishments to Marcuse's credit are many. His indictment of American society is cast at such a depth that it encompasses not just specific policies or problems, but the basic organization of the society and the false consciousness that supports it. This means, of course, that the rules with which it operates are promptly exposed as class-biased, non-neutral instruments of exploitation. Marcuse was one of the first to challenge the dominant orthodoxy's bland insistence upon following its prescribed procedures, and to show that nonofficial violence could be construed as counterviolence and readily justified thereby (if not by the prospective reduction in suffering after a period of change).

For such positions, he was severely criticized, both by sanctimonious defenders of the status quo and by some co-thinkers on the left. But Marcuse's point never was that civil liberties could or should be ignored. To the contrary, he regularly points out that the United States still enjoys certain indispensable conditions of minimal freedoms and for that very reason retains certain possibilities of fundamental change. His argument was to the effect that means are related to ends, and cannot be justified or condemned in isolation; certain values and premises lay embedded in the substance of existing procedures, and should be recognized as such.

The key to the start of a revolutionary process, in Marcuse's eyes, lies in the problem of consciousness change. Until the grip of today's powerful false consciousness is broken, the situation must remain prerevolutionary. Marcuse has devoted a large share of his recent work to the exploration of how new needs may be developed, the ways in which art and culture can promote perception of such new needs, and the importance of self-generated new language forms as means of expressing a new consciousness that cannot be coopted by establishment absorption. He is quite clear on the point that the kinds of new needs that must be experienced must be at a deep and profound level ("biological" is his term) in order to pose a sufficiently fundamental opposition to the existing society. Developments within capitalist society itself are to be the source of such needs. His insights into the role of cultural change as a precursor of consciousness change are probably the most sustained high-level analysis anywhere in political literature today.

As part of his application of Marx's method, Marcuse is an inveterate questioner of every Marxian principle. At several points, this causes him to depart from traditional positions. He does not foresee the traditional working class as an agency of change, for example, on the grounds that they have been too fully incorporated into the dominant system, both materially and through their false consciousness. In fact, part of the disti tiveness of the next revolution will be found in the mixed character of its major agency of change:[10]

> The search for specific historical agents of revolutionary change in the advanced capitalist countries is indeed meaningless. Revolutionary forces emerge in the process of change itself; the translation of the potential into the actual is the work of political practice. And just as little as critical theory can political practice orient itself on a concept of revolution which belongs to the nineteenth and early twentieth century . . . the concept is altogether inapplicable to those countries in which the integration of the working class is the result of structural economic-political processes . . . and where the masses themselves are forces of conservatism and stabilization. It is the very power of this society which contains new modes and dimensions of radical change.

He sees the initial stages of consciousness change as occurring principally among young people and ghetto populations. This does not mean that such groups will expand into a full-fledged agency of change, but that they *can* serve as catalysts for spreading consciousness change.

Marcuse's is a holistic concept of a total process of change, with a long timetable. As cultural and consciousness change percolate through the society, events will add momentum and continue the process of social disintegration. Economic crisis, perhaps a depression, will at some unspecified time add fuel to the fire. Parts may be played also by Third World independence movements which can deny the United States access to needed markets and resources and profits. Fascism is a real possibility, but Marcuse sees only a preventive counterrevolution underway at the present time. Nevertheless, the very social base that could make for constructive fundamental change could also yield fascism, and Marcuse clearly sees much the same proto-fascist syndrome that we have earlier identified.

With all these accomplishments, it may seem ungracious to note some difficulties with Marcuse's current theory of and prescription for change. I should acknowledge immediately that such defects as appear are visible only because of the Marcusian achievement in bringing critical theory to the point where it can be of aid to Americans. The task has clearly not been completed, however, as Marcuse himself would no doubt admit. It yet remains to develop a critical theory fully applicable to the American future and capable of opening that future to men and women able to see it and create it. The points at which the pathbreaking achievements of Herbert Marcuse fall short may serve as appropriate challenges.

To begin with, Marcuse merely assumes socialism as the alternative. Despite reexamining almost every other aspect of Marx's approach, Marcuse invests no effort in asking anew whether Marx's goals might not be better served in this world through other than centralized forms of socialism. Perhaps some modification of this prospective society, or at least more precise definition of its characteristics, would have led to a search for different potential forms and processes in the present society. In other words, we gain our criteria for what to look for growing in today's society in important ways from what we anticipate as the future society. If we are anticipating the wrong things, we cannot find the right things growing nor know how to aid them in becoming the future.

Next, Marcuse seems to be hunting for his new theory in a somewhat ad hoc manner, with some damaging effects. Perhaps this is inevitable in one so much a pioneer, but it leads to an ambivalence and a tendency to opt for whatever is currently topical in an experimentalist manner. Marcuse ends up going several directions at once. For example, he alternately despairs of the traditional working class and terms it indispensable to the revolution. He first sets out the most sophisticated analysis of what is required for consciousness change to occur, and then totally omits the role of social formations in the process, even presenting remarkably Charles Reich-like images of an automatic and all-inclusive process. He takes seriously the most disparate types of change-seeking activity, sometimes whatever happens to be in the headlines, and tries to build upon all equally, much in the image of a "do your own thing" process of change. In part, this may be due to his feeling that conditions now are at so early a stage that everything that makes for chaos is equally constructive. But it does not square with his repeated exhortations to the young to be more self-consciously intellectual and theoretical, or with his concern for the possibility of fascism.

Finally, Marcuse does not appear to have made up his mind about the basic nature of the process that will eventuate in fundamental change. At some points, it appears to be a linear, step-by-step process of pushing through demands within the capitalist framework to a consciousness that cracks the framework itself:[11]

> The radical social content of the aesthetic needs becomes evident as the demand for their most elementary satisfaction is translated into group action on an enlarged scale. From the harmless drive for better zoning regulations and a modicum of protection from noise and dirt to the pressure for closing of whole city areas to automobiles, prohibition of transistor radios in all public places, decommercialization of nature, total urban reconstruction, control of the birth rate—such action would become subversive of the institutions of capitalism and of their morality. The quantity of such reforms would turn into the quality of radical change to the degree to which they would critically weaken the economic, political, and cultural pressure and power groups which have a vested interest in preserving the environment and ecology of profitable merchandising.

And again, in his most recent work:[12]

> To drive ecology to the point where it is no longer containable within the capitalist framework means first expending the drive *within* the capitalist framework.

But at other times, Marcuse seems to recognize that change will take place through a quite different kind of process:[13]

> ... what is at stake in the socialist revolution is not merely the extension of satisfaction within the existing universe of needs, nor the shift of satisfaction from one (lower) level to a higher one, but the rupture with this universe, the *qualitative leap*. The revolution involves a radical transformation of the needs and aspirations themselves, cultural as well as material; of consciousness and sensibility. . . .

This is a crucial question, because it goes to the issue of the nature of the new consciousness and how it is to be promoted. If it is truly qualitatively different, how can it be developed through emphasizing goals and forms that are part of this consciousness and eminently containable within it? By acting within the familiar framework, will not people be even more powerfully held within it? Or at least satisfied (and confirmed in it again) by obtaining the first few results from their efforts? As we discussed earlier, only *new* social forms and unrealizable purposes seem likely to develop a new consciousness.

In summary, perhaps it is fair to say that Marcuse has taken us a very long and promising way, but that he has not fully made the transition. He remains half in each world—the world of Marxism and European critical theory per se, and the world of a modernized, American-applicable critical theory. In some ways, he is still too much the Marxist, controlled and constrained by Marx's questions and expectations. In others, he is too ready to seize any available handle in the American context and try to make it serve the cause for which he has worked so hard and long. We have some immensely useful guidance, but not yet a coherent, appropriate critical theory capable of showing the way to fundamental change in the United States. Perhaps it *is* merely a matter of the stage at which we currently find ourselves. First we experience disintegration, then chaos, then the opportunity for organization and action. And the theory that enables us to transcend our present way of thinking and act appropriately to build the future can only emerge from the processes themselves as they move forward. But if so, we should be about the task of reflecting on where we now are in this process, and what sort of new way of thinking is appropriate to the next stage. In this self-educative effort, we again have Marcuse's insight and exhortation behind us. "All authentic education is political . . . ," he tells us, and that may serve as the text for our consideration of how education fits into the process of fundamental change in the next chapter.

NOTES

1. Barrington Moore, *Reflections on the Causes of Human Misery and upon Certain Proposals to Eliminate Them* (Boston: Beacon Press, 1973).
2. Barrington Moore, *Social Origins of Dictatorship and Democracy* (Boston: Beacon Press, 1969).
3. Moore, *Reflections*, p. 71.
4. Herbert Marcuse, *Reason and Revolution: Hegel and the Rise of Social Theory* (Boston: Beacon Press, 1969).
5. Marcuse, *One-Dimensional Man* (Boston: Beacon Press, 1964).
6. Marcuse, *Essay on Liberation* (Boston: Beacon Press, 1969).
7. Marcuse, *Counterrevolution and Revolt* (Boston: Beacon Press, 1972).
8. Ibid., p. 81.
9. Marcuse, *Essay*, op. cit., p. 87.

10. Ibid., p. 79.
11. Ibid., pp. 27-28.
12. Marcuse, *Counterrevolution*, op. cit., p. 61.
13. Ibid., pp. 16-17.

CHAPTER TEN

Political Change:
Preconditions and Prospects

This chapter is not a collection of "solutions" or "answers" to the questions that have been posed. I do not believe it is currently possible to provide such answers. In some respects, this is inevitable, for reasons to be discussed; in others, however, the fault lies in the fact that the right questions have been addressed only rarely and/or superficially. Up to this point, I have concentrated on identifying these crucial questions, and showing why they are so important. Now, I seek only to indicate some of the necessary characteristics of appropriate answers—in effect, to talk about how the tasks prerequisite to fundamental change might be accomplished. I realize that this is a very modest goal, and I defer gladly to those who will carry the theory and practice of political change on its next steps. But I do insist that such theory and practice will be better if it is approached with the premises that follow, and if it embodies the three major components then discussed at greater length.

The Need for Theory

Perhaps the most important point is still the preliminary one regarding the *nature* of the problem of change in the United States. I have argued from the start that the question of fundamental change is first and foremost a conceptual or epistemological one—a problem of *how to think* and *what to think about*—before it is a problem of social action. The proper answer to the insistent American question, "What do I *do*, right now?" is not a list of strategies and tactics for people to undertake. It is that what you *do* first is to understand why most "organizing" and other activity is either irrelevant or self-defeating, and why some image of a total process, starting with consciousness change as the centerpiece and reaching past the transfer of state power to the construction of a wholly new society, is the indispensable prerequisite.

To fully absorb this point *is* action: one has changed oneself profoundly and achieved the potential to similarly change the world. It is far from inconsequential, isolated, or asocial; it is *doing* in a vital sense, for it initiates the essential continuing process of reflection, action, and reflection. . . . Of course social action is necessary for any individual or societal transformation of this kind, but such action must be within this context—a component in a consciousness change process in which we first see and understand differently, and then reshape our world and ourselves accordingly. There has been no lack of mere action in search of change in the United States. But there *has* been a lack of action in the context of a new consciousness and its associated theory of change. And so the opportunities for fundamental change that have presented themselves every two or three generations have been lost. What we experience today may be the *last* such opportunity, and the price of another failure will be very high.

Education, Freedom, and Consciousness

A second early point, that concerning the reader's use of this essay for self-education in the nature of consciousness and conscious-ness change (or conceptual reconstruction, as then described), may also bear re-emphasis now. Recognition of the constraining effects of one's present consciousness may be possible only after it begins to be supplanted by a new one. But the goal of education-as-it-should-be is to enable one to see these constraining effects more and more clearly. Thus, it should be obvious why, as Marcuse says, "all authentic education is political." Education has no necessary connection with schools or colleges, of course, and it can be a solitary or mutual process as well as a formal, teacher-conducted one. But, to be authentic, education must enable individuals to see the nature and sources of their values and way of thinking, and the implications they carry for the development of human potential. To see these clearly is to be free of all mystification—of all the constraining, system-justifying effects of the dominant consciousness. And that freedom, that moment of opportunity for an autonomous choice, is potentially subversive of the established social institutions and practices. Thus it is profoundly political, and every effort is made within a given social order to see that no such "authentic education" occurs.

Nevertheless, this is essentially what we have been attempting in this essay: to use the potentially constraint-cracking opportunity of thinking about political change to see the nature, sources, and implications of our current consciousness. We have also sought to push past those limitations to gain some insight into the ways in which that consciousness and its associated social order might be replaced.

The Process Concept as an Alternative to Detailed Blueprints of the Future

At this point, we have only the beginnings of a new critical theory and a new consciousness with which to see and understand the future. Both can develop only as people change and develop through acting in the context of changing social conditions. The rest of our current concepts and way of thinking are *this*-society, *this*-consciousness tools. For these reasons, we cannot set forth a detailed image of the future, nor specify what particular forms or actions must be adopted at what moments. These can emerge only through the process of developing and employing critical theory and a new consciousness. Indeed, the felt need for specific instructions for each stage of the unfolding future is very much a *this*-consciousness demand. To yield to that demand, in the context of presently available intellectual tools, organizational forms, and personal identities, would be to project the present into the future and further delay or prevent the arrival of new versions of each.

The concept of *process* is crucial to a new way of understanding. It suggests not only the constant movement of multiple-related parts, but also the necessarily never-finished quality of human and social development. Nothing can be understood if it is viewed as stopped in time, for all is motion. It is tempting to *try* to hold things constant, if only to gain some benefit from previous investments in coming to understand them as they were in their earlier form. But this is disastrous to understanding in any specific area, and most damaging of all when applied to the workings of the human mind. The mind must be constantly in motion, always open to new or changing possibilities. It must seek answers to existing questions, simultaneously with seeking the new questions to replace them. In an important sense, to answer a question fully is to stop things in time, to deny process; questions can properly find their true answers only in the form of new questions—in the process of shifting from one set or range of questions to another.

The Vital Need for Openness

If all is process, it follows that an appropriate critical theory and new consciousness must be completely open and receptive to constantly changing relationships among social forces and people. Relationships between economic conditions, social problems, cultural levels, and individual character and aspirations are *historical* (specific to times and places and societal characteristics), not *immutable* (essentially the same in all societies at similar stages of development). To understand what is happening now, and how to act to bring about a better future, we must constantly absorb new facts, envision new possibilities, and seek answers to previously unimagined questions. An appropriate critical theory is a constantly self-critical and self-reconstructing one. It must be able to see the new growing amidst the old, and then to see how the result embodies both in a different and higher form.

Perhaps the greatest obstacle to this essential kind of openness is the human quest for intellectual certainty. The urge to *know,* to be fully convinced so that one can act decisively, is strong in all of us. And it may be a necessary ingredient in the making of revolutionaries, for few people are ready to sacrifice all in a cause whose merits remain in doubt. But when such an urge leads to a theory and practice which is *closed*—a bundle of eternal truths rather than a method of inquiry and action leading to an ultimate goal—the result can only be self-destructive. The atrophied theory/practice becomes further and further detached from the social circumstances it seeks to affect, leading to greater and greater self-delusion. And it generates abstractions and reifications which appear to justify the harshest and most inhuman actions. Finally, it leads to organizational forms and behavior that in time militate against the very goals that gave rise to the organization in the first place.

A viable theory/practice must learn to live with a degree of uncertainty in order to preserve this essential openness. If that means delay in creating organizations, or deliberate destruction of outmoded ones, the price is not too high.

Connections Between the Individual and the Social

The essence of the concept of process and the principle of openness are embodied in the crucial *connection* between individuals and social conditions—between interpersonal relationships and social institutions, forces, and purposes. People are defined by what they *do* in the world; their consciousness is shaped by their practical social activity. But so is their world made real only by their understanding and actions, which in effect constitute that world. The key to change thus lies in this connection—the mediating, reciprocally defining role played by consciousness—and in the means by which people can deliberately impel themselves toward new identities, consciousness, and the social context coherent therewith. The quality and character of interpersonal relationships, in other words, are both affected by, and shape, the social conditions we experience. Thus, things cannot be "good" in one realm and "bad" in the other. Nor can one area be improved while the other remains the same.

Recall the difference between Parts 1 and 2 of this essay. The first was a description, quite familiar at times, of the "objective" social conditions and problems of the United States today. The second was less familiar, an exploration of the subjective processes and consciousness that give "reality" to that image. The two approaches are quite at odds; it may appear that we are faced with a choice of how to understand our world. But if we realize that they are two parts of the same thing, in a process of constant interaction that demands constantly changing and developing ways of understanding and therefore of acting to achieve goals, we begin to appreciate the importance of the connection between the two. In effect, they merge to create higher understanding, and then are in turn confronted by new problems and challenges, which must next be transcended, and so on.

The Tasks Prerequisite to Fundamental Change

This analysis leads to identification of three closely interrelated components of the process of fundamental change. All must occur together, for it is only as an inseparable package that they constitute the process of fundamental change. The first is the development of a version of critical theory appropriate to the current American context. Primarily the task of intellectuals, it can nevertheless be accomplished only through social involvement and a full commitment to understanding the world in terms that imply the most profound (and political) opposition to it.

The second is the development of a new consciousness on a mass basis. Such a new consciousness ultimately must be consistent with the kinds of people and the character of the social order of the future (and, therefore, with the goals of critical theory as well). It cannot arise instantaneously, of course, nor will all be different as it begins to take shape and gain power. A substantial time and extensive social action are involved in the process, which may well contain ups and downs or false directions within it. But it is essential that the new consciousness begin to spread from the few to the many, and that it gain a genuine mass base.

The third component in the larger fundamental change process is the generation or convergence of social conditions such as to (a) provide both the necessity and opportunity of bringing about the mass-based new consciousness, and (b) enable the transfer of state power out of the hands of the present structure of authority into new forms appropriate to the new society. Along with such conditions must come a new, not-exclusively-empirical way of interpreting these events. In other words, the new critical theory must enable us to see what is happening and what the dangers or potentialities are—and how to act in the developing context to bring about the new society. An adequately creative understanding of the potential for drastic social and political change that may be present in existing or future conditions is just as important as the convergence of those events or conditions themselves.

These interconnected prerequisites—critical theory, beginnings of mass consciousness change, and enabling social conditions—each involve large-scale social forces and purposeful human activity, in varying proportions. We shall now examine some of the ways in which people may act constructively to advance the goal of fundamental change in each category.

A NEW CRITICAL THEORY

Very little has yet been accomplished in the way of creating the kind of critical theory that a viable future demands. American intellectuals have, for the most part, made their critiques of social institutions and practices well within the orthodox American empirical-positivist framework. They have not addressed the vital epistemological and value questions that lie at the base of this social order. As a result, we have almost no American critical theory with which to assess conditions or events, to guide action, or to evaluate developments in the way of consciousness change. This lack stands in sharp contrast to the already-underway process of consciousness change and the clear existence of crisis-level social conditions. Perhaps the best we can do at this point is to state some of the characteristics and functions that such a critical theory would have, if only to illustrate the urgency of the intellectual tasks involved.

In stressing the need for critical theory, we are in an important sense acknowledging our great debt to Marx. From no other source can we draw as much guidance. At the same time, we must be clear as to the ways in which Marx and critical theory as it has evolved are adapted to the American context today. Marx's perhaps time-specific commitment to hierarchical socialism and to a vanguardist process of change, and the unique features of the American social order, are among the problems to be encountered. But what we seek is essentially an extension of the critical theory to which Marx gave birth, and is by no means a rejection of his basic insights or goals.

The new critical theory must be a way of understanding social conditions and human relationships that will lead to the release of as yet unrealized capabilities in people, probably through a non-hierarchical version of socialism. But it must also be appropriate to the United States. Too much can certainly be made of the argument that the United States is distinct or unique, but there is a basic validity to the point that certain special features must be taken into account. Any theory of consciousness change, for example, must address itself to individualism, the cornerstone of American political thinking. It must face up to the deep quiescence accomplished by dominant American ideology. And it must adapt to the level of industrialization, material abundance, size, and decentralization of the United States today. In short, whatever transformative capability critical theory and a new consciousness can generate depends not only on its intrinsic qualities, but also on its relevance to the distinctive features of American life. What is required is a *fully* adapted critical theory.

Thus, we need a way of understanding what transcends our current capacities for knowing. It must be a way of understanding coherent with *both* (a) individuals whose character, not yet known, is nevertheless discoverable by reference to the potential inherent in the human essence, *and* (b) the social order which permits and facilitates the development of such potential in people. By "way of understanding," I intend something broader, more integrated, and far more flexible in regard to the varieties of evidence and logic accepted, than what is now meant by the term *social science*. In today's terms, the major contributors would be philosophy (how we know what we know, and how we might know differently), anthropology (worlds as they are understood by, and shape, people in distinctive evolving contexts, and what people might become in other contexts), and political economy (organizing a social system to achieve desired goals amidst evolving conditions, creating liberating social processes and systems to enable man to realize his potential).

Critical theory starts from the premise that any way of understanding must of necessity be coherent with *some* form of social order; it cannot exist in isolation. Moreover, we know that all knowledge is such only in terms of *some* value base, and therefore we must be assured that our knowledge reflects desirable and appropriate values. The latter are found in the nature of human potential, and in the kind of process by which that is realized. If we seek to consciously shape such a way of understanding, it can only be through keeping constantly before us an image of what people might become and of the kind of social order that would make that possible. That kind of person and that sort of social order are for the present only inchoate in the world around us, and so we must do what we can to create the situations and social formations that enable each to become what they can be, to realize their potential. This process must form the context in which the new way of understanding is developed.

It must also be clear by now that a new way of understanding must be holistic and process-sensitive in character. Nothing really exists, or has meaning, in isolation; its reality emerges only from its relationship to other things, and from the part it plays in the evolving web of mutually affecting changes in those relationships through time. We must seek understanding of any part only in terms of its dynamic relationship to the moving totality in which it is embedded. Nor is there a reality "out there" to be understood by a detached observer: another premise is that subjective and objective worlds are inextricably part of each other, and the observer necessarily an active component of the world that is to be interpreted. It is the *connection* between subjective and objective that is central here—how much and in what ways one defines and affects the other, how a change in one works change in the other, and whether some aspects of each remain impervious to change in the other. Reality is in us as much as it is out there, but even more fully it is found in the process by which people act upon the world, thereby changing both the world and themselves. Reality is becoming— the constantly evolving relationship of parts to whole in which what is today is transformed into something both the same and yet different tomorrow.

Thus, an Americanized critical theory or new way of understanding seems potentially recognizable. The task of constructing it is still a staggering one, but certainly not hopeless. The currently dominant versions of social science, of course, will not give way easily. Indeed, they will draw powerful social support from those with long-term investments in the intellectual, social, economic, and political status quo. Enforcement of orthodox standards of "scholarship" and "professionalism" will seek to discredit those who would build anew. The point is, however, to build both from within and from without the existing social science disciplines—and to build with such scope and quality (and such persuasive values and theoretical sweep) that the orthodox disciplines simply cannot sustain themselves either intellectually or by the equivalent of force alone.

Here is a key role for a reconstructed version of education. People must be aided in the recognition of what lies latent in themselves, and encouraged to discover the potential they have to do and be more than they are. In this process, the main thrust must come increasingly from the people themselves, as they awaken to their own capabilities. They cannot be *told* how to see their world, or submerged with facts, figures, and others' interpretations. This would only be to substitute a new set of externally imposed "truths" (and rulers) for the existing ones, leaving people quite unchanged in any meaningful sense. People can only develop themselves by doing for themselves, by finding within themselves the concepts and language to aptly and critically characterize their world—and then act to change it. The role of the educator is thus to help them see more clearly what is already there in their preconceptual and preconscious capabilities. The educator in effect takes people as they are and merely facilitates their efforts to transform themselves and their world, in order that they become truly free and autonomous first and revolutionary activists second.

Once again, we encounter education in its politically subversive form. To help people to the point of recognizing what they might be, and how their social order and consciousness prevents that, is to strike sparks that may lead to conflagration. Education of this kind *is* action. It is anything *but* theory or abstraction, for it requires the deepest mutual engagement of people and reaches through such relationships to connect with the basic characteristics of the society itself. When people are beginning to awaken, moreover, they will need and seek the insights and strategy that can be provided only by the new way of understanding. In this fashion, new way of understanding articulates with new consciousness, and the two grow together.

TOWARD MASS CONSCIOUSNESS CHANGE

The vital issue, of course, is whether the new consciousness can bridge the gap between the few who have begun the process of consciousness change and the many who are at once the key to fundamental change *and* locked tightly into *this* consciousness. Can such transfer be imagined? Which (if any) of our three models of consciousness change process best fits possible American social circumstances? Which (if any) currently active groups or tendencies offer prospects of success?

Viewed contextually, the classic versions of Marxist revolutionary socialism seem basically unadapted to the United States today.

However inspired to new conceptual capacities, the mind simply boggles at the prospect of this kind of revolution in the United States. And if it did occur, through some now-unimaginable combination of circumstances, the result would probably be anything *but* constructive or liberating fundamental change. The problems in the way of success on the part of such groups have already been reviewed, and there is no need to repeat them here. The strength of American ideology and the support provided by our underlying consciousness make it very unlikely that any revolutionary socialist movement could so develop itself and mobilize enough support to seize state power.

More promising prospects lie within particular tendencies within today's cultural change process. We have noted the multiple moods and directions—some promising, others counterproductive, many destructive—that are swirling about in this process. Our problem is to see the constructive and liberating potential within this process, and how it might be nurtured to grow and become the new society, *in the context of today's other social forces and conditions.* We must try to see the process whole, and in dynamic terms, to uncover its capacity to transform itself into a wholly different social order.

At this time, the minority, women's, young people's, and other limited movements discussed earlier are merely *parts* of a larger whole. They are early, separate manifestations (chiefly—and naturally—within the *existing* consciousness) of the effects of the cultural change process, not in themselves potential agencies of change. They are forecasts of something larger and later, into which they will be absorbed and preserved as the ultimate agency takes shape amidst the rise of a coherent new consciousness.

The United States is now in a process of social disintegration and demoralization, with countercultural value change occurring in sometimes highly visible but sometimes unrecognized ways. At this stage, large-scale organization or extensive social action are simply not yet possible or appropriate. No real alternative currently exists on the left. What is possible, and essential, is the construction of a significant infrastructure of multiplying small groups in which new values and new consciousness can be nurtured and spread.

The nature of this small-group process requires some elaboration, for there are many false starts and dead ends in this direction. To begin with, there can be no withdrawal from this society, either physical or psychic. Change-seekers must remain *in* it, though not *of* it in the orthodox sense. They must act upon it, in order to change themselves and by example to increase their numbers. The vital goal is to begin living lives, and thereby developing wholly new personal identities, that "make sense" only in terms of future conditions and qualities of life. Such identities are in part received from the others with whom one is associated, and consciously new interpersonal relationships of dependence and fulfillment are created—replacing individualism with a new universe of needs and aspirations.

Part of the life and purpose of all such nuclei is to develop a sense not only of what can be realized in the way of interpersonal relationships but also of the social institutions and consciousness that are coherent with such potential quality of life. This implies development of a kind of trajectory, a line of movement and process that leads from the present to that increasingly clear potential future. The trajectory emerges more and more clearly as groups act in terms of their growing insight, reflect upon that action and its impact upon themselves, and so forth. Groups should be inclusive, crossing class and occupational lines as much as possible, so that each member grows from contact with the others and the trajectory of development is one which represents the aspirations that are common to *human* rather than particular wants and needs. But groups should form wherever people begin to see consciousness as the problem, transcending specific issues and causes and existing organizations. This spark of personal awareness and mutual recognition is the key to a new, different, and far more promising process of change.

An immediately visible need, of course, is to multiply. The early nuclei must resist all the temptations and pressures to return to or accommodate with the dominant consciousness and society. Instead, by example, action, and explanation—all of which communicate with the inchoate human wants and needs of others—they must add to their numbers as rapidly as possible. This will be very difficult, for a variety of reasons. One is that all of us begin thoroughly inbued with the dominant capitalist-liberal consciousness, which may rise repeatedly within individuals to derail the process of consciousness change or prevent more than the earliest steps toward identity reconstruction. Every small group will have to constantly struggle against fragmentation, individualism, accommodationism, etc. The way will be very hard, and many groups will fail. Another danger lies in the urge to merely increase numbers, without regard to the level of understanding and purposefulness of such new recruits. A too-rapid influx of people with little or no real awareness of the depth or character of the consciousness change task can disrupt or destroy the fragile process underway in most groups.

But such groups *must* multiply, or the process will end without political consequences. And, as they add numbers and become conscious of each other, communication is essential. What lies ahead is a broad base of many such groups, the latent form of a new society with roots in the most intimate contact with the people. Cooperation among such groups is practical and likely, provided only that all basic directions be established from the ground up by fully participatory democratic processes and all specific implementations be accomplished by the people themselves acting through various local social formations.

ENABLING–OR DISABLING–SOCIAL CONDITIONS

The social circumstances that today cause disintegration and demoralization may lead tomorrow to chaos—simultaneously giving rise to great dangers and great opportunities. As conditions worsen, different forms of organization and action become necessary. But again, they must be appropriate to the specifics of the American context. The most likely drift, as argued earlier, is toward an Americanized version of fascism. This kind of change *fits*—it fits our economic situation, social structure, political consciousness, and familiar political dynamics. It may begin without being recognized for what it is, with every separate act seeming justifiable as such—particularly because done through the legitimate political institutions. As Amerifascism consolidates, however, the process speeds up. Scapegoating, terrorism, and totalitarian organization become harsher and harsher. Some people more or less willingly remake themselves into the fascist mold, while others are coercively reconstructed to become fascist man. The most basic kind of change has occurred, but in the name of preserving familiar American ideals and values. Amerifascism is so likely just because it does *not* require consciousness change at any early stage, and because it already has a broad popular base in the legitimacy of institutions and the patriotic and other fundamentalist values of the American people.

One part of the problem presented by the prospect of Amerifascism is that of failure to recognize its early forms and a tolerance which permits consolidation and forecloses *all* alternatives. The danger is grounded in our basic values and ideology, and particularly in the strong sense of legitimacy that still attaches to institutions and practices associated with fundamental "Americanism." The problem is that fascism is at least in its early stages entirely compatible with capitalism. Indeed, it represents the full and final penetration of government by big capital in order to most efficiently organize the use of resources, control the work force, and maximize profits. It becomes a necessity in times of declining profits, popular restlessness, or serious international economic difficulties. Liberal democracy, no matter how it is bent to serve the needs of big capital, is at some point too slow, too uncertain, too procedurally responsive to too many subordinate interests, to function effectively. And so its forms and rhetoric become the mask for more ruthless organization of the society so that the big corporate and financial sectors of the economy can continue profitable operation. In the case of Amerifascism, patriotic appeals, symbolic reassurances, and repeated assertions of compatibility with the most basic American values—rugged individualism, self-sacrifice, and racism-nationalism paramount among them—will no doubt mark the transition. For these reasons some will actively or passively support Amerifascism, while others will continue to deny its existence long after it has effectively consolidated itself.

Two key processes presage the emergence of fascism, one principally economic and the other chiefly political, in our current terms. The first is the increasingly systematic effort to maximize profits through reorganizing and reducing the real standard of living of the working population in the face of a declining economic situation. Real wages are eroded, either through inflation or joblessness or both, while prices rise. Services to the general public, such as education, medical care, or other social or municipal services, are sharply curtailed. A variety of means are employed to coopt, discredit, or destroy existing social organizations among the population, particularly those (such as trade unions) likely to be economic or political opponents. In their place, employer- or government-initiated organizations provide opportunities to manage people from the top down. The need for sacrifices is stressed—for less consumption, for tolerance of joblessness, for greater production to meet foreign challenges, etc. Associations, formal or informal, of major producers, manufacturers, shippers, banks, and other key sectors of the large corporate economy are increasingly encouraged to rationalize their operations with government assistance and through government enforcement. Risk is effectively socialized or eliminated, while profit remains private. All of these processes may begin under the liberal-democratic state, as economic decline begins. As the latter continues, however, continued profitability requires more and more stringent measures—and at some point the liberal state, no matter how willing, becomes an unacceptably slow and clumsy tool.

The second key process occurs as it becomes clear to increasing proportions of ruling elites that the needs of the evolving capitalist system cannot be met by the liberal-democratic state under the worsening economic conditions. More and more, elections and other participatory opportunities become mere rituals, manipulated from above to provide the facade of consent for policies required in the interests of profitability. Procedural regularity becomes a question of convenience and of the probability of publicity; wherever possible, the most efficient method is chosen instead. The management of news is routinely practiced, both at the source and in the media of communication themselves, so that "the public interest" will be served. The erosion of civil liberties proceeds with the cooperation of the courts, to the point where most "principles" are mentioned only at the beginning of an explanation of why they do not apply in the particular case under consideration. In any event, reasons are regularly found why police and other government investigators should not be limited in their efforts to protect the nation against potentially disruptive or dissenting ideas or actions. The concept of "the national interest" broadens in the context of the times to legitimate a wide variety of government actions, and to stigmatize those who oppose them.

These are *early* signs, the mark of an incipient fascism not yet coalesced into a self-conscious movement nor consolidated in power as such. Coalescence and consolidation can occur very rapidly, however, once these processes are underway and established. The economic conditions and measures inevitably stir resentment and protest, and the political process offers no recourse—only repression. Big capital must come to terms, either with incumbent officials or with protest to the necessary actions to maintain profitability and order. Under an umbrella of soothing and predictable rhetoric, the alliance becomes firmer and its practices harsher and harsher. At first, popular support may even increase, as a result of the appeal of decisive action amidst worsening conditions. Only after the fact will most people realize that Amerifascism has become consolidated, and even then many will endorse it as inevitable or necessary.

The other part of the problem of Amerifascism lies in the nature of the process set in motion as the slide quickens. The nascent infrastructure of small groups developing the new consciousness is no match for the power of fascism as it reaches for control of the society. There is a clear risk of a nearly complete power vacuum, in which fascism would face little or no opposition. But this may be exactly the point at which previous analyses have failed, because they have been searching for the wrong social process, or at least the wrong sequence of events within it. The change-seekers we have analyzed, and the process that they (*and* we) have been trying to visualize, all involve a fundamental change movement acquiring power by taking over an atrophying capitalist-liberal state, a process which requires mobilization of numbers of people to transcend a lifetime of ideologization *and* their existing consciousness in order to move against their government. We imagined the need for defense against fascist reaction only after state power was acquired, or only by means of a new organization somehow constructed by the isolated change-seekers themselves.

But suppose we take seriously two basic premises: (1) social conditions are worsening so rapidly that there is no way that Americans can hold on to the life they now know, and—despite determined resistance—they already realize that fact; and (2) Amerifascism is a real, growing, and immediate threat to take over the liberal state. Then the early form of a fundamental change process would not be an *attack* upon the existing liberal state, but the exact opposite: the *defense* of that state and its unfulfilled promise against those who would convert it to something far worse. In this defense, the prospects of mobilization of numbers of people would be far greater than in any revolutionary movement now visible. It would draw upon the deep well of legitimacy and the natural American defensiveness about holding whatever one can, as well as all of the characteristics of our deepening social malaise already touched upon. Enough apparent traditionalism and support of the status quo would be present to justify militant social action in many doubtful minds, surely many more than would have been ready to attack the state.

We must be clear that those who seek fundamental change cannot merely defend the liberal state, and certainly not in its own terms. Such defense cannot be undertaken within that state's frame of reference, nor managed by its politicians. It must be built in part on new organizational forms, built from the ground up on the basis of new goals—i.e., on the kind of small-group infrastructure just discussed. The defense of the liberal state can only be the means of mobilizing the necessary numbers, taking advantage of their new availability and attentiveness, and delaying fascism until the new social order is more fully developed. *The only true defense against fascism is to make a social revolution,* in the image of the new consciousness and new society growing out of the small group infrastructure. The process by which that infrastructure transforms itself into a new social order, however, is the struggle against fascism.

In certain important ways, the Spanish Civil War of 1936 has much to teach us about this potential process. The defense of the liberal state there failed, as did the social revolution. When key choices had to be made, the leaders of the capitalist system and the liberal state had more in common with the prospect of fascism than with that of anarchist revolution; and for reasons of Russian national interest, the Soviet-managed Communist Party allied with them against the revolutionaries. But the latter's leaders thought that the liberal state could be reformed, or that winning the war required cooperation with it, and so they gave it their full support. Thus, when the liberal-Stalinist alliance moved first to crush them and eliminate the prospect of social revolution, neither they nor their followers were aware or prepared for what happened to them. Ironically, of course, the liberal-Stalinist alliance thereby cut itself off from much potential mass support, and soon had to come to terms with the military superiority of fascism. With a clearer sense of the limits and priorities of the capitalist-liberal system and a more comprehensive theory of change, however, the achievements of the anarchist-revolutionary movement might have been far greater. The liberal state *cannot* be defended, after all—either morally or practically—in the context of evolving social conditions. This realization *must* come to people, as the struggle forces them to examine their purposes and goals anew.

Given the existing malaise and ongoing cultural change process, with all the sense of a need for change generated within it, two things are likely to happen if and when people do rise to the defense of the liberal state against fascism. In the process of struggling against fascism, first through peaceful and civil libertarian means and then by whatever means necessary (emphatically including organized violence or counter-violence), there will develop a subjective class-equivalent. An agency of change will be forged, beginning with the essentially subjective convictions that change is needed and the society must be defended against incipient fascism. People from all existing "social classes" who see or sense such imperatives will fuse into one social group, not a class in the earlier sense but an equally viable social form with a distinctive world view, values, and goals.

Second, once the process of struggle really gets underway, the question of the nature of the post-chaos society will be posed with an increasing insistence. People will want to know what it is that they are fighting *for,* and that it is worth the fight. Moreover, it will seem clearer and clearer that, because we can neither return to the past nor hold on to the present, *some* form of new society must emerge. The focal question then becomes *what kind* of new society. At this point, people are opening and searching. They are committed to each other in wholly new ways by virtue of the joint struggle they are waging. The stage could not be better set for the spread of the new consciousness. And, if it is capable of providing meaning and purpose to the struggle, it should bridge the gap between the few and the many with relative ease.

Because the new consciousness will have grown in pockets within the existing society—mostly in small groups—it will be well represented and scattered amongst the large body of people in the new subjective class-equivalent committed to fighting Amerifascism. It will probably spread by radiation from such small groups and through the formation of others. Under no circumstances could it be inculcated from above, for by definition it must be spontaneous and generated through self-developed awareness of the need for different kinds of relationships with others. An effective national organization is still possible, however, as long as it is a loose and voluntary association of such multiplying units. The formation of more and more such units, the development of the new consciousness, and the struggle against Amerifascism are all related parts of the same process by which the social order may be transformed.

Several subsidiary processes may also contribute to the success of this type of new consciousness-new society development. Of course, we must conceptualize *many* conflicting processes underway at the same time as a result of the deepening crisis conditions. There is nothing inevitable about the success of the one just sketched. Indeed, not only fascism but several other results are probably more likely; it will require knowledgeable intervention by numbers of people to enable apparently discouraging near-chaos to be transformed into the desirable new society. Our problem now is merely to see what might happen to enable such potential to be realized. Essentially, we envision multiple roles for different factors and forces, viewed as parts of a larger envolving whole that is capable of the transformation we seek. In other words, we look at subprocesses not in isolation, as things in themselves, but as parts of what we believe can and should occur. And we analyze them not in their own terms, as *they* understand or interpret what they are doing, but in *our* terms, as our new way of understanding enables us to see and create a future.

For example, crisis-level economic pressures—inflation, depression, unemployment, etc.—are likely to create fissures within the ruling class. One segment may be pitted against another in desperate efforts to save as much as possible for itself out of the coming collapse. Similarly, differences within the ruling class will arise as a result of the advent of fascism. Some segments, relatively less threatened or relatively more sophisticated, will be less enthusiastic about the turn to outright fascism, perhaps even opposed. Cracks in the ruling class may widen to the point of splits, or at least of such conflict as to paralyze major segments from taking decisive action at all. If major segments are opposed or not in active support of the fascist surge, the police and armed forces too may be divided or in basic ways neutralized. The entire weight of American military power can by no means be conceded to the fascist movement, as it would have to be conceded to the defense of the state against attack from the left.

The greatest danger in this process is of course that Amerifascism will not be recognized before it has completely consolidated itself, or that it will in any event be too powerful to be effectively resisted. In part, this is remediable by heightened attention to the potential that groups and practices have, when viewed as a whole and in respect to their possible evolution into Amerifascism, to become components in a process of transformation into fascism. In part, deliberate demythologizing can tear the veil of ideology and legitimacy from the institutions and actions of men in government and aid in subjecting them to informed scrutiny. But, to an inevitable extent, this is a risk that we cannot avoid. We cannot prevent the social crisis that is presently giving birth to both the potential of fundamental change and the growing prospect of Amerifascism. We do not naively seek or condone fascism in order to trigger this process of change; there is no merit to the argument that things should be encouraged to become worse in order that people will come to their senses and rally around to make them better. What happens when things get worse is simply that they get worse and enjoy time to consolidate themselves. The point here is that the growth of Amerifascism is already well underway, and we cannot prevent it. Nor can we foreclose its probable surge toward complete power over the state. Further, the formation of organizations now runs the risk of encapsulating the existing consciousness and projecting it into the future, with the result of delaying emergence of the absolutely essential new consciousness. We must accept the fact that neither circumstances nor people are yet ready for the later stages of the coming struggle. What we *can* do is to develop the new way of understanding, and create the social institutions and reconstructed personal identities that are consistent with the new consciousness and the new society. Most of all, we must constantly think and act in terms of the visible and invisible growth of Amerifascism, preparing ourselves and others to recognize it and fight it, at various levels and with various means, over the next decade or more.

The tasks of developing a new way of understanding and constructing a new consciousness, transferable in a possible American social process to enough people to result in transformation of the society, may still seem insurmountably difficult. This may be the result of the deliberately self-limiting teachings of our current consciousness. Or it may be because each of us assumes that we must individually cope with the problem of reconstructing the whole system or admit defeat, instead of accepting the principle that our first obligation is to reconstruct ourselves and then to contribute as best we can to the larger social project. For the perspective of a new way of understanding, however, neither the new consciousness nor the new society are at all beyond our reach. We have seen one possible version of the process of change, and quite probably more could be generated as the new consciousness develops.

The important point is that a process of change *is* imaginable. It would be much like the American Revolution of 1776 in its legitimacy, defensiveness, and diversity of original goals. It would be much like the Spanish Civil War of 1936 in its grounding in anarchist groupings, rising originally to defend the decaying liberal state against fascism. It would be like both of them in its continuing vulnerability to fragmentation, and in its potential capture or betrayal by hierarchically-organized and self-interested elements in its leadership echelons. But its realization depends entirely on the decisive actions of theoretically prepared men and women—people who see and understand the world as it might be, and act accordingly.

Bibliographical Essay

In this essay, I shall try to provide the reader with a highly selective list of books that deepen and document the analysis or interpretation presented in the text. Because the argument of the text is general rather than specific, page citations have not been employed. Instead, I have sought simply to alert the reader to books that I have found particularly formative or otherwise rewarding with respect to the topics considered in each chapter. Toward the end of the book, references are of necessity either very general or explicitly to opposing views.

CHAPTER ONE

The way we think today is very much the product of our history and the evolution of our political thought. A wide-ranging and authoritative standard interpretation consistent with the frame of this chapter is Louis Hartz, *The Liberal Tradition in America* (New York: Harcourt, Brace & World, 1955). Other classic treatments are Daniel Boorstin, *The Genius of American Politics* (Chicago: University of Chicago Press, 1960), Harry Girvetz, *The Evolution of Liberalism* (New York: Collier Books, 1963), and Clinton Rossiter, *Conservatism in America: The Thankless Persuasion* (New York: Vintage Books, 1955). An excellent recent treatment is Wilson Carey McWilliams, *The Idea of Fraternity in America* (Berkeley, Cal.: The University of California Press, 1973). A provocative little book that says many of the same things as this chapter in a very different way is David Schuman, *A Preface to Politics* (Boston: D.C. Heath & Co., 1972).

Examples of liberal reform writing which make powerful critiques, followed by very limited prescriptions, are numerous. Two may serve as particularly good illustrations: John Kenneth Galbraith, *How to Control the Military* (New York: Signet Books, 1969), and Richard J. Barber, *The American Corporation: Its Power, Its Money, Its Politics* (New York: E.P. Dutton, 1970). Examples of the countercultural side of radicalism, in addition to the celebrated Charles Reich, *The Greening of America* (New York: Bantam Books, 1970), are Charles Hampden-Turner, *Radical Man: The Process of Psycho-Social Development* (Garden City, N.Y.: Anchor Books, 1971) and Theodore Roszak, *Where the Wasteland Ends: Politics and Transcendence in Postindustrial Society* (Garden City, N. Y.: Anchor Books, 1973). On the economic side of radicalism, examples of the many works whose prescriptions fail to match their analyses include Fred Harris, *Now Is the Time: A Populist Call to Action* (New York: Praeger, 1970) and Michael Tanzer, *The Sick Society: An Economic Examination* (New York: Holt, Rinehart & Winston, 1971).

Most of the academic literature on social or political change is too abstract or post-hoc to be much help in framing definitions or theory. See, for example, Chalmers Johnson, *Revolutionary Change* (Boston: Little, Brown & Co., 1966). On the important point of symbolic reassurance, a valuable little book is Murray Edelman, *The Symbolic Uses of Politics* (Urbana, Ill., The University of Illinois Press, 1964).

There is an extensive literature pro and con the existence of a "power structure" in the United States, which will be reviewed in Chapter Two. For general works emphasizing the interests dominant in various eras of American history and the ways in which they operated to channel change, see any of the several books by historians William Appleman Williams and Gabriel Kolko. A revisionist history written from the perspective of anarcho-syndicalism is Jeremy Brecher's excellent *Strike! The True History of Labor's Struggle in the United States* (San Francisco: Straight Arrow Books, 1972), which covers the period from just after the Civil War through the 1960s. A good left-liberal study of the New Deal years is Paul Conkin, *FDR and the*

Origins of the Welfare State (New York: Crowell Collier & MacMillan, 1967).

Along with much hysterical or romantic writing about the possibility of revolution in the United States, there are some very thoughtful academic contributions. Three of these, from quite different perspectives, are Peter Berger and Richard Neuhaus, *Movement and Revolution* (New York: Anchor Books, 1970), Barrington Moore, "Revolution in America," *The New York Review of Books,* Vol. 12 (January 30, 1969), pp. 6-12, and Robert Dahl, *After the Revolution?* (New Haven, Conn.: Yale University Press, 1970).

The problem of conceptual reconstruction is dealt with in detail later, but works of value for the concept of consciousness itself are Robert Hunter, *The Storming of the Mind: Inside the Consciousness Revolution* (Garden City, N.Y.: Anchor Books, 1972), a book which teeters on the edge of sensationalism and triviality but which nevertheless makes the essential early points, and any of the several books by Carlos Castenada concerning his adventures with Don Juan. It should be emphasized that both of these references are useful only for understanding the concept of consciousness itself, and not for what to do about it.

CHAPTER TWO

Overviews of the American political economy, from the same general perspective as this chapter, include Milton Mankoff, *The Poverty of Progress: The Political Economy of American Social Problems* (New York: Holt, Rinehart & Winston, 1972), Ralph Miliband, *The State in Capitalist Society* (New York: Basic Books, 1969), and Maurice Zeitlin, *American Society, Inc.* (Chicago: Markham Publishing Company, 1970). The first of these contains an excellent short bibliography; the second compares the United States with European capitalist systems in useful ways; and the last emphasizes data sources, particularly U.S. Congressional hearings about the banking system.

More narrowly economic analyses include Richard C. Edwards, Michael Reich, and Thomas E. Weisskopf, eds., *The Capitalist System: A Radical Analysis of American Society* (Englewood Cliffs, N. J.: Prentice-Hall, 1972), Gabriel Kolko, *Wealth and Power in America*

(New York: Praeger, 1963), and Howard Sherman, *Radical Political Economy: Capitalism and Socialism from a Marxist-Humanist Perspective* (New York: Basic Books, 1972). The latter contains an excellent bibliography of both economic and other sources.

Liberal-reform works, which make essentially the same arguments on a more superficial level, include Richard Barber, *The American Corporation: Its Power, Its Money, Its Politics* (New York: E.P. Dutton, 1970), John Kenneth Galbraith, *The New Industrial State* (New York: New American Library, 1968), and Michael Reagan, *The Managed Economy* (New York: Oxford University Press, 1963).

The history of the integration of the economy with the state is well portrayed in such as Gabriel Kolko, *The Triumph of Conservatism in America* (Chicago: Quadrangle, 1967) and James Weinstein, *The Corporate Ideal in the Liberal State* (Boston: Beacon Press, 1968).

Sociological aspects are summarized in G. William Domhoff, *Who Rules America?* (Englewood Cliffs, N. J.: Prentice-Hall, 1967) and Richard F. Hamilton, *Class and Politics in the United States* (New York: Wiley, 1972).

The international linkages of the American economy are well developed in Sherman, cited earlier, Harry Magdoff, *The Age of Imperialism* (New York: Monthly Review Press, 1969) and Michael Tanzer, *The Sick Society* (New York: Holt, Rinehart & Winston, 1971), Chapter 6.

The issues of "converged" power structure versus dispersed "pluralism" are argued effectively in C. Wright Mills, *The Power Elite* (New York: Oxford University Press, 1956) and G. William Domhoff and Hoyt B. Ballard, eds., *C. Wright Mills and the Power Elite* (Boston: Beacon Press, 1968), and in Arnold Rose, *The Power Structure: Political Process in American Society* (New York: Oxford University Press, 1967) and Robert Dahl, *Pluralist Democracy in the United States: Conflict and Consent* (Chicago: Rand McNally, 1967). The first is the basic "power elite" text, the second a collection of reactions to it, both pro and con. The last two are well-known illustrations of pluralist concepts and methods. A good review essay on the entire subject, which incorporates the Marxist or ruling class critique of power elite analysis, is that of Milton Mankoff, mentioned earlier.

CHAPTER THREE

Analyses of current American problems are numerically overwhelming, but most treat each "problem" as if it were an isolated phenomenon. Relatively good analyses, though often lacking equally effective prescriptions, include the following:

Inflation-depression issues are taken up in both Sherman and Edwards, et al., mentioned under Chapter Two, above. A somewhat different view of Marxist analysis is presented in Paul Baran and Paul Sweezy, *Monopoly Capitalism* (New York: Monthly Review Press, 1966). A good analysis of the mid-1970s problems may be found in the August, 1972 issue of *Review of Radical Political Economics*, published by the Union for Radical Political Economics at the University of Michigan.

On the distribution of income and poverty, good beginning sources are Herman Miller, *Rich Man, Poor Man* (New York: Crowell, 1964) and Edward Budd, *Inequality and Poverty* (New York: W.W. Norton, 1967). On the role of government, see Frances Fox Piven and Richard Cloward, *Regulating the Poor: The Functions of Public Welfare* (New York: Pantheon Books, 1971).

For issues of technology and ecology, see editors of *Ramparts, Eco-Catastrophe* (San Francisco: Canfield Press, 1971) and Garret de Bell, ed., *The Environment Handbook* (New York: Ballantine Books, 1970), the latter of which includes a good bibliography.

There is also an extensive literature on the situation and needs of minorities, far too extensive to review even selectively here. Let me simply nominate books that I have found to be the most useful of their categories. Robert Allen, *Black Awakening in Capitalist America* (New York: Doubleday, 1969); Armando Rendon, *Chicano Manifesto* (New York: Macmillan, 1971); Vine DeLoria, Jr. *We Talk, You Listen* (New York: Macmillan, 1970) Issues involving the various dimensions of the women's movement are well drawn together in Robin Morgan, ed., *Sisterhood Is Powerful* (New York: Vintage Books, 1970) and Shulamith Firestone, *The Dialectics of Sex* (New York: William Morrow, 1971).

The malaise that grips Americans today is not fully captured in any

single book. A number of survey studies present both general
background and contemporary specifics. For background, see Donald
Devine, *The Political Culture of the United States* (Boston: Little,
Brown & Co., 1972) and David M. Potter, *People of Plenty* (Chicago:
University of Chicago Press, 1954). For specific attitudes, see Lloyd A.
Free and Hadley Cantril, *The Political Beliefs of Americans* (New York:
Simon & Schuster, 1968) and Albert Cantril and Charles Roll, *The
Hopes and Fears of the American People* (New York: Universe Books,
1972). Up-to-the-minute materials may be found in the weekly reports
of the Louis Harris Associates, syndicated to many newspapers, and in
the Gallup Opinion Weekly issued by the American Institute of Public
Opinion Research (Gallup Poll) and available in most libraries.

More impressionistic, perhaps, but deeper treatments may be found
in the work of the psychologist Robert Coles, whose several works
probe the feelings of Americans who moved from South to North. For
example, see his *Children of Crisis* (New York: Dell Publishing Co.,
1964). Studs Terkel has also produced several works amounting to oral
histories of our times, e.g., *Division Street: America* (New York: Avon
Books, 1967) and a forthcoming book on working class attitudes. See
also Todd Gitlin and Nancy Hollander, *Uptown: Poor Whites in
Chicago* (New York: Harper & Row, 1970).

Discussions of the American future do not often include my "real
alternatives." But some do. See, for example, Bertram Gross, "Friendly
Fascism: A Model for America?" in *Social Policy*, Vol. 1, (November-
December, 1970), pp. 44-53, and the discussion in Alan Wolfe, *The
Seamy Side of Democracy: Repression in America* (New York: David
McKay, 1973), Chapter 8.

CHAPTER FOUR

Reform is not usually evaluated as a general process. But on occasion,
authors have argued that liberal efforts at reform have produced
essentially its opposite—the consolidation of the power of business over
the state. Works with this import include Theodore Lowi, *The End of
Liberalism: Ideology, Policy, and the Crisis of Public Authority* (New
York: W.W. Norton, 1969), Grant McConnell, *Private Power and
American Democracy* (New York: Knopf, 1966), and, in a different
vein, Alan Wolfe, cited under Chapter Three, above.

Assessments of the New Deal include Conkin, mentioned under Chapter Two, above; Sidney Lens, *The Crisis of American Labor* (New York: A. S. Barnes, 1961); and Irving Bernstein, *The New Deal Collective Bargaining Policy* (Berkeley, Cal.: University of California Press, 1950). For participants' views, see Studs Terkel, *Hard Times: An Oral History of the Great Depression* (New York: Avon Books, 1971).

Assessments of the specific consequences of the civil rights laws enacted in the 1960s, and the supportive actions of those years and the early 1970s, may be found in Harrell Rodgers and Charles Bullock, III, *Law and Social Change: Civil Rights Laws and Their Consequences* (New York: McGraw-Hill Book Co., Inc., 1972) and Frederick M. Wirt, *Politics of Equality* (Chicago: Aldine Publishing Co., 1971).

On the role of the law generally, see Robert Paul Wolff, ed., *The Rule of Law* (New York: Simon & Schuster, 1971), Robert Lefcourt, ed., *Law Against the People* (New York: Random House, 1971), and Isaac Balbus, *The Dialectics of Legal Repression* (New York: Russell Sage Foundation, 1973). On violence, see Richard E. Rubinstein, *Rebels in Eden: Mass Political Violence in the United States* (Boston: Little, Brown & Co., 1970). A recent collection of materials knitting together the effects of institutions and processes from the perspective of the citizen is Michael Leiserson, *The End of Politics in America: Experience and Possibilities* (Boston: Little, Brown & Co., 1973).

On the self-limiting effects of our political values and ideology, useful works include C. B. Macpherson, *The Real World of Democracy* (New York: Oxford University Press, 1966) and Christopher Lasch, *The Agony of the American Left* (New York: Vintage Books, 1969).

CHAPTER FIVE

The substance of American ideology is discussed in Kenneth M. Dolbeare and Patricia Dolbeare, *American Ideologies: The Competing Political Beliefs of the 1970s* (Chicago: Rand McNally, 1973). A different view, less dominant now than in the early 1960s, is presented in Daniel Bell, *The End of Ideology* (New York: Free Press, 1960). For some thoughts on the origins and substance of ideology, see also Jules Henry, *Culture Against Man* (New York: Random House, 1963). A fresh and lively interpretation is Herbert Reid, *Up the Mainstream:*

Ideology in American Politics and Everyday Life (New York: David McKay, 1973). A more traditional basic work is Robert Lane, *Political Ideology: Why the American Common Man Believes What He Does* (New York: Free Press, 1962). Another empirical standard is Angus Campbell, et al., *The American Voter* (New York: John Wiley, 1960).

The sources of such ideology are analyzed in a number of ways. Representative works, covering the range of such ways, include David Easton and Jack Dennis, *Children in the Political System* (New York: McGraw-Hill Book Co., Inc., 1969), Herbert M. Hyman, *Political Socialization* (New York: Free Press, 1959), James D. Koerner, *Who Controls American Education?* (Boston: Beacon Press, 1968), Richard Hofstadter, *Anti-Intellectualism in American Life* (New York: Knopf, 1963), and William Preston, Jr., *Aliens and Dissenters: Federal Suppression of Radicals, 1903-1933* (New York: Harper & Row, 1963).

The nature of consciousness and its relationship to social sources is more often explored by Europeans than by Americans. Some basic works include G. W. F. Hegel, *The Phenomenology of Mind* (New York: Harper Torchbooks, 1967), Karl Marx, *The German Ideology* (New York: International Publishers, 1965), Georg Lukacs, *History and Class Consciousness* (Cambridge, Mass.: MIT Press, 1971) and Jurgen Habermas, *Knowledge and Human Interests* (Boston: Beacon Press, 1971).

Important works by Americans, the first two drawing heavily on the European tradition for reasons discussed in the text, include Herbert Marcuse, *Reason and Revolution: Hegel and the Rise of Social Theory* (Boston: Beacon Press, 1960), Martin Buber, *Paths in Utopia* (Boston: Beacon Press, 1958), and Robert Lane, *Political Thinking and Consciousness* (Chicago: Markham Publishing Company, 1967). Marcuse's work may be the best starting point for the reader new to this general area.

CHAPTER SIX

The process of consciousness change is little analyzed, and then chiefly within the trivializing perspective dwelt on earlier. A particularly good recent work, however, is Paulo Freire, *Pedagogy of the Oppressed* (New York: Herder and Herder, 1972), which takes up the inner transformation, rooted in language, that must occur. More general and more difficult, but well worth the effort, is Jean-Paul Sartre, *Search for a Method* (New York: Vintage Books, 1968) and R. D. Laing and D. G. Cooper, *Reason and Violence: A Decade of Sartre's Philosophy, 1950-1960* (New York: Vintage Books, 1971).

Discussions of the small-group process are found primarily in the anarchist literature. See, for example, Murray Bookchin, *Post-Scarcity Anarchism* (Berkeley, Cal.: The Ramparts Press, 1971). For more general works on anarchism, see Daniel Guerin, *Anarchism* (New York: Monthly Review Press, 1970), April Carter, *The Political Theory of Anarchism* (New York: Harper Torchbooks, 1971), and James Joll, *The Anarchists* (New York: Grosset & Dunlap, 1966).

The vanguard reconstruction process finds its classic statement in V. I. Lenin, *What Is to Be Done?* (New York: International Publishers, 1969). The mass strike process is analyzed best in Rosa Luxemburg, *The Mass Strike: The Political Party and the Trade Unions* (Boston: Beacon Press, 1971), and next in Jeremy Brecher, *Strike!* (San Francisco: Straight Arrow Books, 1972).

CHAPTER SEVEN

On various possible agencies of change, some useful works are Richard Flacks, *Youth and Social Change* (Chicago: Markham Publishing Company, 1971); Martin Oppenheimer, *The Urban Guerrilla* (Chicago: Quadrangle Books, 1969); Philip G. Altbach and Robert S. Laufer, *The New Pilgrims: Youth Protest in Transition* (New York: David McKay, 1972); Barrington Moore, Jr., *Reflections on the Causes of Human Misery and Upon Certain Proposals to Eliminate Them* (Boston: Beacon Press, 1973), and Robert Allen, *Black Awakening in Capitalist America* (New York: Doubleday Anchor, 1971).

Two excellent collections of varied source materials, pertaining to the process and agencies of change, are Roderick Aya and Norman Miller, eds., *The New American Revolution* (New York: The Free Press, 1971) and William Lutz and Harry Brent, eds., *On Revolution* (Cambridge, Mass.: Winthrop Publishers, Inc., 1971).

For discussions of the problem of organization from a variety of perspectives, see Andre Gorz, *Strategy for Labor* (Boston: Beacon Press, 1967); James Weinstein, *The Decline of American Socialism* (New York: Monthly Review Press, 1967); and Murray Bookchin,

"Listen, Marxist!", cited earlier under Chapter Six. On the problem and importance of generating an image of a total process of change culminating in the transfer of power, no book is better than George Singer, *Prelude to Revolution: France in May 1968* (New York: Hill & Wang, 1970).

CHAPTERS EIGHT, NINE, AND TEN

The most important of the many works authored by Marx or by Marx and Engels together—at least for our purposes here—are probably the *Economic and Philosophic Manuscripts of 1844,* "Theses on Feurbach," in Engels, ed., *Ludwig Feurbach and the Outcome of Classical German Philosophy,* and *The German Ideology.* All of these are available in editions bearing various dates and published by International Publishers of New York. They are also available in many other editions.

Perhaps the best secondary source on Marx's thought is Shlomo Avineri, *The Social and Political Thought of Karl Marx* (Cambridge: Cambridge University Press, 1971). Other valuable works on Marx and the tradition of evolving critical theory include J. Hampden Jackson, *Marx, Proudhon, and European Socialism* (New York: Collier Books, 1957); Louis Althusser, *For Marx* (New York: Vintage Books, 1970); Erich Fromm, ed., *Socialist Humanism: An International Symposium* (New York: Anchor Books, 1966): Georg Lukacs, *Marxism and Human Liberation* (New York: Delta, 1973); Adam Schaff, *Marxism and the Human Individual* (New York: McGraw-Hill Book Co., Inc., 1970); and Roger Garaudy, *The Crisis in Communism: The Turning Point of Socialism* (New York: Grove Press, 1970).

The best starting point into critical theory and its evolution remains Marcuse's *Reason and Revolution* (see under Chapter Seven). Another useful early work is Richard J. Bernstein, *Praxis and Action* (Philadelphia: The University of Pennsylvania Press, 1971). An excellent recent work devoted to the evolution of critical theory is Martin Jay, *The Dialectical Imagination* (Boston: Little, Brown and Co., 1973).

American Marxist groups are represented chiefly by their newspapers and occasional pamphlets, available from their local headquarters, through handouts, or by subscription. There is little theoretical work in book form, however.

Independent Marxists and Marxist scholars, on the other hand, have produced a considerable literature, much of which has been previously cited in other connections. On the specific issue of *how* to bring about fundamental change in the United States, however, there is not much available. The Lerner and Harrington books discussed in the text come as close as any.

Exploration into the development of critical consciousness through analysis of concepts and concept formation could well begin with a collection by Richard E. Flathman, *Concepts in Social and Political Philosophy* (New York: Macmillan, 1973). Another provocative and useful collection is Hwa Yol Jung, ed., *Existential Phenomenology and Political Theory: A Reader* (Chicago: Henry Regnery Company, 1972). Both of these works contain bibliographies that offer multiple directions for further inquiry.

Among the ample literature on the Spanish Civil War, two books stand out. One is George Orwell, *Homage to Catalonia* (New York: Harcourt, Brace & World, 1952). The other is Felix Morrow, *Revolution and Counter-Revolution in Spain* (London: New Park Publications, 1963).

Index